GET REAL

GET REAL

26 Canadian Women Share the
Secret to Authentic Success

Patricia Lovett-Reid
with Jonathan Verney

KEY PORTER BOOKS

Library and Archives Canada Cataloguing in Publication

Lovett-Reid, Patricia

   Get real : 26 Canadian women share the secret to authentic success / Patricia Lovett-
Reid, Jonathan Verney.

ISBN 978-1-55263-878-1

   1. Success—Case studies.   2. Women—Life skills guides.   3. Successful people—
Canada—Biography.   4. Women—Canada—Biography.   I. Verney, Jonathan   II. Title.

HQ1453.L69 2007   650.1'082   C2006-906432-6

The author, Patricia Lovett-Reid, is a Senior Vice President with TD Waterhouse Canada
Inc. While every effort was made to ensure the accuracy of the material in this book, TD
Waterhouse Inc., a subsidiary of The Toronto-Dominion Bank, assumes no responsibility
or liability arising from the use of the material in this book. The material is for information purposes only, and you should consult your own professional advisors.

Key Porter Books Limited
Six Adelaide Street East, Tenth Floor
Toronto, Ontario
Canada M5C 1H6

www.keyporter.com

Text design: Marijke Friesen
Electronic formatting: Jean Lightfoot Peters

Printed and bound in Canada

08 09 10 11 5 4 3 2

CONTENTS

THE INTERVIEWEES

Dr. Nancy Baxter, Surgeon

Natalie Bean-Sole, President of NutritionForeverInc.com

Denise Bebenek, Founder of Meagan's Walk: Creating a Circle of Hope

Major D.M. (Dee) Brasseur, C.M., C.D., one of two of the world's first female fighter pilots

Jacqueline Carroll, Visual and Portrait Artist/Art Teacher and Author

The Hon. Anne C. Cools, Senator, the first African-American female senator in North America

Brenda Eaton, Chair, B.C. Housing

Aimée Israel, Co-founder and CEO of LifeSpeak

Danielle Iversen, President and Publicist of That PR Thing

Lauren Jawno, Speaker, Coach, Trainer, Consultant and President of Personal Health

Pamela Jeffery, CEO of Women's Executive Network

Colleen Johnston, CFO of TD Bank Financial Group

Ann Kaplan, CEO of Medicard

Joan Kelley-Weisshaar, TV Producer and Director, Founder of Hero Media

Dr. Patricia Kmet, Dentist

Kerrin Lee-Gartner, 1992 Olympic Downhill Gold Medalist, Alpine Skiing

Jennifer McNeill, CEO of CipherSoft Inc.

Akela Peoples, President and CEO of Youth in Motion

Karen Radford, Executive Vice President and President of TELUS Quebec and TELUS Partner Solutions

Sarah Raiss, Executive Vice President at TransCanada Corporation

Ann Rohmer, Broadcaster, Citytv and CP24

Lesley Southwick-Trask, President and Co-Founder of Owl's Head Island Retreat

Jacqui Szeto, Vice President and Director, Fixed Income Sales, Debt Capital Markets at TD Securities Inc. and President, Women in Capital Markets

Sarah Thomson, Publisher of *The Women's Post*

Julie Toskan-Casale, Founder of M.A.C. Cosmetics

Linda Wheler, Minister of Pastoral Care

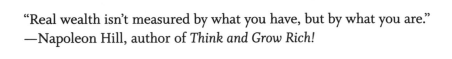

"Real wealth isn't measured by what you have, but by what you are."
—Napoleon Hill, author of *Think and Grow Rich!*

PREFACE

"What we need is less fantasy thinking, more positive role models and more good news stories about women's achievements."
—Darla Campbell, past president of The Canadian Federation of Business and Professional Women's Clubs

ALTHOUGH WE MAY NOT WANT TO ADMIT IT, we Canadians buy far more books than we actually read. That's why I've tried to make sure this book is not only worth reading but worth *keeping*. This book isn't about media-made celebrities living an entourage-protected existence. It's about real women with real names leading really special lives. It's about inspiring yet highly achievable Canadian role models who have found the secret to real success. And best of all, they're happy to share their secrets with you.

I don't know about you, but these women sound like *my* kind of role models.

It's funny how easily shaped we are as children, yet how hard it is to "unshape" ourselves as adults. Women often pride themselves on being a little more self-aware and a little more adaptable than men.

But all of us create some sort of world view for ourselves sooner or later, and once we do, we tend to stick to it whether it's good or bad, realistic or not. It's difficult enough to change a habit. Try making an attitude adjustment. It's a far bigger undertaking.

I've noticed that a certain percentage of women believe their relationships, finances and careers are somehow pre-ordained. Their views are often fixed and fatalistic, and their routines have become so ingrained and so comfortable that they wouldn't dream of changing them unless an external event literally *forced* them to change. These women are set in their ways, rigid, "*conserve*-ative" and *closed* to change.

For other women, however, life is a journey filled with adventure and opportunity. Every day is a new experience, an occasion to test new waters and in the process test and learn about themselves. These women are flexible, passionate, fluid in their thinking and *open* to change.

The latter kind of woman is definitely me. I'm passionate about life with a capital "P." And more important, it's a trait of the women you're about to meet in this book.

My name is Patricia Lovett-Reid, but everyone who knows me calls me Pattie. I work on being open to new things, but I live my life according to a certain moral code. My mother taught me to be resilient. When I stumbled, I was told to dust myself off and move on. Believe me, I've had my share of slip-ups. A number of years ago I left TD Bank Financial Group to become the morning news anchor at Business News Network (formerly Report on Business Television). I had to get up at 2:30 each morning and left the house while my husband and the kids were still asleep. I loved interviewing CEOs and business experts, but initially I was a terrible teleprompter reader. I worked at it and soon became pretty adept at reading the flashing screen. I wasn't a terrible anchor, but I knew I wasn't Barbara Walters either. I had (and still have) a great relationship with the folks at Business News Network. But when a few months later the bank offered me a new position—one which would really allow me to play to my strengths—I decided it was a better fit and moved on.

Yes, I've tripped up at times, but I've also enjoyed each new experience and as a result have had some success. I'm occasionally in the public eye, whether on television or presenting at financial seminars across the country. Whatever I've achieved has happened because I'm passionate about everything I do, whether it's writing or giving financial seminars or hosting *MoneyTalk* on Business News Network. Although I'm a financial broadcaster, my goal isn't to be the best financial broadcaster in the world. Although I'm a writer, my goal isn't to be the best writer in the world.

What's my goal? Simply to be the best *I* can be.

I attribute many of the things I'm most proud of to my values and my attitude. I wondered if other successful women were similar to me in any way. That's part of the reason why I wrote this book. Not to find out if other women shared my *views* (after all, people are different and should be different), but to see if there might be a common underlying theme. Something that could be of value to other women and to you, the reader. And, after talking with them, I discovered there was.

Now I'd like to share that discovery with you.

Although I'm the author of five personal finance books, I've always wanted to write a lifestyle-oriented book for women. Having advised on money issues most of my adult life, I know firsthand how powerful money and lifestyle issues can be to women. One day, after I'd finished giving a financial seminar to a few hundred women on the East Coast, one of them came up to me and whispered in my ear.

"Pattie, could I talk to you about something?" she asked.

"Sure," I said. "What's on your mind?"

She continued whispering: "It's kind of awkward. Could we talk in private?"

It turns out she was totally uncomfortable talking about money, but not because she hadn't saved very much. Just the opposite, in fact. She didn't want people to know how well off she was! Like many women, she had developed an intensely complicated relationship with money. It was both a boon and a burden. She reconfirmed for me just how many personal boundaries money crosses. Money is never just money. For some it's a status symbol or a scorecard or a reminder of unmet needs; for others it may be about freedom and independence; and for some it may be about self-worth. Some of the women attending my seminars even have what I call a submissive relationship with money. It controls them, not the other way around. And that's unhealthy. I know in my heart these women need to find some positive role models. But that's often hard to do.

I went looking for stories of women who had a positive relationship with money—especially Canadian women—but I must confess I didn't find much at the bookstore. This country has published precious few stories about successful Canadian women.

It wasn't until I read Napoleon Hill's bluntly titled book, *Think and Grow Rich!*, that my thoughts on the subject really crystallized. Packed with pearls of wisdom, Hill's book is filled with inspirational stories profiling the greatest men of his era. Although first published way back in 1937, even today many consider *Think and Grow Rich!* the greatest self-help book of all time.

There's just one problem with Hill's excellent book.

Throughout its 350 pages, there's not a single story about a great *woman!* Pages and pages on business executives and inventors and scientists—all male. Not a single woman to be found! Sure, it was written only twenty years after women received the right to vote in the United States and Canada, but there were lots of successful women in those days. Examples? Here are four from Canada:

- Social activist Nellie McClung was one of the leaders of Canada's Famous Five who fought for women's right to vote.
- Wife and mother Laura Secord became a true Canadian heroine when she risked her life to warn the British of a planned attack by the Americans during the War of 1812.
- Lucy Maud Montgomery wrote a classic that was beloved by millions across the globe—*Anne of Green Gables*.
- Mary Pickford was not only a Hollywood star, she was an astute businesswoman who co-founded United Artists with Charlie Chaplin, D.W. Griffith and her (at the time) soon-to-be husband, Douglas Fairbanks.

Since then, of course, women have entered the workforce in huge numbers. The workplace is changing as a result. And women's attitudes to work and life have changed dramatically. Or have they?

In a March 17, 2004, *Calgary Sun* article entitled "Girls Just Wanna Have Husbands?", Valerie Gibson highlighted an intriguing

U.K. study. The study claims that when one thousand English women aged 18 to 34 were surveyed about their workplace ambitions, more than four in ten of the 25- to 34-year-olds said they "would leave even a highly successful and powerful position to live a life of luxury with a guy who would pay all the bills."

In the article, Darla Campbell, past president of The Canadian Federation of Business and Professional Women's Clubs, responded to the study by saying she found the poll results "shocking."

"What we need," she says, "is less fantasy thinking, more positive role models and more good news stories about women's achievements to inspire them."

I couldn't agree more!

Through their actions even more than their words, the inspirational women featured in this book are telling the world that if you want success and happiness, you need to be real. And you need to stay real.

How do you do it? And is it easy to do? Read on and you'll learn what these successful women already know—that the secret to a happy and truly successful life is yours for the taking

You just have to know where to look.

Patricia Lovett-Reid
Oakville, Ontario
April 2007

INTRODUCTION

IMAGINE YOU'RE DRIFTING on a raft in the middle of the ocean. You've got supplies to last you at least a month, and the sky above is clear and blue. The raft is your protection against drowning and being attacked by the creatures in the sea beneath. The gentle waves caress you, and you feel safe and secure. Yet you have a vague sense of unease as you wonder where you are and where you're drifting to.

Most of us have constructed our own "life" rafts—a job, a place to live, food on the table. It's our foundation against drowning in a sea of debt. There's just one problem with a raft: it won't get you anywhere. Sure, you won't drown, but you'll drift with the current and the winds—rudderless, directionless, lost—until someone rescues you.

Or will they?

What would happen if the skies darkened and the wind started to howl and the rain came at you sideways, and suddenly the gentle caress of the waves became a terrifying succession of sickening, roller-coaster-like freefalls and wood-wrenching jolts?

Would your raft still make you feel safe and secure?

In life, bad things can happen, and at a moment's notice. You may be restructured out of a job you do well or you may lose your husband in an accident or your life savings may disappear by way of medical bills stemming from a critical illness. Suddenly you've gone from drifting to drowning.

Now imagine a slightly different scenario. Imagine that while you were drifting on your raft, you decided to look underneath the wooden planks.

Of course, you'd find those big metal drum flotation devices but, strangely enough, two of them are loose. You roll one up onto the raft and discover it's filled with sailing equipment and an easy-to-read instruction manual. You roll up the other to find tools and a compass and a map. You suddenly realize that, with a little effort, you can turn your raft into a sailboat equipped with a rudder and sails and maybe even an engine. What do you do? You get to work building your home-grown vessel. And when you're done you pick a direction and, guided by the sun and the stars and your compass, you set sail. You've not only stopped drifting, you're heading for dry land.

This is what this book is all about: charting the course of successful Canadian women who've found a way to build their own "sailboat" and have set sail for a richly authentic life. What do these women have in common besides success? Among other things, they're honest about themselves, they believe in themselves and they have a remarkably clear sense of direction.

Every one of us wants to be successful, and many of us are looking for the magic key to get there. But each of us defines success differently. What energizes my life and makes me feel successful may not be of any interest to you, and vice versa.

Some of you might want to be the next Martha Stewart or Margaret Atwood or Karen Kain or Shania Twain. Not the women I talked to.

They want to be who they are, only better! They're a diverse group, from artists to business people to fundraisers to broadcasters to athletes. They come from all parts of Canada. Most of them are not household names. They love what they do and they do what they love. All of them found success in different ways, but all of them were passionate about their work and their life.

As a child, I grew up with anything but an entitlement attitude. Instead, I grew up with a passion for life, a good work ethic and a healthy respect for the value of money and savings. My father died when I was only 9 years old. As I watched how Joyce, my mother, managed the finances and took care of me and my brother, I learned early on that women are survivors. Mom was entirely on her own until she remarried a few years later. And by the way, the man she married—Les—is not only my stepfather but is a terrific role model.

When I was a teenager, I had two or three part-time jobs and then, when I was just 18, I made a momentous decision to leave school after getting my Grade 12 diploma. I was impatient to get into the work world and I wanted a career in the financial arena, so I started as a bank teller. I was thrilled to have financial independence and my own apartment at the age of 19! Having money gave me choices, which was great, but my mom always said: "The last thing anyone should want is to die the richest person in the graveyard." She was right, and I took her advice.

The way I see it, money and lifestyle and success and happiness are really just part of the same package. I'm a mother of four, I have a loving husband with a high-powered career, and I also happen to be a Senior Vice President at TD Waterhouse. I'm a people person but, just as important, I'm a realist. A realist sees the world for what it is, not through rose-coloured glasses. But I'm also a *positive* realist because I see the world as a place of hope and change, a place where good things can happen if we have a clear sense of direction. I try hard to lead a balanced, meaningful life. In our family, lifestyle issues are addressed openly and honestly. And of course those issues include money.

Like my mom, I'm a survivor. I don't spend much time dwelling on the past. Am I perfect? Hardly. That's why I'm always learning, always striving to get better. I have self-doubts like anyone else, but I've learned to acknowledge the negatives and focus on the positives. I don't know it all and I know I never will. I'm always evolving. But I know one thing for sure: As my life has evolved so have my goals, but my principles and values have always remained the same.

Okay, I can hear you saying—"Hey! Hold on, Pattie. I thought this was supposed to be a book about lifestyle. Don't tell me it's just another *money* book!" No, it's *not* another money book. This is a book about real women who live real lives, all of them making a difference in different ways. But from years of giving educational and financial seminars to Canadians of all ages (more than half of them being women), I've found that money is at the root of a million and one issues people have with their spouses, their jobs, their relationships and their lives. That's why my goal, and the goal of the women interviewed in this book, is to inspire you to get real with yourself and your own life.

Yes, money can be frustrating. But it can be mastered. Hey, life can be frustrating, but it, too, can be mastered. It's no coincidence that money and life are so tightly interwoven.

I'm fortunate to have very few frustrations in my life. But a really big one is talking with people who seem to have given up, who feel powerless, who don't feel there's anything they can do about their financial situation. Often, their feelings are masking a deeper issue. Whether it's their marriage or their career or their finances, they've convinced themselves that, "*it is what it is.*" What do I advise people who feel like this, who feel helpless, out of control? I tell them it's time for them to *get real*!

And now it's time for us to get real. So let's get started.

ONE

GET REAL ABOUT FINDING YOUR PASSION

IN A WORLD WHERE THE DESIRE to keep up with the Joneses and the availability of easy credit is driving us into unprecedented levels of debt, it's not so easy to get real. The women in this book know that. And they also know that getting real is only half the equation. If you want to be successful, you need to stay real. And as you're about to find out, passion is one of the two driving forces to getting and staying real.

Finding your passion in life can happen early and easily, but more often it happens later and laboriously. But whenever and however it happens, passion becomes the critical ingredient to success. As our interviewees will tell you, passion has the power to drive us through brick walls and hurdle life's biggest obstacles.

THE WORLD'S FIRST FEMALE FIGHTER PILOT

Society puts undeniable pressure on us to conform, to chart the safest course and follow the beaten path. But the safest route is seldom the smartest one. Dee Brasseur, the world's first female fighter pilot (along with fellow Canadian, Captain Jane Foster), knows this all too well. She never followed the beaten path, despite the huge challenge of being a woman in a man's world.

Born into a military family (her father is Lieutenant Colonel Lyn Brasseur), Dee joined the Canadian military at the age of 19, and began work as a typist for a dental office. Dee soon realized that being a clerk was not what she wanted to be or do, so she signed up for the Officer Candidate Training Plan program.

"My parents were fantastic role models with sound values and a solid work ethic. They taught me there was no such thing as 'can't,'" Dee says. "Thanks to them, gender roles meant nothing to me. Although my father was a traditional male and my mother was a homemaker, my sister and brother and I were raised in a very egalitarian family environment. I did the dishes, cleaned the car and helped put up the storm windows, just like everyone else in my family."

There were few women serving in the Canadian Armed Forces when Dee Brasseur joined in 1972, and their roles were restricted to areas like administration, nursing and food services. But in 1978 a golden opportunity opened up. The Forces initiated a trial program called SWINTER (the Study of Women in Non-Traditional Environments and Roles) to expand opportunities for women in the military. "I chose pilot training," says Dee, "and made Canadian military history by becoming one of only three women to get my wings."

"I think I'm most proud of how I've lived my life. That's why life is my passion."
—DEE BRASSEUR, the world's first female fighter pilot

Later, she made another key decision—she asked to stay on as a Flight Instructor and became the world's first female instructor after signing on with the Forces flight school in Moose Jaw, Saskatchewan. She was now front and centre on the fast track, or so she thought. But it wasn't until seven years later, at age 35, that the opportunity of a lifetime was offered to her. She was asked to train as a CF-18 fighter pilot.

"I've always been a high-energy person, with a dream, a solid work ethic and a good sense of myself as a person," Dee explains. "So here I am in Cold Lake, Alberta, I've just been given the opportunity to train to become the world's first female fighter pilot—heck, I've been dreaming about this for ten years—and guess what starts to flit through my head?"

Could it be visions of fame and fortune and wild-eyed success, I wondered? It turns out I was dead wrong.

"What if I failed?" That's what Dee was thinking. "Can you believe it?" she says to me now.

Driven, confident and now an acclaimed motivational speaker, Dee Brasseur was plagued by self-doubt.

"What if I said yes, decided to train, decided to grab hold of my lifelong dream, and then I *failed*?" she asks aloud.

It was October 1987, and this "gift" had suddenly turned her life upside down. She didn't know what to do, so she took her dog out for a walk. It turned out to be a very special night: "I remember that night so vividly it could be yesterday. The Northern Lights filled the autumn sky, and it felt like there was a magic presence all around me. But I was still very much confused. So I looked up into the night sky and said, 'Listen Dude, I need some inspiration!' I guess I got it. Suddenly, I realized the only way I was ever gonna know for sure if I would fail or succeed was to do it!"

And boy did she do it. The first female fighter pilot in the world at age 36. She passed the test with flying colours and the rest, as they say, is history. Yet when she looks back on her life, Brasseur is not as proud of her achievements as she is of something else. "I think I'm most proud of how I've lived my life. That's why life is my passion."

CAN PASSION MAKE US HAPPY?

What is passion, exactly? Passion originally came from the Greek word for suffering (thus, the Passion of the Christ). Today, its more common meaning is much different. It can mean many things—great emotion, fervour, determination, boundless enthusiasm. In the context of this book, finding your passion means developing a lifelong purpose or vocation that keeps you connected and true to yourself. Passion will help drive you to accomplish your goals and, even more important, it will help get you on the road to happiness.

BROADCASTER ANN ROHMER: ON PASSION AND ENERGY

We often talk about high-energy people with a certain admiration and maybe even envy. Broadcaster Ann Rohmer of Citytv is certainly one of those people.

"I've been an extremely high-energy person ever since I was a gleam in my father's eye," she says proudly.

One of two daughters of author Major-General Richard Rohmer, Ann has been a mainstay on Toronto television for more than twenty-five years. She hosted Citytv's *Breakfast Television* for twelve years and is a news anchor on CP24, Toronto's number one, 24-hour news channel. She also hosts CP24's *CityOnLine*, *Hot Property* and *Animal House Calls*.

Ann is also an ardent supporter of animals. She has twice co-hosted the show *World Wildlife Fund: Countdown to Extinction*, with actors Kelsey Grammer and Kevin Bacon. In the show, the World Wildlife Fund and Hollywood celebrities tell stories of endangered animals and their struggle for survival.

You might think Ann was born to be on TV and probably didn't have to look very far to find her passion. But that was certainly not the case. When she was young, her parents made her take a career aptitude test.

"Flight attendant and lawyer were the two answers," she tells me.

Ironically, the first answer (flight attendant) was the job she'd dreamed about since she was a child, and the other (lawyer) was what her parents always wanted for her.

"It may seem a little silly to say in retrospect, but I always loved uniforms," she says. "I became a flight attendant while I was at university and the experience proved invaluable. I was very shy, and only my parents knew it! But I grew out of my shyness on airplanes."

Ann is known for her boundless work ethic. If she could choose one word to describe her approach to work, it would be "professional." She attributes her attitude and approach to life to her biggest role models—parents Richard and Mary-O.

"They always led by example, they never preached to me or to my sister," she explains. "My mother is the essence of grace, and my father is the most forward-thinking man I've ever met. They are my greatest supporters and my best friends."

Has Ann found her passion in life?

"Absolutely," she says. "I wake up every day and say, 'Yeah!' I've always been a people person and I'm fortunate to have a fabulous job, interviewing interesting people every day. I'm doing what I love and it inspires and energizes me. I'm so lucky."

Not everyone is a high-energy person like Ann, although I've discovered that many of my interviewees are.

> "My mother is the essence of grace, and my father is the most forward-thinking man I've ever met. They are my greatest supporters and my best friends."
>
> —ANN ROHMER, Broadcaster, Citytv and CP24

But having passion for your work and your life can provide a huge energy boost. I've seen passion create lifelong energy in those who aren't naturally high-energy people—an energy that can help level the playing field.

PASSION AND ATTITUDE

When Oprah Winfrey hosted a show called "How to Find Your Passion" back in March 2001, she said that true happiness comes when you do what you're most passionate about. She also made this intriguing comment: "Thousands of you recently took an online poll, and more than 70 percent of you told us you have no idea what your life's passion is!"

Our view of the world—our attitude—has as much effect on our happiness as the nature of the events themselves. With that in mind, I wanted to find out what my interviewees' mindset was, and I also wanted to see if they shared a common world view.

Their answers proved fascinating. In virtually every case, they said they were optimists who see the glass as half-full, and they were realists who didn't see the world through rose-coloured glasses. In other words, they were *positive realists*—a great combination to aspire to. Positive realists see the world for what it is, yet continue to have hope. That's exactly what I am too. And interestingly enough, that describes the personalities of many of my most successful colleagues at the bank.

There's no one magical step to authentic success. It's a process. I know this because that's what my interviewees have told me, and because I've always tried to follow this path in my own life. If what you're really after is success, not passion, it will show. What's worse, both success and passion will likely elude you. That's because authenticity must be the goal, not success.

"If you love something or have a true passion for it, it doesn't feel like work because it's so easy to spend time doing it."
—LAUREN JAWNO, Speaker, Coach, Trainer, Consultant and President of Personal Health

That means you have to define what is really right for *you*, not for someone else. Success and happiness aren't goals so much as by-products of the passion with which you work, engage and play.

A lot more women are drifting than are sailing, according to my interviewees. Some of my interviewees believe as many as 90 percent of us are adrift, and the figure may be just as high for men. Is passion that elusive? Let's see what our interviewees have to say on the matter.

THE LUCK OF THE IRISH
Akela Peoples, the dynamic CEO of Youth in Motion, sees a definite link between passion and attitude: "I don't know if it's my Irish background or not, but I've always enjoyed what I do, whatever it is. And a lot of that came out of my attitude. The media spends a lot of time focusing on the negative, but I always see the glass as half-full. If you choose to seek out the things you like to do and spend time with people you enjoy, then it's very easy to be inspired and passionate."

When I asked Akela to define what passion meant to her, she said, "It's ultimately about doing something that makes my heart happy, you know, with my eyes closed. It makes me feel good. However, I do think passion is different for most people."

Akela's company, Youth in Motion, is a national, not-for-profit organization dedicated to preparing Canada's youth for the job market by empowering them to make meaningful life and career choices. She found her passion in a purely serendipitous way.

"I was hired right out of university by a wonderful man named Russ White, who was the Arts Director at the Peel District School Board," says Akela. "I'd gone to teachers' college and had plans to go to med school because my father was a doctor. I'd done some summer camp work, and people spoke highly of me. So along came Russ, and he offered me a great opportunity to help set up an arts program in Ontario. The chance to be part of an exciting team, to be creative and truly innovative, and to actually produce something, was too alluring to pass up."

After six years, Akela left to set up another program that integrated business and technology into every high school course. Then, in 1997, she left the school system to set up a regional organization called Women in Motion Career Education. "We subsequently rebranded it as Youth in Motion (YIM), a national organization established to inspire and educate youth. But I have to tell you, it took a lot of courage to set it up because I had no formal business training."

From the time she was a child, Akela always saw herself in a leadership role: "I liked to organize things at school, and my parents were incredibly encouraging. They always said I could do anything or be anything I wanted to be. So now I've found my passion in life, although for me there was no master plan."

> "The chance to be part of an exciting team, to be creative and truly innovative, and to actually produce something, was too alluring to pass up."
>
> —AKELA PEOPLES, CEO of Youth in Motion

For some of the women in this book, serendipity is a close friend. And for others, the plan was set into motion early. It's fascinating how closely intertwined these three words are—success and passion and happiness. It reminds me of something a friend of mine told me recently.

THE SECRET TO HAPPINESS

Let me tell you a story. I had a friend who decided to visit his aunt and celebrate her 90th birthday in Manchester, England. When he got on the plane, he sat beside a youngish Buddhist monk decked out in his formal crimson robe. The monk, an American from Colorado, was going to visit a spiritual retreat and training centre near Manchester. Now my friend, being the curious intellectual type, soon got into a lively philosophical discussion with his seatmate. It turns out the Buddhist had a sense of humour about his chosen vocation. He said he was in the happiness business, and actually called himself a "happiness guru."

My friend laughed and asked him whether he thought happiness should even be a goal in our hedonistic society. The monk said: "Definitely, yes! I believe happiness is a sense of well-being, an inner peace. It is a very worthy goal, a goal we should all strive for."

Hearing this shocked me because I grew up believing something entirely different. I was taught that happiness was a by-product of working hard at the things I loved to do. Chasing happiness? Couldn't be done. That was a mug's game, better left to hard-core dreamers and gamblers and racetrack enthusiasts and lottery ticket buyers. And buying happiness? Even more far-fetched.

Then, a couple of days later, I happened upon an article in Princeton University's News@Princeton newsletter archives quoting a study by two Princeton professors, economist Alan B. Krueger and psychologist and Nobel laureate Daniel Kahneman. They collaborated with colleagues from three other universities to see if happiness was linked to income. They gave daily diaries to nearly two thousand women, and made sure they were completed in detail by all the respondents. Their study found there was little connection between happiness and income. But in my opinion, of greater importance were some other survey results the professors quoted. According to U.S. Bureau of Labor Statistics, men making more than $100,000 per year spend 19.9 percent of their time on passive leisure, compared to 34.7 percent for men making less than $20,000. Women making more than $100,000 spend 19.6 percent of their time on passive leisure, compared with 33.5 percent of those making less than $20,000. Leisure activities were defined as socializing or watching television (which the respondents viewed as more enjoyable). Interestingly, the survey found that people with higher incomes devote relatively more of their time to work, shopping, childcare and other "obligatory" (non-leisure) activities.

Intrigued by this concept of studying happiness, I discovered that one of the world's leading experts on happiness is Professor Martin Seligman. Seligman has devoted his life to the study of positive psychology, and heads up the world's first graduate program in Positive Psychology at the University of Pennsylvania. The author of *Learned Optimism* and of *Authentic Happiness*, Seligman says on his website that "there are three distinct kinds of happiness: the Pleasant Life (pleasures), the Good Life (engagement), and the Meaningful Life. The first two are subjective, but the third is at least partly objective and lodges in belonging to and serving what is larger and more worthwhile than the just the self's pleasures and desires." Seligman sees authentic happiness as synthesizing all three traditions.

Richard Handler, in an excellent article for the CBC entitled "The Science of Happiness" (December 21, 2006), does a good job of summarizing the current state of happiness research: "Happiness, the literature now says, resembles a three-legged stool. The first leg is what psychologists call 'affect,' meaning how you feel, your day-to-day mood. That's different for everyone. And here's the bad news: It's mostly inherited."

Apparently, all of us have a happiness set point. We can tinker with it, but we will always revert to the mean (our normal range). The second leg of the happiness stool is called "flow"—the ability to lose ourselves in our work or outside activity. The final leg is "the meaningful life," which means being involved with something bigger than ourselves (it may mean religion, or it may mean giving back or giving of ourselves to a cause or movement).

Seligman and his colleagues have discovered that the secret to happiness lies in small things. And these things are attainable by just about anyone who is willing to enjoy them. The key ones: being grateful for what we have; maintaining ties to our friends and family; giving to others. And when all the results of their surveys were consolidated, the number one conclusion they came to was ... Yep, you're right.

Money can't buy happiness.

But we all know that, don't we? Maybe. But as we shall see, our interviewees have some fascinating things to say on the matter of happiness. For example, visual artist Jacqueline Carroll has found a way to give back to others through her job, and as a result she feels exceptionally good about herself. Is that what true happiness is all about?

GOING AGAINST THE GRAIN

There's a saying on the lovely island of Barbados: "Rain is just liquid sunshine." When Senator Anne Cools left Barbados for Canada at the tender age of 13, she brought with her a personality full of warmth and sunshine. "I did well at school, I had many friends, but there was always a bit of a cultural divide," she remembers. "When I came to Montreal—this was back in the 1950s—my perspective was completely reshaped. In those days, Canadian society wasn't multicultural like it is today. Yes, there were plenty of Eastern and Western European immigrants, but very few people of colour. Everybody looked when I walked past."

"I got a taste of social reform from the many discussions heard at the dinner table, and to this day as a Senator, I fight for social justice and fairness for both sexes."

—THE HON. ANNE COOLS,
Senator

Although Anne was raised a Catholic because of her father, her mother was a Methodist who instilled in her the principles of duty and public service—the cornerstones of the Methodist Wesleyan tradition. Anne's education in Barbados was based on the finest British schools.

"There was an enormous emphasis on discipline and concentration and logic," she says. "I studied Latin, and read Shakespeare, Dickens, Robert Louis Stevenson and John Buchan (author of *The Thirty-nine Steps*). I actually made my first Canadian connection through reading John Buchan. Most people don't realize that Buchan was the pen name of Lord Tweedsmuir, who had been a Governor General of Canada."

Growing up in a family involved in the politics and social issues of Barbados had a major impact on her thinking and shaped much of her world view. The slogan, "One person, one vote," was on everyone's lips as universal suffrage finally came into being on the island. "My father was a pharmacist and my mother owned property. Before universal suffrage came in, only property owners could vote—which meant that

if you were a woman *or a man* without property, you were disenfran-
chised. I got a taste of social reform from the many discussions heard
at the dinner table, and to this day as a Senator, I fight for social justice and fairness for both sexes."

When Pierre Trudeau appointed Anne to the Senate in 1984, she
became the first black person ever appointed to that august body—
and she also became the first black female senator in North America.

Senator Cools has always gone against the grain. "I am a non-fem-
inist, I do not denigrate men and I do not denigrate parenting," she
says firmly. "I see men and women as equals who are on the same pil-
grimage or journey together. I see life through the lens of a woman
and as a Member of Parliament. To me, finding your own passion is
critical to success, whether success for you means being a great parent, a great hairdresser or a great statesman."

But Senator Cools has her feet planted squarely on the ground,
and a lot of that came from childhood experiences.

"I learned about sorrow early on in my life," she says. "There were
eight of us children, but two of my siblings died when I was very young.
I was only four years old, but I understood how painful and crippling
it was for my parents."

How does a person deal with life's setbacks? Anne tells me you must know yourself and the world because "life can be a pretty stern taskmaster." Anne was a social worker before she became a senator,

"To me, finding your own passion is critical to success, whether success for you means being a great parent, a great hairdresser or a great statesman."
—THE HON. ANNE COOLS,
Senator

and she ran shelters for abused women. What drew her to the field
was "my overwhelming sympathy for people who suffer. I learned
very early that the role of love in mending and healing human beings
was a very great one."

To the Honourable Senator Anne Cools, the simple pleasures are
life's deepest joys. "You want to see happy people?" she laughs. "Spend
forever cooking a Thanksgiving meal. Serve it with your finest crystal
and silverware, and then observe the appreciation, the give and take
of love at the dining room table."

PEOPLE NEED PEOPLE

Of all the findings in the field of happiness research, the most powerful one may be that most people feel happier when they're with other people.

Happiness experts like Martin Seligman and Mihaly Csikszentmihalyi (author of the book *Flow: The Psychology of Optimal Experience*) say that most of us are "people persons," and people persons need (you guessed it) people. However, there are other ways to be a people person even if you're an introvert, because introverts sometimes have to face the public if they want to be successful. Just ask Olympic gold medalist Kerrin Lee-Gartner.

A GUTSY YOUNG INTROVERT GOES FOR THE GOLD

Kerrin Lee-Gartner grew up competing in downhill skiing with the Rossland Red Mountain Racers Ski Academy in British Columbia. Her determination and natural ability allowed her to move quickly through the junior racing ranks. But her real competition had always been her sister.

"My older sister Kelli was my role model growing up," says Kerrin. "She was so active, energetic and totally fearless. I wanted to be like her and do the things she did. When she joined the Nancy Greene Ski League (I was too young to join then) I'd follow her training runs and even travel to races. When I started racing, sure I was motivated to beat her, but I really just wanted to be *my* best. I learned early on that if I tried to impress others, I always did worse."

Kerrin was chosen for the Canadian Women's Ski Team at age 16, but her hopes for a successful World Cup tour were dashed after a skiing accident in 1985. She underwent reconstructive surgery on her knee. In February 1989, another accident kept her off skis for six months, but again she came back.

She spent countless hours rehabilitating her body and soon returned to the top of the women's world ski rankings with a superb 1991–92 World Cup season.

"I had a dream the summer before the Olympics," Kerrin reveals. "I saw myself winning the Val D'Or (the gold medal) for Canada. I'd really got into a zone during the 1992 season by allowing my trust and my talent to coincide, and then executing. My confidence was at an all-time high."

And then it happened.

"The night before the race, I slept very peacefully without any dreams." The next day, in Albertville, France, Kerrin Lee-Gartner won Olympic Gold in the women's downhill.

But after Kerrin reached the pinnacle of her skiing career, she faced a wrenching transition. World-class athletes are asked to routinely speak spontaneously in front of the camera. That's okay for Kerrin, who sees TV interviews as "an audience of one," but it's a completely different story

"I think you need to go after what you love and do it. Don't be afraid to try new things, live every moment of life and your passion will grow from there."
—KERRIN LEE-GARTNER, Olympic gold medallist

when one becomes a celebrity on the speaker circuit. Now the stakes are raised. They are asked to give often lengthy, prepared speeches in front of hundreds of "live" people.

THE COURAGE TO SPEAK

"I was always a shy, quiet person, but I had a lot of determination," says Kerrin. "When I became a celebrity, the necessity to speak in public came along with it. I vividly remember the first time I was in front of an audience. I was terrified. But I forced myself to look inward and then, somehow, I found the courage to speak."

In answer to the question, how does a person find her passion in life, Kerrin has this to say, "We have a lot of choices in life. Some might say too many. I found my passion early in life. I grew up in Rossland and skied every weekend with my parents and my four siblings. I think you need to go after what you love and do it. Don't be afraid to try new things, live every moment of life and your passion will grow from there."

I find it interesting that Kerrin said our "passion will *grow*." Passion isn't a ready-made treasure chest that you're either lucky enough to find or you're not. It needs to be nurtured and developed and fed like a puppy or a beautiful but delicate flower. Passion seems to blossom when we work hard at something we love to do.

Former entrepreneur Julie Toskan-Casale knows exactly how Kerrin felt in front of all those people that night. After selling her company in 1997, she became a Toronto philanthropist at the tender age of 33.

"Although my first speaking engagement wasn't going to happen for two months, I was deeply afraid. In fact, I couldn't stop thinking about it. I practiced and prepared what I was going to say but I always wondered if it would be of any interest or value to my audience."

So what happened that fateful night? "When I finally got up and spoke, I actually loved it," she said. "I'm a people person. I made eye contact with the people in the audience before I spoke, and they actually seemed interested in me and what I was about to say. That energized me, and away I went!"

Although I myself have been speaking in public for many years, I remember when I gave my first speech in a public forum. I had a definite case of the jitters. I solved the problem by breathing deeply for several minutes, to the point where I was dangerously close to hyperventilating. But I got through it, so have countless others, and so can you.

When I asked Julie about finding her passion, her response was interesting. "When I was a teenager working as a cashier at No Frills, I wasn't thinking about finding my passion in life. I think passion finds you." She isn't the only one who feels this way. When Danielle Iversen was a young girl, she was told she was a natural born publicist. And guess what? That's exactly what she is today. More on Julie's and Danielle's stories later. Right now I'd like you to meet a small-town girl who has learned that you have to be willing to be wrong if you're going to succeed in life.

FROM SMALL TOWN GIRL TO BIG CITY SURGEON

Toronto surgeon Nancy Baxter knows first-hand that geography can thwart ambition. She grew up in small-town Ontario, and while it had its attractions, it was a rather small stage for an insatiably curious mind like hers.

"There weren't a lot of role models, but I remember as a teenager I was kind of hooked on watching *St. Elsewhere* on TV," she says. "I think that it piqued an early interest in medicine, and the urban setting and excitement helped spur me to leave town so I could pursue my dream of being a doctor."

Life doesn't move in a straight line, however. When Nancy graduated from University of Toronto (U. of T.) medical school, she did her internship and residency in Toronto. But she remembers a period of failure and frustration that happened long before

"I learned a lot from the early ups and downs in my life."

—DR. NANCY BAXTER, Surgeon

she found ultimate success as a specialist/researcher and colorectal surgeon at U. of T./St. Michael's Hospital.

"After finishing my general surgery residency, I couldn't get the fellowship I wanted in the specialty I coveted at the time—surgical oncology," she explains. "I was bitterly disappointed and I remember crying on the streetcar. I felt just awful, and for at least a month I would wake up thoroughly depressed about everything."

But Nancy was keenly aware that failure is part of the scientific process. "Eventually I regrouped and did a fellowship in a different specialty—colorectal surgery—at the Mayo Clinic," she says.

Unfortunately, she couldn't get a job anywhere in Canada so she went back to the United States, found a job in Minneapolis and worked there for four years. With a sparkling new resume in hand, plus some sage advice from mentors she'd connected with south of the border, opportunities opened up back in Canada. She took advantage and returned to her Ontario roots—but this time at a much bigger venue, the city of Toronto.

"I learned a lot from the early ups and downs in my life," Nancy admits. "After all, you have to be willing to be wrong

"You have to decide what you're going to do and be great at it."

—DR. NANCY BAXTER, Surgeon

as well as right if you're to learn from the trial and error process of proving a hypothesis. It's not much different with your life, so I guess you could say I'm a realist. As far as finding your passion, I don't know if there's some sort of epiphany. I personally searched for a long time while I was in medical school until I found out what turned me on, what truly fit."

Nancy believes focus (along with intensity) is the key to career success. "You have to decide what you're going to do and be great at it." As a successful surgeon, she's already proven herself in a man's world. "Fighting for the underdog gets me jazzed." She helped overturn a government policy proposal in 1998 that would have imposed school tuition on medical residents. At the time, residents routinely put in eighty to one hundred hours or more per week with no compensation for overtime. This small-town girl seems to have found her passion after all.

WHAT REALLY MAKES US HAPPY

Visual artist Jacqueline Carroll has a lot of friends, but what lights the fire inside her heart comes through a combination of meditation and creativity, and through helping to empower others to find joy in what they're doing. Jackie is a successful artist, teacher and writer. Her original images in oil, pastel and watercolour can be found in many private art collections.

She believes real happiness—not the false, temporary kind—comes from within. "Most people know if they're happy on the inside," she says. "If they're not, hopefully they take the steps to alleviate their situation. I know it's been heard a lot lately, but it's true: happiness is living mindfully in the present. The journey is far more important than arriving at the destination."

I'm learning from these amazing women that passion, happiness and success are intertwined, weaved together like the strands in a piece of rope.

"How would you define passion?" I ask.

"Passion is being true to yourself," says Jackie. "Having it lights the inner fire so that you reflect outwardly what is true about you. It's your truth."

"What about success, how would you define that?" I ask.

She pauses for a moment.

"Success is being true to yourself and helping others be true to themselves. I believe if we're living our truth we can work beyond our physical limits. There's never any sacrifice if you've found your passion and are in alignment with the inner stirrings of your heart. To me, this is success. In my case, it is helping others tap into their authentic self."

As I noted earlier, the happiness experts say that giving makes you feel good about yourself. And Jackie has framed her job in just those terms, of giving and "helping others be true to themselves." How did she come to this place in her life?

"From a very early age, I was aware that whenever I was creating, be it painting or drawing, I experienced a sense of completion, an inner contentment," Jackie says. "I found, too, whenever I visited art galleries, I knew that I had an inner calling to create. However, when I graduated from high school I was encouraged to go into a profession that offered more financial stability and ended up in the teaching profession. I regretted this decision until I started to paint again and then, in later years, teach what I believe in wholeheartedly, teaching art as a meditation."

> "Success is being true to yourself and helping others be true to themselves. I believe if we're living our truth we can work beyond our physical limits."
>
> —JACQUELINE CARROLL, Visual Artist and Author

"Do artists have a special talent, a genius that us mere mortals can never understand?" I ask.

Jackie doesn't look at creativity that way, as being exclusive. "Most athletes, musicians and other artists have learned there is 'magic' produced when you let go. You can't force it, but you can create the conditions that allow flow to take place. I believe there's a flame in everyone's heart, but igniting it depends on your environment, on how carefully you listen to the voice within, and on your values and your intuition."

Jackie has already written one book, *Muskoka Boathouses*, which features forty of her original pastel paintings and a written history of each subject. She's currently writing a book on the power of personal discovery through the creative process and meditative techniques.

"I believe everyone is creative, but your creativity has to be nurtured," she explains. "I developed The Creative Heart art classes because I look at art as a meditation. Through the freeing power of meditation my students reveal and realize their creative gifts and abilities. It gives me tremendous joy when my students begin to see and feel the magic inside them."

A LAID-BACK GO-GETTER

You won't ever persuade Pastoral Minister Linda Wheler that being positive is a bad thing. A self-described "laid-back go-getter," Linda has a 24/7 job as a pastoral minister that involves visiting and comforting the sick and dying.

"I'm an optimistic idealist," Linda tells me. "I think I always have been, ever since I could remember. My father was my role model. He was a tool designer and he took great pride in his job; he was always grateful, and he looked forward to work. He was also a very faithful Christian. He and I were the only ones in the family who would go to church on Sunday. My searching led me at first toward the study of early childhood education. Then I determined it wasn't my field, I got married, had my first child and went back to university. I had two more children while studying yet continued to seek my passion. Now I have it all, including three lovely children (23, 20 and 17)."

Linda is a loved and respected United Church minister, serving a large congregation in Toronto's west end. She seems to have always "had her act together," yet when I asked her how she found her passion, Linda said this: "I think I was constantly looking for my passion, ever since I was a teenager. In my twenties, I got married and had my first child. I worked at Consumer's Gas in accounts receivable, but I really wanted to be at home with the children. My husband and I found it rough in the beginning. Every time he got a raise, I would cut back on my hours so I could be with the children. I took a bank teller job, then worked in a hospital, then drove a school bus. That job allowed me the flexibility to stay at home with the children. But as a result, our lifestyle never changed for the better."

"I'm an optimistic idealist. I think I always have been, ever since I could remember."
—LINDA WHELER, Pastoral Minister

When she was in her late twenties, she broke her ankle and had to stay at home. Linda read *The Road Less Traveled* by Scott Peck. "The first line of his book—'Life is difficult'—hit me like a ton of bricks. Those words were a huge relief because it made me realize I was not alone. That's when I started to do a lot of soul searching."

In her thirties Linda had her third and last child.

"By now I had developed a real sense of needing more in my life," she reveals. "I had a recurring dream that I was standing, talking to a group of people from a pulpit. A minister at the church suggested it was a calling to the ministry—I tested it out by taking an interview at the Centre for Christian Studies. Then my husband lost his job. It made me question whether I should still be doing this—being a school bus driver."

Linda had a lot of help in ultimately reaching her decision.

"The Minister at the church I was attending encouraged me to believe in myself and my leadership skills," Linda explains. "She really helped me to grow and to understand my strengths more clearly. I ended up getting my Masters of Divinity. Fortunately, my boss gave me one day a week off to attend Emmanuel College. A teaching assistant at the school, David Zub, encouraged me to keep on going to school. So there I was, a school bus driver, a divinity student and a full-time mom."

Linda is a tenacious woman, and her story of courage and quiet determination is genuinely inspiring. She is one happy and fulfilled woman. So what's her advice to women who can't seem to find their passion?

"Keep trying until you find it!"

Linda works hard at what she does because she loves her work. She has found inner peace. Having found her passion, the need to find something more in her life has evaporated.

THE HIGH FROM WINNING THE LOTTERY DOESN'T LAST

According to a January 3, 2006, BBC report entitled "Why Hard Work Makes People Happy," the world is full of temporary happiness, but the lasting kind is harder to find. Researchers from Gothenburg University in Sweden studied masses of published data on what makes people happy and concluded that while winning the lottery or achieving a goal at work might give people a temporary high, it didn't last. Ultimately, working hard to achieve a goal (rather than actually attaining it) made people more satisfied and fulfilled.

For those of us who are not fortunate enough to be geniuses, persistence seems to be a secret weapon for success. Not all of us persist, however. Even though most of us strive to be happy, not nearly as many of us are willing to put in the work that is often required to be happy in our jobs and our relationships. Many of us prefer to spend our time worrying about things, especially things we can't control.

Worrying just makes a bad thing worse. We should be *concerned* about our careers and our family and our retirement plans—but worried? That's a more negative word, something we should reserve for graver things, like for example, worrying whether a critically-ill friend is going to die or not. "Don't worry, be happy," is sage advice for those of us whose greatest obstacle is ourselves.

Psychologist Richard Wiseman also believes lucky people create much of their own luck by noticing chance opportunities that others miss. On his website (www.psy.herts.ac.uk/wiseman) he says that people create self-fulfilling prophesies via positive expectations. Wiseman carried out a simple experiment to see if this was true. This is what he discovered.

"I gave both lucky and unlucky people a newspaper, and asked them to look through it and tell me how many photographs were inside. I had secretly placed a large message halfway through the newspaper saying: 'Tell the experimenter you have seen this and win £250.' This message took up half of the page and was written in type that was more than two inches high. It was staring everyone straight in the face, but the unlucky people tended to miss it and the lucky people tended to spot it."

In our own lives, we can choose to think and react negatively, neutrally or positively about the events that happen to us. If you read any of the literature in the burgeoning field of cognitive therapy, you'll soon discover that our thoughts affect the way we perceive the world and the way the world reacts to and perceives us.

WHAT DO YOU REALLY LOVE DOING?

If you think back to your childhood and teenage years, what did you love to do? Play games? Of course. Read? Perhaps. What were you good at? Organizing things? Speaking? Acting? Were you good with your hands?

Finding your talent or skill is an important endeavour. But it's a tricky one. How much of your talent was talent and how much of it derived from parental encouragement, how much was situational and how much was pure enjoyment?

What do you love to do now, whether you're paid anything or not? That is usually called a hobby. But who's to say you can't turn a hobby into a career? Who's to say that work shouldn't be play, and play be work? But remember, I'm a realist. Many people I know have been passionate about hobbies they couldn't turn into workable careers. Ask yourself: Can I find a way to actually make a living from my passion? And if I can, should I? Is the timing right? For some, it won't be. What if you're a 38-year-old single mother of two with a mortgage, for example? Can you afford to make that move if it means retraining yourself and going with a cut in income for a year or two? Remember to always be realistic.

WHAT ABOUT THESE THINGS CALLED VALUES?

These days, everyone seems to be talking about finding their passion, but why is it that so many of us never find it? Is it really that elusive? Is it in such limited supply that what little there was has already been snapped up by the fortunate few? Maybe, just maybe, we're looking for it in the wrong place.

The pace of life keeps accelerating and technology keeps pushing us toward that great ideal of über-productivity. So on and on we go. But sometimes—maybe lots of times—we just don't want to go there! Those are the times when we take stock of our lives, see where we come up short and resolve mightily to do something about it. We begin to tackle new tasks, think new thoughts and make new plans, and maybe something good happens for a while.

But then we backslide, we regain our senses and get back to the daily grind, never the worse for wear, never feeling we've sacrificed much.

Or have we?

Most women are loathe to sacrifice them, but sometimes they do. They're our *values*. And the more women I interviewed, the more I heard that values come first. If our values are aligned with our life and our work, then our passion will be allowed to bloom. The Code of Ethics of the College and Association of Registered Nurses of Alberta (CARNA) defines a value as "a belief or attitude about the importance of a goal, an object, a principle or a behaviour... that is desirable in itself and not simply as a means to get something else." Values, therefore, are the standards we uphold, the codes we live by. And if your job isn't aligned with them, it's going to be very hard for you to be happy. That's why we can't talk about passion without also talking about values.

I said at the beginning of the chapter that passion is one of the two driving forces to getting and staying real. Values are the other. Passion is the fire we bring to the things we do because we just love doing them. *But values are the fuel that makes the fire possible.* Put them together and everything just "fits."

CHANGE REQUIRES COURAGE

Sometimes things happen that dramatically shift your thinking or even shift the direction of your life. Sometimes events result in you making the change yourself. It takes courage to make a major change. I call them turning points. A screenwriter friend of mine told me that in film stories, there are usually two or three pivotal moments that swing the story in another direction. In our lives, these events shift our experience level, change our attitude and in some cases change our life course. They seem to happen as quickly as a shift in the wind on an open sea.

In reality, they happen much slower, often over weeks and months. And because turning points are often such life-changing events, because they are so momentous, so upsetting at times, the feelings that we have around these events accelerate and deepen the experience, almost out of proportion to their reality. Notice I said "almost." That's because turning points happen so rarely in our lives that their authenticity goes unquestioned. And rightly so, by the way.

I asked the women in this book what were the two biggest turning points in their lives—outside of getting married and having children. They were all different, naturally, but a constant response was that you must be open to change.

Julie Toskan-Casale, co-founder of a great Canadian success story, M.A.C. Cosmetics, says her life changed dramatically when she and her business partners sold the company eight years ago. "M.A.C. was a family business with family values, and when the Estée Lauder Group bought us out, they brought in a completely different value structure." Although she knew they were a public company with different constituencies and objectives to follow, she still found it unnerving to "watch our baby" get restructured for presentation to a strange new corporate world. The sale of the business left her wealthy but rudderless.

"I still had fairly young children to look after, but I kept wondering, '*What am I going to do with myself?*'" she reveals to me. "When we were running M.A.C., we developed the M.A.C. AIDS Fund to create awareness for AIDS victims. We gave all the money from sales of one of our lipsticks to local AIDS organizations. Years later, we thought, 'How about starting a foundation? But who will we give money to?' There were so many worthy causes, but a decision had to be made. And that decision led to the second turning point in my life."

> "*I've always wanted to make a difference in this world, but the issues seemed so big I began to wonder if I really could do anything to help.*"
> —JULIE TOSKAN-CASALE, Founder of M.A.C. Cosmetics

Julie became the first Canadian to enrol in the Rockefeller Foundation's Philanthropy Workshop. Part of the program entailed a visit to Buenos Aries, Argentina, and when she was led to the shantytowns just outside the city, for the first time in her life she felt overwhelmed.

"The children were drinking rainwater, they had no shoes," she says. "It was worse than anything I'd ever seen on TV. I've always wanted to make a difference in this world, but the issues seemed so big I began to wonder if I really could do anything to help."

It took another six months before she could completely come to grips with the issue. She and her husband decided to create an initiative targeted at Canada's youth—the Youth and Philanthropy Initiative (YPI). In her mind, YPI would give youth the opportunity to make their own choices about where YPI's philanthropic dollars should go. With choice comes responsibility, and that was a good thing for kids who might have squandered their energy on other, less constructive endeavours.

"We're encouraging young people to become active agents of positive change through education and practical experience. YPI students learn the fundamentals of philanthropy and how charitable organizations should function with respect to finances, ethics and accountability. Most importantly, student participants of the course are required to research and identify a charity in their community which, based on research and analysis, is in need of funding. The students are then required to present their findings to a school-appointed judging panel, and based on the most compelling case, a charity is awarded $5,000 by our foundation (the Toskan-Casale Foundation)."

WHERE DO VALUES COME FROM?

Julie's desire to give back to the community illuminates one of her most cherished values: integrity. Values are as varied and complex as the people we know and meet throughout our lives. Values can include honesty, commitment, dependability, creative excellence, thoroughness, harmony, team-building, initiative, interpersonal needs, building a sense of vision, loyalty, caring, compassion, empathy . . . The list is almost endless. Values can be shaped or picked up from parents and other family members, books by and about famous men and women, colleagues and role models at work, friends, sports heroes, in fact just about anywhere—including yourself. But values have to be internalized and developed over time so they become a part of who you are. And then they have to be carefully guarded so they will not be compromised by external conflicts and pressures.

Each of us has a value system, but values can sometimes get mixed up with goals. For example, if we want to achieve a comfortable life or have freedom, that is really a goal. On the other hand, honesty, integrity, loyalty and compassion are values.

But where do our values come from? That is a difficult question to answer, and even the sociologists and social psychologists are not in complete agreement. I like what Julie Toskan-Casale has to say on the subject. She believes values are a combination of nature, nurture and experience. "I think we are born with a base," she says. "And then our parents and our family add layers. Then, as we go out on our own, our life experiences and relationships either reinforce or re-mould them."

AN EXTROVERTED WALLFLOWER

As a child, Sarah Raiss, Executive Vice President at TransCanada Corporation, had so much energy her father used to call her "Sarah McBoing-Boing-Jump-Jump Raiss." She was always on the go then, and she hasn't stopped since. Her early role models were her father and mother. Her businessman father was a very intelligent, logical thinker and an intense communicator who was highly focused on his career and always gave to the community. In contrast, it was her mother's sunny personality and energy that gained her the respect and love of her community through the not-for-profit organizations she led.

Believe it or not, Sarah used to be a wallflower. An *extroverted* wallflower, to be precise. How is that possible? As she tells it, she always wanted to be with people but there was a disconnect in her life because she was so heavy. She called herself one of those "very likeable extremely chubby kids who was always eating sweets." As we'll see in the chapter on fitness, as an adult, Sarah was to find a much more healthy lifestyle and a brand new self-image.

While Sarah's schooling in Applied Math followed later by an MBA was of enormous importance as she worked her way up the ranks in a telecommunications

> "Over the years, the feedback I've received from my colleagues and friends and family has been invaluable. It helped me identify my strengths and confirmed my own gut feelings."
>
> —SARAH RAISS, Executive Vice President of TransCanada Corporation

company, her values ultimately made the difference. They helped her find the courage to make the biggest decision of her life as she switched gears from the technical side into Human Resources (HR).

"Over the years, the feedback I've received from my colleagues and friends and family has been invaluable," Sarah explains to me. "It helped me identify my strengths and confirmed my own gut feelings. I always knew I was a people person. Despite this, I often found myself guided to more technical positions because of my background."

Nevertheless, Sarah always knew her goals and her values. And eventually, they won out.

"It took courage to make the change," she says. "But I've wanted to be an executive so I could have influence on people, to give back to the community, to help others. Although I'd wanted to get into HR for some time, it was considered a dead zone for many years. Frankly, I was discouraged from thinking about it too seriously. Then, while I was living in Chicago and working at Ameritech and at my own consulting firm doing merger integration work, I was offered a fabulous job in Calgary as Executive Vice President of Corporate Services (which included HR responsibility). I knew and loved Calgary because my parents often took us through the city and Banff and Jasper for vacations when I was a kid. I jumped at the opportunity to leave engineering, operations, marketing and strategy—this was about seven years ago—and I've never been happier. To make things even sweeter, I met my husband because of the move."

Sarah has found her passion and is fulfilling her potential. But for many of us the pressure to conform is immense, and the drive to keep up with the Joneses affects us more than we let on. Sarah's advice is direct and unequivocal: "It does take courage to follow your passion. Don't pursue it if you don't have the courage."

How can someone find the courage if they're really stuck?

"Pay attention to feedback from others," Sarah says. "Get support from your friends and family. Find your strengths. Learn what your true obstacles are. Often it comes down to money. If income issues are enough to prevent you from following your passion, either recognize and accept them, or find a way to overcome them."

Values come from our families, and our genes. They come from our role models and our friends and the mentors we seek out. They develop and change through experience. But one place values don't come from is a messy household or a dysfunctional working environment. They don't come pre-packaged from your television or radio or magazines. They're developed and nurtured inside of us, and over time they're allowed the freedom to grow and flourish. Or not.

"THE PLUCKY LITTLE OPTIMIST"

Brenda Eaton knows all about the power of values. Since she was a child, she's been fascinated by the big issues that affect people on a massive social scale. She found her passion a long time ago when she was a little girl and participated in frequent family dinner discussions with her firefighter father—discussions which were often about public policy issues. They fuelled her ambition to make a difference someday—in fact, under Brenda's high school yearbook photo are these words: "I want to be premier of the province."

Today, Brenda is the Chair of the B.C. Housing Commission with province-wide social responsibilities, and the power and the budget to get things done.

"I think a lot of what shaped me were the expectations of my parents," she says. "They encouraged me (and my siblings) to be anything we wanted to be. Initially, I didn't have any career aspirations, but I was always interested in public policy. My father was a firefighter, but at some point when I was growing up he decided to pursue a degree in economics and political science. I guess that really got me interested."

Brenda acknowledges she's found her passion, and then some. She was fortunate enough to be given the chance to create her own job when soon-to-be-Premier Gordon Campbell recruited her and asked her what her biggest interest might be.

"I told him I wanted to take a look at the role of government in society, to find a way to prioritize limited resources and become a kind of strategic planner," she explains. "He agreed, and I later became his deputy minister. I've been in public service a long time and I've never lost my enthusiasm. In government circles, I'm known as that 'plucky little optimist.' I kind of like the term."

As a child I was a good student—very skilled at math and literature—and I think my teachers were also role models for me, especially in high school. I was interested in the way they taught. I can still remember some of their names. My Grade 10 teacher was Paul Smith, in computer science it was Sheila Cardon, and my homeroom teacher was Cory Reagan. By the way, my apologies to them if I've misspelled any of their names.

Although based in Victoria, B.C., Brenda travels extensively to Vancouver and the mainland. She sits on the boards of B.C. Hydro, Canada West Foundation and Phillips, Hager and North Centre for Financial Research. Finding a balance between work and home life is not always easy, but Brenda is tremendously focused, and her husband Brent is very supportive.

> *"I believe the key for any leader is to have a clear sense of direction."*
> —BRENDA EATON, Chair of the B.C. Housing Commission

"I believe focus is the number one secret to success," she reveals. "I like to put my heart and soul into all my projects. My true north keeps me focused and I always keep an eye on the big ball, not the small obstacles and barriers. I believe the key for any leader is to have a clear sense of direction."

Not only is Brenda a leader, she's also a mentor and role model to many young women in the public service. As we'll see in Chapter 3, women mentors are in short supply.

A LIVING DEFINITION OF SUCCESS

Sarah Thomson, Publisher of *The Women's Post*, found her passion a long time ago. She wanted to be a writer from the time her father "forced" her to write letters as a little girl. Whenever she and her twin brother had a fight, her father would make them go to their room and write a letter to each other. Over time, the exercise fostered a skill and a passion that Sarah has never lost.

"My father was a real role model for me," she explains. "He was an artist, a philosopher and an architect. He believed in giving back to the world. People came to him for advice and—like Socrates—he never forced his opinions on them, but led them to their own conclusions. My father was also very strong-willed. As a teenager, I rebelled against him because we were so much alike. But as I grew older we became close. Sadly, he passed away on September 14, 1999. He was the one who taught me that the answers are within. He's still my role model, and always will be."

Strong-willed though she was, the push that eventually led Sarah to running her own newspaper came in a highly serendipitous manner.

"I dropped out of high school, truth be told," she admits. "I was bored with school. I travelled around North America, but I just couldn't find myself. So I came back home and pumped gas, full-time. I was 17. When I was 18, I purchased my own gas station through a line of credit that my aunt signed. I owned three stations by the time I was 20. Oil and gas is a male-dominated industry, so I know what it's like to be a woman in a man's world."

At 26, Sarah decided to sell the businesses and run for alderman in the Hamilton region. At the time, she had fifty employees. The lone paper, the *Hamilton Spectator*, ran an article that misquoted her. She was furious, and it made her realize that Hamilton needed two newspapers. At age 28, she set up and ran the *Hamilton Examiner*.

"It was a huge learning experience," she says. "I learned layouts, distribution, editing, writing, selling ads, the works. I hired people by feel, based mainly on my experience with employees when I ran the gas stations."

After five years at the helm, she was bought out. Then, in 2003, Sarah became the first and only female publisher of a national newspaper in Canada when she started *The Women's Post*. But her goal was not to create a paper dedicated solely to women's issues.

She wanted to counterbalance what she calls the "gender-biased communication" that is so prevalent in many newspapers.

"I believe the traditional just-the-facts style of reporting is outdated and lacks the emotional pull and intimate narrative that women connect with," she states.

"I know what it's like to be a woman in a man's world."

—SARAH THOMSON, Publisher of *The Women's Post*

Sarah is quick to point out that *The Women's Post* is "the only newspaper that teaches our writers (both male and female) to communicate in a style of writing that women prefer. Our goal is to provoke an emotion, to give more description and context, and to provide the best judgment we can on global, national and local issues."

What is she up to now, you ask?

"I'm working on a bunch of new ventures that tie into the newspaper, including a women's economy summit for CEOs and an awards event for businesswomen. I spend a lot of my days meeting CEOs and discussing what their needs are, and I'm enjoying every minute," she reveals.

Anybody with that kind of focus and determination and vision is destined for success. And with a supportive husband and two young kids, Sarah is truly happy. She's making a difference, and she's become a role model for an entirely new generation of aspiring Canadian women. In short, she is the very definition of success.

We all aspire to be successful, but just what that means is very personal for each of us. If you haven't found your passion in life, perhaps the marvellous women appearing within these pages will inspire you to find it. And if you've already found your passion, kudos to you! This book is not only about finding your passion, it's about *focusing* it and *sustaining* it once you have it. So relax. If you haven't yet found your passion, please remember something. It's never too late to find it.

TWO

GET REAL
ABOUT YOUR
RELATIONSHIPS

HMM. . . . RELATIONSHIPS. What a powerful, mystical, highly loaded word, especially if you're a woman. Relationships draw us in like a warm, calm, inviting sea. If they're healthy, we float as if on air. If they're troubled, the sea grows turbulent and drags at us like an anchor. The nineteenth-century orator Henry Ward Beecher believed that love grows sweeter with age: "Young love is a flame; very pretty, often very hot and fierce, but still only light and flickering. The love of the older and disciplined heart is as coals, deep-burning, unquenchable."

I think the same could be said about the connective strength of short-term versus long-term relationships. Long-term relationships have a solid foundation that is deep and difficult to break. Relationships, to me, are the foundation of who I am. Whether they're with my husband, my children, my colleagues or friends and family, every good relationship is different, yet it feels the same. It's about giving of yourself to others. It's not about what's in it for you.

According to an article for Yahoo personals written by Professor David Niven of Florida Atlantic University, author of *The 100 Simple*

Secrets of Great Relationships, a volume in his 100 Simple Secrets series, "Traits we otherwise think of as very important, such as our age, income, and education level are completely unrelated to the likelihood of finding a satisfying relationship."

So what *does* matter, then? What's the secret to a great relationship? Different women have different beliefs regarding what makes a "great" relationship, but many of my interviewees say respect is a key starting point.

IT TAKES TIME AND EFFORT TO MAKE IT WORK

As a Pastoral Minister, Linda Wheler is also a spiritual advisor and professional caregiver. Many years ago, when she decided to specialize in the caring side of the ministry, she developed a friendship with one of her mentors, David Zub.

"He was my teaching assistant, and we also sat on several committees and attended group sessions together," she explains. "We both lived north of Toronto and we even commuted downtown together. He was a very learned theologian and a good man, and I got to know him and trust him personally and professionally. I started to rely on him as a confidant, and we developed a relationship of great respect. After my mentoring period concluded, we continued to phone each other. We both knew what we said would be held in strictest confidence. He saw me as a great listener and encourager, and I saw him as a gifted teacher, theologian and friend. But it takes time and effort to build a strong relationship—it's an investment by both parties."

SAY WHAT YOU MEAN AND MEAN WHAT YOU SAY

Registered Nutritionist, Certified Personal Trainer and Life Coach Lauren Jawno says being able to have fun and laugh together is very important. But there's something else more important in the long run. "In the long term, mutual respect and trust play a bigger role. It's important to say what you mean and mean what you say. People treat us the way we treat ourselves—we attract what we reflect. If we don't respect ourselves we'll attract people who won't respect us. We create the situations and relationships we have in our lives—they don't just randomly appear. Many people don't want to hear this because it means they'll have to take responsibility for their lives."

Lauren brings a fresh perspective to life in Canada because she's an immigrant.

"When I left South Africa thirteen years ago I was an elementary-school teacher and sports coach," she reveals. "South Africa is a beautiful country, but I just felt there were so many more opportunities for me here. The violence was also an enormous factor." Making the move would require a lot of courage, because when she arrived in Canada she didn't have a job and she didn't know anyone!

"People treat us the way we treat ourselves—we attract what we reflect."
—LAUREN JAWNO, Speaker, Coach, Trainer, Consultant and President of Personal Health

"Fortunately, I was connected with cousins in Toronto that I didn't even know about. They have been amazing to me. I initially took a job at a physiotherapy clinic. Because of my background as an athlete and my passion for sport, after three years I decided to make health and fitness a career. I went back to school while working at a fitness club. Once I had all my designations and qualifications, I started my own health and fitness company, Personal Health. That was ten years ago."

Lauren has experienced many challenges, the hardest being the passing of her mother in South Africa from breast cancer five years ago.

"Over a period of about six years I would go back home two or three times a year so I could spend time with my mom," she explains. "Sadly, it was only after she was gone that I truly understood what an incredible role model she was. She was a spiritual person, always in a good mood, always positive, kind and humble. She never ever complained, even when she was at her sickest. Interestingly, my relationship with her grew the most after I emigrated. She helped me become a more patient, understanding and accepting person. Every day, I'm grateful for the legacy that she has left me."

Artist and teacher Jackie Carroll sees the ideal relationship as a balance: "To me, an ideal relationship is when the people in the partnership have a healthy degree of self-love and self-respect. Both are confident and happy within and share the same values. Both are able to reflect back to the other person who they truly are and affirm what they want in life. In an ideal relationship, each person is present to empower the other toward enlightenment."

ys she's had the good fortune to attract relationships into ...re real, because the people are real.

...re very special friends, and it's quite an exciting stage in my life," she says. "But as I've grown older, I've also become very comfortable in my own skin. I'm not self-critical any longer. My whole approach now is to just step aside, so to speak,—in other words, just get out of my own way. For example, as an artist you cannot create if you're entangled with negativity and self-criticism."

> *"In an ideal relationship, each person is present to empower the other towards enlightenment."*
> —JACQUELINE CARROLL, Visual Artist and Author

Nancy Baxter thinks empathy makes a big difference to the quality of our relationships.

"We all want to feel we are understood, and the empathetic listener has real advantages because of this," she reveals. "People like to talk to people they feel are listening. Women tend to be empathetic listeners, which is good. But I think in relationships we can go too far. Sometimes it needs to be about you, it can't always be about the other person."

> *"I think everyone needs to be validated. It's part of what makes relationships so necessary in our lives."*
> —DR. NANCY BAXTER, Surgeon

Nancy knows herself well. She will never be a doormat in any relationship.

"I'm a confident person—it takes a lot to get me down about myself," she says. "I know what my abilities are, and expect to achieve in the areas where I know I am skilled. It enables me to focus, and eliminates destructive self-doubt. Having said that, I don't expect to be perfect—I don't make those kinds of demands on other people so I don't make them on myself."

Nancy believes good relationships are also validating experiences. Validation is defined as the communication of respect for one's partner and acknowledgement that the other's opinions are legitimate. "I think everyone needs to be validated," she says. "It's part of what makes relationships so necessary in our lives."

University of Victoria Professor F. Ishu Ishiyama wrote an interesting article on this point in 1993, in the Athabasca

University–supported *Trumpeter Journal*. In the article, entitled "On Self-Validation," Ishiyama wrote, "Life is a process of self-validation . . . Being criticized or ignored is one of the most self-invalidating experiences, since our life revolves around social relationships and self-concept."

I agree, but I think there are times when we need to validate ourselves *outside* our relationships and our careers. Sometimes, at crucial points in our lives, we have to stop and take stock of ourselves. We need to face the music and do some deep soul-searching. And as adults, we have to do it alone. When those times come, input from others is crucial, but ultimately, only *we* can make our choices in life.

What about destructive relationships and activities? How do we avoid these negative, corrosive and ultimately energy-draining situations? Ishiyama says our lifestyle choices are key: "It is important for us to develop a well-rounded lifestyle for validating our self-worth and meaningful personal existence without solely relying on one kind of activity or on a relationship with one significant person as the only available sanctuary for emotional and spiritual safety."

Former fighter pilot Dee Brasseur agrees that mutual respect is critical.

"People in healthy relationships understand there's a process," she says. "They know what respecting one's 'self' really means and how to do it. It may seem obvious but if you don't know yourself and respect your 'self,' then who will? Perhaps most important, if you don't know how to respect yourself, how will you know when someone else is not respecting you?"

> *"If you don't know how to respect yourself, how will you know when someone else is not respecting you?"*
> —DEE BRASSEUR, the world's first female fighter pilot

Good question. Many of us have known people in abusive relationships, for example, and it is always surprising how long they last. It truly *is* about self-respect, and self-respect begins with self-knowledge.

IT'S A LIVING THING

Senator Anne Cools believes that great relationships must begin with mutual affection and caring.

"Long-term relationships are work," she says. "Both parties must be willing to self-reflect. Love and industry are essential in relationships, as they are for most things in life. A relationship is a living thing that needs constant care. I did much counselling of couples, and to me the key is what I call 'love-work.' If an argument happens, avoid the he-said/she-said route. You need to create willful action. Go to the other person. Give them a gift and apologize. Take full responsibility."

> *"Long-term relationships are work. Both parties must be willing to self-reflect."*
> —THE HON. ANNE COOLS, Senator

WE SELDOM COMMUNICATE WITH WORDS

Dee Brasseur believes many people think they are listening empathically but in reality are not. "When we listen and hear the words that another is speaking—what is really being said or what we understand from our listening is likely a fair distance from what is actually intended. According to practitioners of neuro-linguistic programming, our words represent only 7 percent of our communication."

So what comprises the other 93 percent?

Dee says, "The tone of our speech forms 38 percent of the process. And physiology—body language—constitutes the remaining 55 percent. In other words, 93 percent of the communication process is out of most people's conscious awareness when they attempt to listen empathically."

No wonder people are misunderstood so often.

> *"Empathy is critical to developing great relationships."*
> —DEE BRASSEUR, the world's first female fighter pilot

"A great relationship is a dance between two individuals developing and discovering rapport skills," says Dee. She believes relationship skills like empathy must be learned. "I think that empathy is critical to developing great relationships. How and when to use empathy, and the ability to turn it on and turn it off as required is a direct result of mastering the skills required in establishing exquisite rapport. A great relationship is a dance between two individuals developing and discovering rapport skills."

According to Producer and Director Joan Kelley-Weisshaar, "If you want to get to know someone, you need to really *be* interested, not just pretend to be. You won't learn anything if you don't listen and pay attention."

Growing up in a farm community in Saskatchewan, Joan's parents were uncomplicated people with solid core values. They taught her to be respectful of others from an early age. She says that keen listening skills and paying attention to details make the difference between developing good and great relationships.

"It's very respectful to care about what someone is sharing with you," she says. "Eye contact is important. You learn a great deal more by listening and asking questions than by talking."

Wilcox, Saskatchewan (population: 200), was a good place for a bright and ambitious young girl like Joan to be from. Athol Murray College of Notre Dame—the high school she attended—inculcated a strong value system and an independent streak into both the boys and the girls. "The school taught us to strive and work hard. They created an environment where you could dream big, whether you were a girl or a boy. I remember the school motto was 'Struggle and Emerge.'"

Interestingly, the school's high academic standards were matched by a strong devotion to the Notre Dame Hounds hockey team—a team which counts NHL stars Vincent Lecavalier and Brad Richards as alumni.

Along with respect, she learned something else about interacting with people: "I believe self-respect is a crucial element in healthy relationships. If you treat yourself and others with love and gentleness, relationships will just naturally be much easier. Others will treat you as you treat them. The Golden Rule definitely applies."

> "Self-respect is a crucial element in healthy relationships."
> —JOAN KELLEY-WEISSHAAR, TV Producer and Director, Founder of Hero Media

She says self-respect involves "being realistic and honest about one's self, and realizing and accepting one's weaknesses." It also means celebrating strengths in a comfortable way, not in a show-off way. "It should be the same kind of respect that you give to others, kind and supportive."

When she graduated from high school, Joan travelled to Toronto and went to Glendon College part-time to study art. She had no clue what she wanted to do, but she knew a career wasn't going to happen in Wilcox. She found a "little room in the Annex" (a midtown Toronto neighbourhood) that cost her $200 a month, got a waitressing job, and did some modelling and promotional work. "I figured I would just keep busy until I figured out what I wanted to do." She got into radio and TV in her twenties and became a makeup artist and spokesperson.

"The first person I ever made up was Pierre Berton," she says proudly. "I guess I had a knack for the business, but I worked hard and I had a bit of luck, too. Robin Periana, who was a Director of Photography at the time, gave me a huge break. He taught me how to do time code notes that are used for script continuity, so I learned that side of the business as well. As a result, I was able to market myself as a makeup artist and a continuity person. Lots of corporate video producers needed to save money so I became very valuable."

How Joan went from makeup to directing will be revealed in Part II of Chapter 3. But let's jump for a moment to what happened to Joan later on in her life. In her thirties, she was courted by, and later married, a prominent Toronto businessman. But instead of becoming a stay-at-home mom, she kept herself busy working, but only on projects that were interesting to her. In fact, she was seven months pregnant when she did production on an NHL All-Star Game spot for NHL Productions and Ken Rosen.

It all took place on a frozen pond in the town of Uxbridge, Ontario. Several NHL greats, including Mario Lemieux and Wayne Gretzky, passed the torch to three up-and-coming hockey stars.

The way the public loved the piece and the huge international exposure was a fascinating experience for her. Today, she has her own company, Hero Media, but she's still mindful of her values and her farm roots.

"You need to make sure the people you choose to help are not just using you— they must be trying to help themselves."
—JOAN KELLEY-WEISSHAAR, TV Producer and Director, Founder of Hero Media

"Often I've had long conversations with people who've never once asked about me and my life," she says. "I think it's easy to talk about one's self and risky to ask a stranger about themselves. That's part of the reason we don't listen as well as we should, but effective listening can be learned."

Although Joan believes that empathy is critical in developing great relationships, "one also has to be careful not to be too empathetic." What does she mean by this?

"This may sound harsh, but from experience, I feel it's important not to get drawn into dealing with someone else's problems," she says. "Of course, it's good to help people and be supportive, but there are people out there who seem to find individuals to take over their problems—the 'broken wing syndrome' I call it. You need to make sure the people you choose to help are not just using you—they must be trying to help themselves."

I don't think that's harsh at all. There's only so much time and energy in this world and I think we have to pick our spots when it comes to the charitable organizations we help and the people we support. Joan notes the importance of listening in the business world. "If you're listening with empathy while developing the relationship, you can carefully assess the person and situation and decide to go further into friendship or business with that person."

For today's working woman, personal relationships are just half the equation. Job-connected relationships are also very critical to her sense of self. Yet at the same time, she is keenly aware that the workplace is an ocean of cross-currents and undertows. Authors and researchers Patricia Ohlott and Marian Ruderman have been studying high-achieving women for many years.

"In traditional Western society, a woman defines her identity through attachment and intimacy, organizing and developing her sense of self in the context of her important relationships," Ohlott and Ruderman write in their excellent book, *Standing at the Crossroads: Next Steps for High-Achieving Women*. "Women are expected to act as supporters, caretakers, mothers, maintainers of relationships."

Ohlott and Ruderman argue that as maintainers of relationships, women have become expert at maintaining the ties with their own family and friends and those of their spouses. Both clinical observation and psychological research prove this, and the authors argue that much of a woman's value system develops out of this experience.

The cross-currents occur when these relational and networking skills are transported to the workplace. Ohlott and Ruderman interviewed sixty-one women and discovered that these skills are not in high demand, as they note on page 40 of their book:

"All the women struggled with the fact that in most organizations, the type of relational work that women have typically been responsible for is not valued. Instead, they and the men they work with are encouraged to strive for individual achievement, often at the expense of other people."

I personally think this is changing. In my experience working at TD Bank Financial Group, I've found that collaboration and teamwork are highly valued, and relational skills have always been important. My senior management team, as a group, is very team-achievement oriented. Any individual achievements always arise from the success of the team. The old cliché is true. There's no "I" in team.

What do the women I interviewed have to say on this subject? Are so-called "female values" like inclusion, openness, relationship building and collaboration infusing into and changing today's workplace, making it more humane and multi-dimensional?

"I think the old boys' club is pretty well dead or dying," says Ann Kaplan, CEO of Medicard, a highly successful medical finance company. "Most leaders, be they men or women, have to have these empathetic and communicative traits you're talking about in order to be successful leaders. Male leadership has dramatically changed over the last twenty or thirty years. The reasons include women's empowerment, ease of travel, communications technology, the Internet and the fact that the nuclear family is dying."

"I think the old boys' club is pretty well dead or dying."
—ANN KAPLAN, CEO of Medicard

Unlike most of the women I interviewed, Ann is not an optimist. But she *is* a realist who is passionate about life.

"From a young age I knew there would be no white knight to rescue me," she says. "I learned fast about life and when I moved out at age 14, I swore to myself that I'd never have to cap my income. I survived financially on my own. I began as a 14-year-old waitress, and I lived on tips. Today, I have kids of my own, I have my own company and I'm working towards my Ph.D."

Ann's parents divorced when she was young. Of her mother she says, "She sees the world through rose-coloured glasses and never had a bad word to say about anybody in her life." Her father was a radiologist and a specialist in internal medicine. "He was eccentric and intelligent and he always challenged me, but in a good way. He taught me a lot." Ann's life was not an easy one, but she learned to be a survivor.

"When I was 17, my father got ill and moved in with me," she reveals. "I got married and had kids, but he lived with me on and off for nineteen years. Absolutely the biggest turning point for me was when my father died. He died in my arms. He was my best friend and you can never replace that. I was divorced at the time and extremely alone. I guess I was in shock for at least six months. But I knew my children had to see a happy person, so I regrouped, got my act together and started a business (Medicard Finance Inc.) in 1996. It was the best decision I ever made."

Medicard offers financing to Canadians seeking elective medical procedures. It is now the largest medical finance company in Canada. Over 4,500 plastic, reconstructive and dental physicians are Medicard-registered to offer financing to their patients.

Of course, not everyone has the same workplace experiences as Ann Kaplan. Some economic sectors and job types are skewed heavily male—as we witnessed with fighter pilot Dee Brasseur in Chapter 1. The oil and gas sector still tends to be "old-boys'-club" driven, while the IT sector might be said to be driven by the "young boys' network." Whatever the case, a few decades ago, it was definitely male-dominated, as Jennifer McNeill, CEO of CipherSoft Inc., can attest.

"I think women are shot down a lot, unlike men," says Jennifer. "I remember when I finished university and got hired as a computer systems analyst by the manager of a local software company in Alabama. His name was Kenn Walp, and he took a lot of flak for paying me the same salary as the men. I guess he saw something in me and stuck to his guns. Anyway, his confidence in me was rewarded because I was promoted to marketing manager at the age of 27."

Jennifer was married at the time with one child. She would continue to build her career while raising four kids. As you can imagine, life wasn't all peaches and cream for her, but the cream quickly began to sour when her relationship became abusive. She divorced her husband, and at 41 years of age, she uprooted her kids and moved to Canada.

"When I moved to Canada, it was a bit of a shock, but in a pleasant way. I found people here had a lot more humility, and they just treated each other better." Jennifer always had a strong belief in herself, and some of it definitely came from her upbringing.

"I was fortunate to be raised by a father I admired intensely. He was a consulting engineer for forty-five years, and he was a business owner with integrity. On his death, we received so many wonderful, heartwarming letters from his business colleagues. It really resonated with me. I admire people who have resiliency and a passion to build. Oprah Winfrey is one of those people. And believe it or not, Donald Trump is another. Although Trump might not make most people's list of authentically successful people, I admire his tenacity and his will to succeed and his fierce, unshakable belief in himself. I think he truly, passionately loves what he's doing—and it shows in his work ethic."

> *"I've found my passion. But finding it was a trial and error process."*
> —JENNIFER MCNEILL, CEO of CipherSoft Inc.

Jennifer has since (happily) remarried and her husband works at the company which, not incidentally, is growing by leaps and bounds. CipherSoft services blue chip companies by converting older, legacy-type computer systems to Java. But to her, the business isn't technical, it's all about relationships.

"I'm a passionate person by nature," Jennifer says. "I can't do something unless I give it absolutely 100 percent. I've worked hard to build what I call 'partnership relationships' with many of the Fortune 500 companies. I've found my passion, sure. But finding it was a trial and error process. And now that I've found it, I still need to work hard at it every day."

She's certainly beaten the odds because only 7 percent of CEOs are women. But the numbers are growing, and Jennifer is an inspiration to the women who work for her. A five-person shop only four years ago, CipherSoft now employs over twenty-five people in its Calgary and Las Vegas offices, making it one of the fastest-growing software companies in the west. She's still working in a man's world, but there's a sea change coming and Jennifer McNeill is already making waves in the most positive sense.

Jennifer may be a hard-working CEO, but she values her personal relationships more than ever. Her children are all in their twenties now and live away, but they have dinner together every week.

"I generally work a twelve-hour day, but I get to have lunch with my husband most days, and most of my workday is spent interacting with clients and colleagues," she says. "On weekends, I spend at least two-thirds of my time with my husband, and working and shopping takes up the other third. My only regret is that I don't spend enough time with friends."

UNDERSTANDING, RESPECT, CONNECTION: THE PATH TO GOOD RELATIONSHIPS

I can totally relate to what Jennifer is saying. Just like most of you, I have lots of *different* relationships in my life. Some are intimate, some are casual, some are business-based and some are purely social. But I like to think all of them share one thing in common: a level of "connectedness." I believe strong, healthy relationships should contain three elements: understanding, respect and connection.

1.   UNDERSTANDING is about empathy and listening with compassion; it's also about being understood, about compatibility and communication.
2.   RESPECT is about clarity and openness and honesty.
3.   CONNECTION is about trust and intimacy.

In his classic book on personal leadership, *The 7 Habits of Highly Effective People*, Stephen Covey offered us a powerful message that still resonates today. In communicating and developing relationships with others, we need to "seek first to understand, then be understood." Covey says that most of us do the reverse. Rather than listening with the intent of understanding the other, we listen with the intent of replying. We're either speaking or preparing to speak.

Lauren Jawno says we need to learn to listen better.

"We need to really hear and understand what someone is saying, and be able to convey our thoughts across in an unthreatening, clear way," she explains. "Our body language and tone should be congruent with our words. This is why e-mails can be so easily misunderstood—we're missing the audio and visual part of the message."

From my own experience, and from talking with others, I've noticed that when people develop strong relationships, the following process has usually happened in one form or another:

- We start by trying to understand the other person (the empathy or listening part). At about the same time, we try to be understood by the other person by communicating and eliciting some kind of response. (*Understanding*)
- If the above two things are happening, and both parties are in a healthy state of mind, over time, mutual respect should evolve. (*Respect*)
- If there is respect and compatibility and understanding, then a real connection begins to grow, and there is trust and openness on both sides. (*Connection*)

The above steps can happen to us sequentially or simultaneously or even a combination of the two. If they happen simultaneously, there is "instant chemistry." Many people say that communication is the key to our relationships, yet it is one of the hardest things for us to do effectively. True communication is hard work. To have healthy relationships, we need to understand people, not just communicate with them. To do that we need to listen empathetically to the people in our life. We need to become aware of other people's emotions and values and goals, not just our own. Covey says listening "empathetically" is about listening with our ears, our eyes and our heart.

Empathy goes much deeper than sympathy. Empathy is defined by the American Psychiatric Glossary as "awareness and understanding of another's feelings and thoughts." In other words, seek first to understand, then be understood.

"I WAS TAUGHT TO BE SELF-SUFFICIENT"
Relationships are Publicist Danielle Iversen's lifeblood. A public relations consultant with a flair for the dramatic, Danielle is always on the go with an attentive assistant or two beside her.

"Growing up, I always worked for whatever I got," she says. "My parents never gave me money—they believed I should be self-sufficient. I rented and furnished my first apartment by myself, and to this day my job and learning are my prime motivators, not money. I never cared about the Gucci bags and all the trappings of success. Work to me is like breathing. I couldn't live without it."

Multiple cellphones squawk in the background as she says hello to the guests at her latest party. President of Toronto-based That PR Thing, she knows how to put on a corporate party, and she knows how important parties are for people to connect. But today's companies are changing the way they do business. One of the changes is how they hold their holiday parties.

"In times past, the company party was a key way to get employees to bond and stay connected. They became bigger and bigger, a kind of status symbol. Not any more," she says. "Companies know you don't build a strong community by putting hundreds of people into a convention centre.

"People continue to scale back," she says. "Christmas parties are often combined with charitable giving, and it seems women's fashions are following suit. We're now into 'comfort glam' where shoes are designed for walking, not just standing. All the top designers are getting into the act with their black suede shoes and little black dresses. As far as business lunches go, business is booming, at least here in Toronto. There are lineups for lunch on Mondays and Tuesdays. The drink of choice at lunchtime is sparkling water or a glass of white wine, and all the restaurants are serving very healthy meals now. It's definitely a trend. And I see it gaining momentum," she says. "I'm totally okay with the leaner lifestyle. That's how I've always lived my own life."

Danielle knows she's a perfectionist. She can even be self-critical at times, but she seldom worries about what other people are saying or thinking about her.

> "Work to me is like breathing. I couldn't live without it."
> —DANIELLE IVERSEN, President of That PR Thing

"Today, I'm my own role model," she says. "I believe it's important to lay down the groundwork for others, because others did for me.

When I was a teenager, I used to babysit Linda Smith's kids. Linda is the Executive VP, Senior Partner and General Manager of Fleishman-Hillard Public Relations in Canada. I got to know her well, and I talked to her all the time. She helped me get summer jobs, and in the process I learned an awful lot about the PR business. I'm still in touch with her. Susanne Courtney of the Courtney Group was another mentor. I always got a kick out of planning parties at school and when I graduated from university, Susanne helped me get my first real job. I was an account assistant with Cosette Advertising."

After just a year, Danielle entered the profession which would become her passion.

"Actually, I didn't find my passion," she says. "My passion found me."

She became a full-time PR person with CFTO, where she assisted with the Sick Kids Telethon, and since then she's never looked back.

"I probably have over 13,000 names in my Rolodex and Palm Pilot. Sure, there are celebrities on that list. But I've never been a star-struck type of person—celebrities are just regular people to me," she states.

"I keep my word, I'm honest, I deliver and I love what I do."
—DANIELLE IVERSEN, President of That PR Thing

She's made a name for herself and her company by working hard and totally focusing on one client at a time. People count on her because "I keep my word, I'm honest, I deliver and I love what I do."

RENAISSANCE WOMAN

Getting a kick out of meeting new people every day is fine if you're a super-extrovert like Danielle. But what if you're a self-described "high-energy introvert"? At least, that's what Lesley Southwick-Trask, Co-founder of Owl's Head Retreat, calls herself.

"I'm an introvert, but I'm also a people person," she says. "I need to be away from people for periods of time so I can recalibrate, and think about things. Don't get me wrong, I focus on being with my family as much as I can, especially on weekends. But during my workdays it's different. Some days I spend 100 percent of it with colleagues, but other days I'm entirely alone and I love it! I get excited by the prospect of writing some in-depth e-mails or some reading or some deep thinking. I've always been an intensely curious person."

Lesley is a Renaissance woman in every sense of the word. Strategist, anthropologist, builder and artist, she doesn't fit into any stereotype.

"I don't work in roles, I work in outcomes," she says. "My immediate goal is to transform the way our clients think, act and perceive the world around them. My ultimate purpose is to see them apply their newfound knowledge to change the way society operates."

Among other activities, Lesley runs Owl's Head Retreat, an oasis of calm near lovely Mahone Bay on Canada's East Coast. "Strategic thinking and transformational change rarely occur in the chaotic environment of our day-to-day business and personal lives," she says. "My business partners and I founded the retreat for individuals and small groups seeking personal and corporate growth and change."

It's fitting, then, that the facility's mascot is a West Coast Haida totem pole depicting an eagle and a man, because it is said that the eagle guides humankind. Lesley is at heart a cultural anthropologist because she loves people and the societies they've created.

"Ever since I was a child I loved going to documentaries and watching history unfold on film," she states. "I've always

"I don't work in roles, I work in outcomes."

—LESLEY SOUTHWICK-TRASK, Co-founder of Owl's Head Retreat

had a passion and an intense curiosity about how society has evolved. I would stand in a cathedral and imagine what it would be like to have lived with the people who went to the church when it was first built. Sometimes I'd think about meeting the people who were buried or memorialized inside. I entered the change consultancy business as a result of this societal curiosity."

Weaving modern Western business insights with ancient transformational wisdom, Lesley's unique solutions help CEOs and their leadership teams clarify and reframe their most pressing needs— whether this involves the need for double-digit growth or a complete strategic turnaround. But relationships are the most important product she creates, and they always fire her up.

"Some days our strategy sessions go from morning till night," Lesley says. "When I come home to my family on days like that I'm tired but I'm never exhausted. The only thing that exhausts me is if people won't make a decision and abdicate accountability by sending things off for 'consensus.'"

Architect and implementer of change interventions in hundreds of large-scale organizations, Lesley doesn't even mention business when I ask her what she's most proud of: "Learning what love is. That's what I'm most proud of."

She goes on to explain: "I've always loved my children and my husband, but I went through a mid-life crisis a few years ago. I was flying back from Vancouver and I realized I'd spent fifteen years running my business and yet we were no further ahead as a sector. How do we evolve our businesses to serve better? How do we overcome all the NIH (Not Invented Here) issues? I felt there was nothing sticky or sustainable, and I began to question my motives—I even wondered if I was being driven by pure ambition. Where did love fit into all this?"

Lesley came out of her crisis stronger and wiser. "At one level, love is easy. But as an intellectual, I live in my head. I did some soul searching, and I began to realize what true love was—unconditional love, tough love."

Lesley's biggest inspiration is her husband.

"My husband is quite ill, and he has been for a while now. But he's a tenacious person, perhaps the most determined man I've ever known. He's completely reframed his life to focus on the things that truly matter. He drives our youngest daughter to school every day and makes a point of seeing our older children every week. The family has become stronger and richer because of him. I'm just so proud of him. It's hard to articulate, but I've developed a deep love for myself and my family that I'd never really had before."

"Learning what love is. That's what I'm most proud of."
—LESLEY SOUTHWICK-TRASK, Co-founder of Owl's Head Retreat

Many people are uncomfortable admitting they love themselves. It's considered narcissistic. But if we don't love ourselves, aren't we going to have a tough time truly loving others? That seems like common sense to me. I'm referring to healthy self-love, not the kind that psychiatrists call pathological narcissism. In a November 1, 1988, article in the *New York Times* by Daniel Goleman entitled, "Narcissism Looming Larger as Root of Personality Woes," Dr. James Masterson is quoted as saying: "Normal narcissism is vital for satisfaction and survival; it is the capacity to identify what you need and want." Masterson is author of *The Search for the Real Self*, and a psychiatrist at Cornell University Medical College.

Forget narcissism. Lesley Southwick-Trask thinks we need to be clear about what we mean by self-respect.

"Self-respect requires embracing our unique strength as it collides with our vulnerabilities," she says. "Self-respect requires us to strip back the layers that we have used to mask ourselves to the world and most importantly ourselves. By the way, we are quite talented at hiding ourselves from ourselves."

She calls relationships a "creation process."

"It means being in a dimension with another party that transcends the individuals and forms a space of true exchange," she explains. "Only in this dimension can we create thoughts, ideas, actions and so on—which is the very purpose of having a relationship. This requires an awareness of the other person that goes deeper than what they are wearing and saying, feeling or hiding."

Lesley makes a clear distinction between true listening versus "active" listening: "I think empathetic listening is different for different people, and it heavily depends on their own state of awareness. For some, empathetic listening means listening intently to what the other person is saying and demonstrating this with the right paraphrase or question such as, 'What I hear you saying...' and 'I appreciate how you are feeling.' To me, however, this is not true listening. I believe a truly empathetic listener holds the space for someone to experience and express what is important to them."

My interviewees are saying healthy relationships involve understanding, respect, self-respect, communication and connection. But isn't all of this common sense? Of course. But common sense only seems to become inner wisdom when we reflect on it and absorb it deep into our bones. Otherwise, it's just lip service. That's why common sense is not always that common. Dictionary.com defines common sense as "sound practical judgement that is independent of specialized knowledge or training." I don't know if that is really an adequate definition.

I think training and discipline and knowledge gained through experience and trial and error are all important factors in developing common sense. A simple example proves the importance of training: Why are we better speakers than listeners? I think it's because few of us are trained in the art of listening, but many of us are trained in the art of speaking.

"If you want to be understood...listen," says a character in writer-director Alejandro Iñárritu's movie, *Babel*. The title of the film comes from the ancient story of the Tower of Babel in which a thousand voices spoke but no one understood each other. And true listening is all about empathy. "Empathy is about putting yourself in another person's moccasins," says Lesley Southwick-Trask.

WHAT ABOUT ME?

Do you want to get real about *your* relationships? Then start with yourself. It's absolutely the most important relationship of all. Without a healthy amount of self-respect, it's going to be hard for us to attract the right people into our lives. And if we don't listen well or know what our values are, we're not very likely to have healthy relationships. Successful people thrive by maintaining networks of healthy relationships, says Akela Peoples, who believes relationships were critical early in her life.

"I've always had a good level of self-respect and a positive attitude, but earlier in my life and career, I wasn't as self-confident as I am now," admits Akela. "Looking back, I realize how crucial it was for me to have a network of people around me—friends, family and colleagues—who not only recognized my strengths but told me what they were."

Nearly all of the women in this book have told me they deal with negative thoughts from time to time. But they also tell me they work through them as quickly as possible. They're not negative people, and they don't surround themselves with negative people. If you were to take a cold, hard look at any negative experiences and behaviour patterns that have happened in your own life, what would you find? I'd bet they came when you yourself were negative for some reason.

Your negativity may have resulted because of a broken relationship or a failed job, or you may have been under a lot of stress or change, or you might simply have been bored and disillusioned with your life. Whatever the reason, you weren't your usual positive self. Whether we like it or not, our attitude—positive or negative—is usually mirrored back to us in spades, especially by the people closest to us.

The vast majority of the women I interviewed in this book said they had a positive attitude to life. All of them said they enjoyed very healthy business and personal relationships. Is it any coincidence they're happy and successful and "connected"? People simply don't like to hang around people who are negative. Physicists tell us there's a finite amount of energy in this world, so who wants their energy sapped by negativity?

Negativity is bad and positivism is good. Fine. You knew that. Norman Vincent Peale's famous book, *The Power of Positive Thinking*, was well intentioned but perhaps limited by its mixture of religious faith and positive affirmations. Sure, we have to look inside ourselves from time to time, but even the best of us need outside help as well, whether it comes from mentors and teachers who guide and inspire us, or from our parents and friends and partners who love us.

Whether they're with yourself or with others, healthy relationships carry special obligations and expectations. And there's no bigger obligation than being true to yourself. After all, if you don't keep the promises you make to yourself, how are you going to keep the ones you make with others?

KNOWING YOURSELF

Some wise person said that no matter how old we are, we never fully know ourselves. I tend to agree. I think people who say they know themselves completely are a little delusional. Having said that, the overwhelming majority of the women I interviewed are aware of who they are and how they fit into the world. They know what they stand for—their values—and they're clear about how they see the world—their world view. So, do the above two statements contradict themselves? Only on the surface.

Almost all of the women I interviewed pointed out that they had yet to realize their full potential, and many suspected they never would. In fact, these high-achieving women felt they were on a life-long journey of self-enlightenment.

Like them, I haven't achieved my potential, and I doubt I ever will. But just think about it for a moment. What would there be to look forward to if you had? How could you continue to grow? I think life's rewards come from the effort we make. In many ways, the effort *is* the reward. My goal in life is to always *strive* to achieve my potential, and hopefully never reach it. Why? Because I have the feeling that during this lifelong process I'll discover my true meaning.

"I LOVE HELPING PEOPLE"

Years ago, at Willoughbrook Public School, a young girl struggled with her life when her parents' marriage fell apart. Natalie Bean-Sole felt alienated and alone, and she became an emotional eater.

"I was compulsive and out of control," she reflects. "At school, I would sit in the cupboard eating everyone's treats while everyone was out at recess. I became obese."

Years later, Natalie lost the weight, gained back her self-esteem and became healthy again. She is now a professional nutritionist and President of NutritionForeverInc.com.

As a child, Natalie was always high energy with an outgoing personality. "From day one I guess you could say I was a high-energy, Triple-A extrovert. I got energized by people and from doing the things I loved to do. I think mental energy is more important than physical energy because your mind can control your body. Getting a second wind, having adrenalin kick in—I think these are mental, not physical phenomena."

It seems that many of the women in this book are high-energy people. But Natalie herself has lots of successful clients who are quiet but determined, so being high energy is clearly not the only road to success. For proof of that, just take a look at Kerrin Lee-Gartner who was profiled in Chapter 1. What matters more, perhaps, is how nurturing one's family environment turns out to be. For many young kids, role models are often their parents or older siblings. In Natalie's case, her father motivated her to run her own business.

"He would always say to me, 'You don't need to work for someone else.'"

But an even bigger role model was her older brother, Elliotte Friedman, who works for CBC sports.

"Elliotte is two years older than me, and he is such a tremendous listener," she says. "He ran the newspaper at the University of Western Ontario, then he went to *The Score*, and then to CBC. The qualities I most admire in him are his passion, his ability to listen and his desire to always seek the truth. If you watch him when he interviews an NHL star after a game, he asks real questions. And because he listens so thoughtfully, he gets real answers, fresh takes on things. He doesn't get the usual pablum that most sports stars drop on the press."

Natalie loves people, and it shows.

"My childhood ambition was to become a doctor or a counsellor, because I wanted to help people," she says. "But when I developed my weight problem, I decided I wanted to be a nutritionist."

"I think mental energy is more important than physical energy because your mind can control your body."

—NATALIE BEAN-SOLE, President of NutritionForeverInc.com

But there's more to relationships—especially business relationships —than being a people person. Because nutritionists are not registered (at least in the province of Ontario), they have to develop an extra level of respect and trust with their clients.

"I think with me, a lot of the trust comes from going through such a long ordeal with my own weight as a child, and some of it comes from going through the tortuous trial-and-error process of coming up with a weight-loss solution for myself as a teenager."

Natalie is proud to say she lost 70 pounds, and she's kept it off for ten years.

"Before I started NutritionForeverInc.com, I worked at Jenny Craig, so I learned the business side of it, and I ended up being their top producer," she states. "So all of these factors help bring credibility to me and my company, but especially to me as a person. I think my clients relate to that."

I ask her about her family. How have marriage and having a baby changed her life? As always, she answers truthfully and without hesitation.

"Marriage changed everything. Marriage is work," she reveals. "Now that there was someone else in my life, I had to incorporate his needs as well as my own—everything had to be considered. It was more work, but it was a lot more fun! And much more rewarding. My husband Bobby works, but he is a big supporter and a big motivator to me."

When I asked her what she was most proud of in her life, she joyfully cried out, "My baby girl! Earlier, I had suffered through a miscarriage and then a miracle happened. I had a child."

"Life is too short for negativity."
—NATALIE BEAN-SOLE, President of NutritionForeverInc.com

And how do you balance the demands of your business with those of your friends and family?

"During my work day, I speak to my husband at least once a day, and I talk to my close friends almost every day, although I don't see them as often as I'd like—maybe once every couple of weeks." She has a nanny at home now, which is a huge help, and she usually doesn't work weekends. "I try to be with my parents and siblings and grandmother once a week. It's really important to me to reconnect. You know, the relationships with the people in my life are very healthy. If they weren't, I wouldn't have them. Life is too short for negativity."

THE DESIRE TO UNDERSTAND

Some of the biggest misunderstandings occur between men and women, and it's all because of our different communication styles. Men often get frustrated when women ask for advice and then don't take it, and when they seem to take forever to make decisions. Women counter that men don't listen, and dismiss their feelings by being too quick to step in and solve problems.

I'm reminded of a conversation I recently had with a male friend who has entered an excellent long-term relationship after a long relationship drought. He says he's "coming to grips with my girlfriend's need for connection and intimacy." Apparently, the concept of connection is something he hasn't understood or valued the same way she does. To his credit, he's beginning to realize that from a communications standpoint, men are from Mars and women are from Venus. As a result of his male-pattern behaviour, he gets accused of not listening and thus invalidating his girlfriend's feelings. But understanding our differences is the key to acceptance by both sides.

THE DESIRE FOR CONNECTION

In general, women (more so than men) are masters at connecting with others. Women understand the power, support and emotional well-being that come from team-building and collaborative relationships. *Standing at the Crossroads* authors Ohlott and Ruderman studied the attitudes and behaviours of sixty-one high-achieving women who attended The Women's Leadership Program, a five-day leadership development course offered through the Center for Creative Leadership (CCL). In their book, they point out an interesting change:

"In the 1980s women attending the [CCL] leadership program were focused on fitting in and breaking through obvious barriers. They tried hard to be accepted by men. . . . Today, women spend less time on fitting into a man's world and more on the lifestyle choices they confront—choices about how to be a woman leader. Choices about whether or not a particular assignment is the right opportunity at the right time."

Ruderman and Ohlott note that many organizations actually discourage connectedness by overemphasizing individual autonomy and accomplishment. These organizations encourage the male value of individual achievement above the more traditional female values of cooperation, compassion and connection. Women—who value connection—tend to use participative management.

As part of my research for this book, I picked up a book called *Never Eat Alone*, by Keith Ferrazzi. Admittedly, it's more of a "networking" book than Ohlott's and Ruderman's, but it was interesting to see how these two books intersected and diverged when it came to the subject of relationships.

Never Eat Alone was written by a man; *Standing at the Crossroads* was written by two women. Why is this important? I'd wager that two more different approaches to the subject of relationships couldn't be found. Ohlott and Ruderman break their chapters into broad themes such as "Wholeness," "Authenticity," "Making Connections" and "Self-clarity." Ferrazzi's chapters are headed with phrases such as "Build Your Brand," "Warming the Cold Call," "Managing the Gatekeeper" and "Be a Conference Commando."

While both books are well written, perhaps women might be more comfortable with Ruderman's and Ohlott's advice. Their book is couched in terms women intimately understand, while Ferrazzi's book is written in a more hyper-aggressive style.

WHAT MAKES A GREAT RELATIONSHIP?

I believe the greatest romantic relationships happen when two people become passionate friends. But there's much more to it than love and affection, as Brenda Eaton points out.

"Successful relationships are about trust and respect and valuing your partner's contributions," Brenda says. "They're about growing together and sharing new experiences, which creates a formidable bond. Over time, those shared memories become irreplaceable."

I couldn't agree more. But we all know that relationships have their ups and downs. What happens when one partner is going through tough times? What if money troubles or other conflicts develop? Brenda says we should help in the tough times, but don't take over.

"Your partner needs to solve his/her own issues," she continues. "As far as money goes, you have to avoid financial traps, like taking out too big a mortgage. This is a stress that relationships don't need! When there is a difference of preferences and a win-win isn't possible, I try to think about compromise in the sense of 'who cares about this the most?' It's not necessary to win all the battles—only the ones you really care about. If two people take that approach, it's amazing how many things really don't matter a lot in the scheme of things. However, it takes two to do this tango."

Great advice for all of us. Many people walk an uncomfortably fine line in relationships: on the one hand, they are learning to compromise; on the other, they sometimes feel like they're losing their identity. At times like these, it's important to remember: It's not about your ego or his ego—it's about something else. Brenda puts it very well.

"To me, the acid test of a great relationship is two independent individuals who are even stronger as a team."

I think she's absolutely right. Long-term relationships are about teamwork. If they weren't, why bother getting into one? Just stay single. That way you won't have to compromise, and you won't have to work at things. You won't get the joy and deep satisfaction that comes from sharing and growing together—but life is about choices. I've made my choice and I'm very happy about it. And I never forget that my key to a great relationship is to keep things fresh—and have fun together!

A HEALTHIER RELATIONSHIP WITH YOURSELF

I think support networks are an essential part of life, and it's not because I'm an extrovert. I've been fortunate to have a good support network in my life, and my family and friends and colleagues have been invaluable in helping me get through the inevitable tough times.

Have you ever noticed how some people are hard to "read," even after two or three meetings? I like to believe I'm pretty honest and open with others. And I think that most other people are that way with most of the people they meet—to a certain degree, of course. Perhaps people are closed and unreceptive and "opaque" due to shyness or have been badly burned by a former relationship (social or business). They are just naturally shy or reticent with strangers. Or it could be something else. It could be their values don't include openness, honesty and trust. If their values don't include these things, then clearly those values will not be shown to others. But even more important, it will be hard for them to have a good, open and honest relationship with *themselves*.

It could be they're not that comfortable in their own skin. A lot of people have trouble being alone, but not the women in this book.

These women have good relationships with the people in their lives because they tend to have a very positive relationship with *themselves*. They aren't self-critical, except in a positive, motivational sense. They know themselves well and, interestingly, they are comfortable being alone.

They have a clear sense of values—they know what's important to them and what makes them feel good about themselves. As a result, they know what choices they need to make and never let others make those choices for them.

"I think self-belief is critical if you're in any type of leadership role," says Brenda Eaton, Chair of the B.C. Housing Commission. "Unless you believe in yourself, no one else is going to believe in you either. People have a sixth sense about this—they know. They won't follow your lead if they know you don't have confidence in yourself. This doesn't mean you need to have all the answers; just that you have confidence that if we give this thorny problem our best shot, we have as good a chance as anyone of cracking it. And if you learn to believe in yourself, you'll be comfortable taking risk. Only by taking calculated risks can you achieve more than the average Josephine."

What are some of the elements of a great relationship?

"Absolutely you need mutual respect," says Brenda Eaton. "I recently read the book *Blink* by Malcolm Gladwell and was struck by how certainly and devastatingly the lack of mutual respect will annihilate a relationship. But self-respect is only half of the equation."

"Most important to me is respect and trust," she continues. "Empathy adds to those critical elements. It really helps if someone can put themselves in your shoes. Empathy allows for better understanding and better dialogue and that ultimately leads to a better relationship."

So empathic listeners provide agreement and support?

"I'd be careful not to confuse empathy with agreement or consensus," she says. "Empathetic, active listeners will hear and understand our issues better, but that doesn't require buy-in to our point of view. In fact, my empathetic mentors often have very different perspectives than mine—that is one of the things I value about them. They listen carefully and respectfully, think broadly, offer insights—and then often have a completely different but valuable take on a subject."

People who know themselves know their values. They've usually done a fair amount of soul-searching or self-analysis. They quietly project their values for others to see, and insist that others respect them for having those standards. And they generally avoid falling into the "superwoman" trap. Marjorie H. Shaevitz, author of *The Superwoman Syndrome*, described the syndrome as a "range of physical, psychological, and interpersonal stress symptoms experienced by a woman as she attempts to perform perfectly such multiple and conflicting roles as worker or career volunteer, wife, mother and homemaker."

I can't help thinking that maybe what we *really* need to do is get out of our own way.

STOP THINKING AND JUST . . . *RELAX*

Nearly all the world's top athletes use a "mental coach" to help them perform at the highest level. Why? They know the difference between winning and losing is often a microscopic line. Mental focus and toughness, not physical prowess, usually tips the balance.

Professional athletes ultimately want to reach what's called the "zone." When a person is in the zone, there is a heightened sense of reality, an alert calmness where the intellect is temporarily left behind, and intuition and instinct and feeling take over. A broader term for the zone is "flow." Whatever you want to call it, it seems clear that if we want to optimize our experiences, whether at work, at play or in relationships, we need to stop thinking, get out of our own way and . . . relax!

DON'T FORGET TO FLOSS
Patricia Kmet, a dentist in her mid-thirties, lives and works in the Greater Toronto Area, so she might be tagged as a young, urban professional. One of two daughters of Croatian immigrants, she's worked hard to prove herself and make her parents proud. Boomer? Yuppie? Gen-Xer? Gen-Yer? Trish is just herself. She refuses to be labelled. On

the other hand, if you were to ask her what she does for a living, she would proudly say she's a dentist with a strong work ethic.

"I grew up with a very supportive and motivational family," she says. "My parents were definitely my role models. My father's a successful businessman, and my mother was a stay-at-home mom who worked for my dad part-time. My mom was affectionate and she was always there for us. She was a great motivator who told us we could do whatever we put our minds to. My dad was a hard worker, and the two of them taught us the importance of family, cooperation, education, honesty and hard work."

> *"Look at the circle of people around you—don't go looking at a celebrity, or the unattainable for inspiration."*
> —DR. PATRICIA KMET, Dentist

Trish knows how important relationships are, and not just with friends and family but with the "people you meet along the way who you admire for one reason or another." As a student at Tufts Dental School in Boston, Trish got to know and bonded with many of the professors.

"My clinical instructor, Dr. Chen, was head of Prosthodontics. He was inspirational and also fun to be around. My cousin, Dr. Mauro Stuparich, was also a clinical instructor there. He inspired me but challenged me as well. He wanted me to be the best I could be."

She also has a mentor now.

"Later on, a colleague of mine, Dr. Ken Serota, became a kind of mentor to me," she explains. "I met him approximately seven years ago through another colleague and we have worked together ever since. Dr. Serota was very much interested in technology and the use of the Internet as a means of interoffice communication and education."

He inspired her to develop a more high-tech approach to her own practice and enabled her to provide the best care and education to her patients.

What's Trish's advice for young women looking for their own mentors?

"Look at the circle of people around you—don't go looking at a celebrity, or the unattainable for inspiration," she says. "Find out what you're passionate about, and then find someone who already shares that passion. I like to think that I am a mentor for my younger sister. She's also a dentist, and although she is an excellent one clinically and personally, I still enjoy offering advice and being a sounding board for her."

As Trish points out, "When it comes to relationships, what goes around comes around."

PARENTS AT WORK

Companies around the world are beginning to realize that their employees' work-life conflicts are not going to go away. And more important, it's costing them a lot of money. Double-income working parents are becoming the norm, not the exception. But they are not better off, say Elizabeth Warren and Amelia Warren Tyagi. In their book *The Two-Income Trap: Why Middle-Class Mothers and Fathers are Going Broke*, they say these same two-income families have *less* money to spend than one-income families did thirty years ago.

But it's not just the parents who are suffering financially. A Health Canada report estimated that work-life conflict costs Canadian organizations roughly $2.7 billion in lost time due to work absences. Aiming to change that is Parents At Work, an innovative program of workshops and seminars paid for by employers that enables employees with children to get valuable information and practical strategies from Canadian parenting experts. The Parents At Work program is the brainchild of an ex–corporate lawyer and mother of three named Aimée Israel. Along with business partners Michael Held and Alexis Wise, Aimée's goal is to provide information and expert counsel to frazzled working parents across Canada.

"It was a strange constellation of events that led me to start the program," says Aimée. "It began when I became pregnant with my first child. I was working as Corporate Counsel at Cadbury, and I needed to know everything I could about having a child. I bugged my older sister for information, since she'd already gone through the process. And then I realized that if I needed someone to talk to, there must be lots of other women who did, too. That's when a friend and I decided to invite six to eight expectant mothers to my house for a series of classes, and have subject experts come and talk to them. The program was a huge success, and I got lots of callbacks. The amount of sharing that goes on at the sessions is amazing. Women would call and say: 'I'm having my second. Can you put together another gathering?' The business has gone from two to over twenty clients across the country in virtually every corporate sector from pharmaceuticals to financial services to oil and gas."

Parents At Work evolved into LifeSpeak (www.LifeSpeak.ca). In addition to the Parents At Work program, LifeSpeak now offers two other programs relating to health and aging, respectively: Vitality At Work and Generations At Work.

It's been quite a ride for Aimée so far, but she's handling it well.

"Making the switch to being an entrepreneur was a real turning point in my life. It's so different than being a lawyer on a salary," she says. "I feel overwhelmed at times because as an owner you take everything so personally. The highs are really high and the lows are really low. I think I'm handling it all right. My father's a doctor, he was my role model growing up and I never saw him get flustered. His advice has been invaluable. He said, 'How do you eat an elephant? One bite at a time.' And that's the way I deal with the business. One day at a time."

> "[My father's] advice has been invaluable. He said, 'How do you eat an elephant? One bite at a time.' And that's the way I deal with the business. One day at a time."
> —AIMÉE ISRAEL, Co-founder and CEO of LifeSpeak

Maybe we should take more time to listen to the voice inside. That's what some of my interviewees have told me. Call it what you will—conscience, intuition—this little voice helps us identify our core needs and values. Once we know ourselves better and understand our values better, we can work at behaving according to those values.

BELIEVE IN YOURSELF

Self-belief seems like such an obvious value to possess, but it's amazing how many people, women included, lack this essential quality. Sarah Raiss, Executive Vice President at TransCanada, says believing in yourself is critical to success in any endeavour.

"If you want to do what is in the best interest of the organization as a whole, if you want to be a great selfless leader and help people develop beyond even your own capabilities, and if you want to give the most possible in everything you do that is a priority—it is very difficult to do this without believing in yourself," says Sarah. "This belief can be supported by family, friends and co-workers who provide feedback, and from your own experiences as you develop yourself, and from your upbringing. Self-belief has helped me countless times in my career as I have taken on good risks and new career challenges without the requisite technical skills, and when moving into ever more increasing leadership roles."

Does she ever have any self-doubts?

"Honestly, at this point in my career it is very rare that I have anything but belief in myself. If it happens, it pops up for only a tiny amount of time. I address it by reminding myself of the countless times I've taken on something new with positive outcomes, and by reminding myself of all the support I have in my life."

"I believe you need to focus your energy outward, not inward, to give as much of yourself as possible to others," Sarah says. "You need to know who you are, respect yourself and like yourself if you want to have the maturity to be a partner in a relationship and yet still retain your individuality. I believe that to have the best chances of long-term success, relationships should be formed on the same values and priorities that one has in life. Differences beyond these critical values and priorities make a relationship interesting but quite workable, as long as both parties are self-assured."

> "I believe that to have the best chances of long-term success, relationships should be formed on the same values and priorities that one has in life."
>
> —SARAH RAISS, Executive Vice President of TransCanada Corporation

WHEN YOU'VE LOST A CHILD, EVERYTHING CHANGES

Denise Bebenek, the founder of Meagan's Walk, sees things a little differently.

"Self-confidence is essential when spearheading anything—be it a business or volunteer organization or committee," she says. "If one does not believe in themselves, or what they stand for, how can one believe in others and what they are standing for? With regards to Meagan's Walk—if I didn't have the confidence in the importance of this message, then I couldn't deliver it. If you believe in your message, then your confidence comes out during the process. This helps create positive interest and positive results in whatever you're doing."

Denise established Meagan's Walk for two reasons: as a loving tribute to the memory of her daughter Meagan who tragically passed away at the age of 5, and to raise awareness and research funds for pediatric brain tumours so that other children might avoid this deadly affliction.

> *"If you believe in your message, then your confidence comes out during the process. This helps create positive interest and positive results in whatever you're doing."*
> —DENISE BEBENEK, Founder of Meagan's Walk

The Human Hug was established when Denise had a vision and realized that in the absence of a cure, the next best medicine was human compassion. She went to the city with her idea, to the people who run public events. They told her, "It's a lot of streets, a lot of people." But Denise was undaunted.

"So the public officials agreed to let us do the walk," she explains. "And at the end of the walk, the true power of the message would be expressed by the hug at the end—the Human Hug—where we all come together. The hug represents the world at that moment. The officials told her there was only one day when this could happen— Mother's Day! It was like a tapestry—I don't believe in flukes."

Denise is a positive force for all of us because despite her tragedy, she sees happiness as an important goal.

"Peacefulness, clarity, contentment are great goals," she says. "If you're not happy, people are not going to want to be around you."

When I learned that Meagan's Walk has raised over $800,000 so far, I asked her how she defines success.

"Success means an awful lot of things. Was Meagan successful in her five short years? Absolutely. She touched so many people's lives. Does success mean having millions of dollars? Not at all. Some millionaires have come to me and said that Meagan's Walk really changed their lives. That makes me happy."

Denise believes in herself, her family and her cause because for her, happiness "is measured in terms of our hearts and souls and where we want to be as people."

"WHAT I NEED IS A WIFE!"

That's the opening line of a July 21, 2006, lifestyle article by Valerie Gibson in the *Calgary Sun*. She's referring to the need for career women to have some help around the house. In the article, entitled "Alpha Female & Mr. Mom," Gibson says, "What I need is a wife! It's a complaint heard quite often, not from single men, but, quirkily, from WOMEN—especially high-powered, stressed, single, successful female professionals. Alpha females to be exact. What these women really mean is they need someone in their lives who will take care of them, be supportive of their careers, do household chores and, oh, heaven, maybe have supper ready when they get home from another hectic day.... Younger men, having grown up in an era of equality, tend to be more accepting and celebratory of a female partner's successes."

What do some of our high-achieving women have to say on the subject?

B.C. Housing Commission Chair Brenda Eaton has this reaction: "I think there is some truth to this article. But the bigger issue in my view is not about husbands and wives—it's about the difference between one or two high pressure careers in a family. Most people I know manage two jobs and a family admirably well. It might not be their preferred lifestyle, but it's pretty much the way our society works these days, and if they have a strong and sharing relationship, life hums along pretty nicely. Women often carry a disproportionate share of the load, but that is slowly changing and women are pretty good at organization and multi-tasking. That's not a great solution, but it's manageable."

But what about Brenda's own situation?

"A situation like my own works pretty well, too," she says. "My job requires irregular, sometimes long hours and a lot of out-of-town travel. We have no children and my husband is retired. We share the housework and the yard work pretty evenly, but he looks after much of the day-to-day stuff like laundry; we have a housekeeper who comes occasionally to keep the grime at bay; and, most importantly, when there is something that unexpectedly pops up—such as a broken water-pipe when I'm about to head out the door on a three-day business trip—he looks after it. Because he does not have a day job, we can arrange holidays around my schedule. And if anything crops up where I need a hand in an emergency, he can usually help out."

"It's not a wife you need, it's surge protection!"
—BRENDA EATON, Chair of the B.C. Housing Commission

So it's not the housework, yard work, family time, fitness schedules that are relationship killers?

"No. The impossible scenario is two high pressure jobs that result in two sets of non-routine hours, unexpected demands, significant travel, crowded calendars, etc.," she states. "Trying to accommodate one of those is bad enough; two is almost impossible. There is no room left for surprises—either the emergency kind or the happy kind. The stress from the smallest things going off the rails rises exponentially. So it's not a wife you need, it's surge protection!"

RELATIONSHIPS ARE A PROCESS

What have I learned about relationships from these women I spoke to? Relationships are a process. Relationships are essential to heath and happiness. And above all, the process of developing a good, strong, long-term relationship begins *before* any contact is even made.

We have to go "inside" and get to know ourselves better before we can venture out to mating-heaven. And we have to be honest with ourselves and with others about what we see there. It comes down to developing self-respect. We have to make that commitment to ourselves before we can get respect from others.

The process of building a great relationship is usually multi-stepped. As I mentioned earlier, we usually begin by trying to understand the other person by making the effort to listen empathetically. At the same time, we are trying to make ourselves understood by the other person, and to do that we speak to them to elicit some kind of response. I believe the ratio should be 90 percent listening and 10 percent talking. If we are communicating well and understanding each other, and both of us are in a healthy frame of mind, a sense of mutual respect should quickly develop. Out of this respect and compatibility and understanding, a real connection should begin to grow.

For me, connection means trust. It also means there is openness and honesty on both sides—there's no sense that either of us is withholding from the other. I give my trust to others and will not take it back unless it is betrayed.

Jacqui Szeto, Vice President and Director at TD Securities Inc., and the President of Women in Capital Markets, works fifteen feet away from her bond trader husband, Brad. The noise level and the overall pace on the trading floor is usually intense, so when she wants to communicate with him, she shouts that she's about to send him an e-mail. He waves back to show her he's heard, and away they go.

Jacqui loves her job and her husband. To her, the basis for building a great relationship is trust and honesty.

"If that line is crossed, it's difficult to get it back," says Jacqui. "Communication and respect are the other keys to our relationship. I admit I do get jealous, but it's very rare. I'm confident in our relationship but I need to know what's going on. For example, if I was to hear he'd gone on a business trip with some single women and he didn't tell me about it, I might get pretty steamed. That's about it."

"What keeps a great relationship going?" I ask.

"Making the effort," she says. "Showing respect for others, never getting lazy or complacent. Relationships are my support system. They're my community, my network. I need close relationships in my life for a lot of reasons. I need to get input when I make big decisions, I need to hear another point of view to balance my own. In business especially, having a network of trusting relationships is crucial to success. No woman is an island, at least not me. If I were alone, I couldn't survive, let alone thrive, for very long."

> "Relationships are my support system. They're my community, my network."
> —JACQUI SZETO, Vice President and Director at TD Securities Inc. and President of Women in Capital Markets

I agree with her in many ways. When I married my husband, Jim, a part of me felt I was losing my independence. He was really understanding. He said, "Pattie, I'm not taking away your independence. I want us to be *interdependent*. I want you to rely on me, and I want to be able to rely on you."

It's interesting, this word *interdependent*. I work in the corporate world—which means I work in a very interdependent world. Collaboration and teamwork are essential for success in any world where relationships exist. Lone wolves don't succeed as well as managers and leaders unless they are exceptionally brilliant. Relationships are important because two heads are better than one—the sum product of two healthy minds is always more dynamic and revealing.

Every person is different, which is why every relationship is different. But the key starting point, as always, is to know yourself as best you can. As my high-achieving interviewees watch their younger Canadian counterparts build their own careers, they see themselves in strange and wonderful new forms. They see a need for these women to challenge themselves, as they once did themselves. And (as the next chapter makes clear) to be successful, they need to get real about who they really are. If not, they're going to have a hard time matching their expectations with reality.

THREE

GET REAL ABOUT YOUR CAREER

PART I

KNOWLEDGE

WHAT WOULD IT TAKE FOR YOU to get real about your career? I'm talking about *more* than just making a living. I'm talking about creating a career that will reward you for a lifetime. For most of us, finding a great career is a very complicated question. In fact, for many people, it's *THE* question—the million dollar question. But then again, if money is your main driving force, I think you could be asking the wrong question.

The question isn't, how can I find an organization that will take care of me? The right question is, how can I find a place that will let me make a difference? Each of us defines "making a difference" differently. It could be advising people on financial issues or emotional issues, it could be designing a brochure or designing a will, managing people or managing processes. It could be building a house or building a business, developing government policy or developing third-world infrastructure.

That's what makes finding the right career path so complex. But it might surprise you to know that many of us make the process worse by 1) *overcomplicating* and 2) *underpreparing*.

1) We overcomplicate things *before* we start working by believing too much of the so-called conventional wisdom. We listen to

career experts and read countless career counselling books that say the first job is critical to long-term success. Pick the wrong job—or too narrow or too technical a job—and you're doomed to be stuck for eternity. So we often opt for the safe choice rather than the right one.

I say baloney.

I'm a Senior Vice President at TD Waterhouse but I started my career working as a teller at Bank of Montreal. Did that early career choice hurt me? I don't think so.

2)   The second big mistake we make is to under prepare for success while *on* the job. Recent research says the average person will have 3.5 different careers and work for ten employers. So if we fail to upgrade our skills and stretch ourselves (which, unfortunately, too many of us do) we are severely undercutting our career choices. I read somewhere that if managers leave people in the same job for too long and allow them to become too comfortable, they lose the capability to refresh themselves and stay creative. That hurts everyone.

There are no shortcuts to finding success. And women often have to dodge the shattered remnants of the glass ceiling as well. But there are ways to rejuvenate your career or kick-start a new one. There's no magic bullet, however. It's a process. Fortunately, the women I've interviewed have been kind enough to provide us with a few guideposts along the way.

How do you get real about your career? First, competence in your job is a must—it's really the bare minimum. And if you don't have it, you had better get it by trying a little harder. Second, you have to get real about yourself.

GET TO KNOW YOURSELF

If you want to get real about your career, you need to get real about yourself. There are several useful steps to self-clarity.

1. Know your inner "you." Are you a risk taker? Someone who likes pressure or dislikes pressure? Likes or dislikes structure? Gets bored easily? Do you live in your head or prefer to interact with people?

2. Know your work values. Do you have a strong need for accomplishment, for a high salary, for team-building, travel, a desire to be creative?

3. Know your strengths. Is it communicating? Influencing? Managing people? Are you detail-oriented or big-picture oriented? Are you socially skilled, tech-savvy and so on.

4. Know your situational needs: family commitments, commuting time, where you want to live, how much time you are happy to spend away from home.

Competence is necessary but not sufficient for career success. Too many women focus on being ultra-competent at the expense of other equally important skills. Ultimately, we can have all the technical smarts in the world, but if we can't communicate appropriately and assertively with our peers and bosses, what good are such skills? Schools spend far too little time on teaching their students to communicate and sell their ideas. That goes for men as well as women.

ONLY 20 PERCENT OF US MAKE USE OF OUR STRENGTHS

How well do we know ourselves and our strengths? To succeed career-wise, we have to know our workselves on an intimate basis. We have to drill down to our core strengths, weaknesses, skills, passions, values—and then shine a big fat light on them. Once we've done that, we have to start putting the focus on our strengths, not our weaknesses. Make it a priority, because in an interview by the Gallup Organization, only 20 percent of 1.7 million employees said they were using their strengths every day! Okay, so now that we've gotten clear about ourselves, it's time to ask some key people for advice to help focus us even further. This is the platform, the foundation. But the process really begins to expand exponentially when preparation meets opportunity and we start to develop that uncanny ability to "catch serendipity in a bottle." Some people call this luck. But the "lucky" ones don't see it that way. They believe it is the end result of preparation, tenacity, flexibility, creativity and the occasional willingness to leave one's comfort zone.

Okay, that's a lot to absorb, I know. But as you're about to discover, what separates the high-flying eagles from the head-in-the-sand ostriches isn't so much talent or drive, but attitude and self-awareness.

UNDERSTAND YOUR STYLE AND MAKE IT YOUR OWN

Brenda Eaton has spent a lifetime getting to know herself and mentoring many of the people she's worked with over the years. She offers this sage advice: "Values are critical, but they may be too broad to offer realistic career direction. I might believe in honesty or helping people or sustainability, but those can come into play in so many fields that it doesn't offer much help in thinking about where to start career-wise. So I start with two questions. What am I good at? What do I like to do? These are so mutually reinforcing that they can become one and the same. Then I overlay my values; that is, I take those talents and use them in a way that is consistent with my values. Talent and interests are more useful screens because they're not so broad that you can drive a truck through them."

"Can you give us a specific example?" I ask her.

"In my case, this is what happened," she explains. "First, I was good at numbers, I have a logical mind, I liked really big and complex puzzles, and I was interested in how big systems work. This led me to schooling in economics, and a leadership career in finance. Second, I fundamentally believe in democracy, the greatest public good and a strong social safety net. This led me to take my talents to the public sector."

So your career choices started with your talents and interests, but how you came to use them was guided by your values?

"That's right," she tells me. "I didn't start with the public sector and narrow it down to economics; I started with economics and narrowed it down to the public sector. One of my friends I asked about this told me her own life story. She was brought up in a family that believed in helping people, and that's what she wanted to do. But, she said that could have been science, or teaching, or plumbing, or medicine or any number of fields. However, she was good at business and enjoyed it. She got her degree and ultimately used her business acumen to become executive director of a hospital foundation. Her talents and interests honed her career skills; her values guided where she would employ them. And she's phenomenal at her job."

As you can see from Brenda's story, it all starts and ends with self-awareness.

Karen Radford is acutely aware of herself and the world around her.

"As an older sister, I had responsibility helping to run the household," Karen says. "My parents were very family-oriented, and were heavily involved in the community. I adopted many of their values. But people in Atlantic Canada are naturally supportive of each other."

As Executive Vice President, and President, TELUS Quebec and TELUS Partner Solutions, Radford is already one of Canada's most powerful executives, and she's still in her thirties. Her career is almost a Hollywood version of the fast track, and it all started in the notably unpretentious city of Moncton, New Brunswick.

"When I was in high school, I ran for President, and for the first time in my life I said to myself, 'I really want to win.' The experience pushed me to work on my speaking skills, and made me realize that I loved to lead."

Karen doesn't always follow the rules. Early on in her life, she decided to attend one of the job fairs that start before Christmas. She was told that she must wear a blue or black pantsuit. So what did she do?

"Make sure you understand your personal style."

—KAREN RADFORD, Executive Vice President and President of TELUS Quebec and TELUS Partner Solutions

"I showed up in a red pantsuit!"

Apparently, her very first interview was the best one.

"The interviewer had a great attitude, a vision for her company and she even sent bios of team members to my home!"

But Karen's fledgling career took a surprising turn when she was riding an elevator from the first to the twenty-sixth floor.

"A woman from TELUS made a pitch to me. She wanted me to redesign their entire customer service process! And shortly after that meeting, TELUS merged with B.C. Tel."

Today, Karen works with telecom partners across North America, providing carrier and operator services, and consulting services to smaller telecom companies. She also hires and recruits, and buys and sells technology, and she oversees all of TELUS Quebec's business and consumer, wireless and wireline customers. In other words, she wears a *lot* of different hats.

What career advice does Karen have to share with us?

"Find out what you love to do when you're young, if possible. The risk is lower then," she offers. "Try different things; find mentors and friends who can give you advice and support. And maybe most important, make sure you understand your personal style. It's a tough nut to crack; it's definitely a trial and error process. But from experience I can tell you it's well worth the effort."

BE WHERE YOU WANT TO BE

Senator Anne Cools is someone with a similar take on career success. She believes the secret to having a great career is to be where you want to be.

"Early in my life I knew I wanted to work directly with people," she says. "I decided that being a doctor was not for me so I went into social work. By the way, I think 'values' is a strange term, a relative term."

Anne makes it clear to me that she prefers the term "principles" or "ideals" to the term "values." And she's equally clear about how to achieve success.

"For me, the key to success is to work in an area that is satisfying to you; to build up the necessary viscera [guts] to face the inevitable challenges from colleagues and other organizations; and to be industrious so that when someone asks you to do something, they know that you are going to do it well."

When Colleen Johnston, CFO of TD Bank Financial Group, was younger, she was a perfectionist and a bit of a lone wolf. She was ambitious, highly skilled and wanted to become a manager. But when she finally became one, she found out there was something important missing in her resume.

"When I was younger and less experienced, I found my work really interesting, but for the first eight years of my career I had gained little leadership or managerial experience—and that frustrated me," she says. "So I went to a position as an Assistant Vice President at a trust company where I had a staff of thirty people. I learned that no one wants to work for a perfectionist. I had to change my philosophy. I had to become more tolerant, and I did. I found out I had a flair for leadership, and I've never looked back."

Today, Colleen is the Chief Financial Officer of a multi-billion dollar group of companies, the TD Bank Financial Group. But her story reminds us that even the most successful must learn to change and adapt, and sometimes even ditch a cherished value if it doesn't work in the real world—like Colleen did with her perfectionism. She offers this advice for women aspiring to leadership positions.

> *"Be consistent, be positive and be relationship-driven."*
>
> —COLLEEN JOHNSTON, CFO of TD Bank Financial Group

"Be consistent, be positive and be relationship-driven. I've always prided myself on doing the right thing, having integrity and being grounded. I'm a real person, down to earth and loyal. I have an abiding respect for people. I'm not quick to judge and I don't see the Machiavellian in others. That's why I've always avoided getting mired in office politics."

VARIETY IS THE SPICE OF LIFE

A May 1999 *Maclean's* magazine article entitled, "Jobs: Best and Worst," quoted a workplace survey that concluded we have a strangely ambivalent attitude to this thing called work. The 1999 survey of 2,000 Canadians provided to *Maclean's* by Aon Consulting Inc., a human resources consulting firm, revealed that, "Canadians are committed to their employers and are willing to work hard, but will do so only if they feel the organization values them as much as it cares about customers and shareholders."

It works both ways. What do today's employers and search consultants expect to see on an applicant's resume? Many of today's executive search pros want to see resumes that are dotted with frequent job shifts. Why? If someone has worked at the same place for twenty or thirty years, it can suggest a shortage of the varied experience often needed for today's multi-faceted jobs.

This view is interesting, especially from my perspective, because I've spent virtually all my career with one company: TD Bank Financial Group. In my case, the company gave me plenty of opportunity to change and grow *within* the organization. I didn't have to go anywhere to spread my wings. But still, there was a point earlier in my career when I wasn't sure about myself and my future.

Many years ago, I managed and budgeted the training program in TD's Human Resources department. I felt I was spinning my wheels and not really getting anywhere. Ultimately I think I lost my way— and my confidence. I knew something was holding me back but I wasn't sure what it was. I did some soul-searching and began to realize I'd lost track of my core skills and my core desire. I've always had good interpersonal skills (heck, I like people!), and I've always wanted to make a difference by helping people. When I remembered this, I started to regain my equilibrium and knew it was time to refresh my job. I met my future husband, Jim, about that time, and he was extremely supportive of my decision to refocus my career.

I had a simple mission: I wanted to help women become independent financial partners. Once I was clear about that, I set about charting the steps to make that a reality. I worked hard, and senior management was very supportive. They inspired me to "think outside the box," and over time I was actually encouraged to create my own job. I became a financial spokesperson for the bank with a focus on educating women about their personal financial issues. I began to develop and present seminars and workshops all over the country. Later on, I approached management and asked them if I could do a TV show on personal finance. They agreed, and my show *MoneyTalk* was born. Yes, I was lucky that the bank was very supportive, but the harder you work, the luckier you get. I worked hard to prove myself and I was rewarded.

WHY BE A SOMEBODY WHEN YOU CAN BE YOURSELF?

How well do we really know, like and trust ourselves? These are critical questions, according to oil executive Sarah Raiss.

"Sometimes we're our own worst enemies," she says. "Negative beliefs can really hurt us. Early in my career, the first few months, I thought I was stupid and couldn't do the job, and on top of that I was extremely heavy, weight-wise. I was an electrical engineer and it was definitely a man's world. So I tried to be like a man, but I'm not. And it didn't work. But then I began to like myself and follow my passion, which was dealing with people."

Sarah has some simple but important advice for any woman about to embark on a corporate career, especially in a male-dominated field.

"My advice to any woman entering the corporate world is to be clear about yourself—I'm a big believer in taking the time to figure out who you really are, what you really like and what your strengths are. Have the courage to be able to laugh at yourself—it will get you out of a lot of jams. And don't be afraid to ask questions."

WE UNDERVALUE OURSELVES

As women, the need for us to know ourselves is doubly important because we tend to undervalue ourselves. This long-held perception is beginning to be validated by research. When John Jost, Assistant Professor, Stanford Graduate School of Business, investigated why women value themselves less than men, he asked 132 college students—64 women and 68 men—to write an essay on computer shopping. He then asked how much they would pay an author to write that same essay. As a group, the women paid themselves 18 percent less than the men paid themselves for the same work. You can find a summary of his conclusions on the Stanford Graduate School of Business website (http://www.gsb.stanford.edu/) Key in: "Women Undervalue Themselves in Setting Pay Rates."

Dee Brasseur has personal experience with that issue.

"I retired after twenty-one years, but I came back after 9/11 because I knew the Department of National Defence needed people," she says. "We develop many important skills in the military, but we often undersell ourselves when it comes time to enter the corporate world."

NEGOTIATING YOUR WORTH

In an October 3, 2005, CNNMoney.com article entitled "Want More Pay? Some Disturbing News," written by CNN/Money senior writer Jeanne Sahadi, Carnegie Mellon Economics professor Linda Babcock is quoted as saying, "Women are 2.5 times more likely than men to say they feel 'a great deal of apprehension' about negotiating, and they tend to undervalue their work more than men." In her study, Professor Babcock found women's salary expectations are up to 32 percent lower than the expectations of men in the same job. Based on this study, Babcock went on to coauthor a book: "Women Don't Ask: Negotiation and the Gender Divide."

Brenda Eaton tends to agree with Babcock's findings. She says most women accept the first compensation offer that is made.

"I've done it myself. But others see the first offer as just an opener. You must have enough confidence to go after what you want and ensure your terms are met. It costs nothing to push the envelope and it usually yields a win-win that recognizes your contribution and achieves a fairer resolution. Even if you don't get it all, you will get respect."

Whatever the underlying reasons may be, career women need to know themselves better, become more realistic (in a positive sense) and take on a more assertive view of their value in the workplace. An excellent article on how to negotiate a higher salary, called "Six Steps to a Higher Starting Salary," can be found in the career advice archives at CareerBuilder.com.

FOCUS ON YOUR STRENGTHS

For years, organizations and their managers have focused on identifying the weaknesses rather than the strengths of their employees. Why? Perhaps because people believed that weaknesses could be "fixed" through training, and strengths should be left alone. But that philosophy has become a little outdated. Today's flat organizations work in teams—so each member of the team brings their own strengths to the table, thus any weaknesses are less of an issue. My view is, you should accept your weaknesses and continue honing your strengths. Akela Peoples says it's common sense.

"We often like things we're good at, and we're good at things we like," she says. "If a woman wants to carve out a great career in any field, I would advise her to find an area where she can be passionate about the work. If work doesn't feel like work, you almost can't help but succeed."

Artist and teacher Jackie Carroll believes focusing on our strengths is even more critical if you are an artist.

"It's absolutely huge for the artist to focus on their uniqueness and allow their self to be authentic and original when they create," she says.

Dee Brasseur says too many women dwell on their weaknesses.

"They say 'I can't,' as opposed to 'I can.' Women need to find their core skills and strengths," she says. "I didn't recognize my sense of curiosity and 'just do it' attitude until I was close to 30."

"If work doesn't feel like work, you almost can't help but succeed."

—AKELA PEOPLES, CEO of Youth in Motion

Brasseur believes the military world is a lot like the corporate world, "except there's a stronger level of commitment in the military."

"I've discovered new aspects of myself through my career as a motivational speaker," she says. "I've had a great many wonderful experiences and helped transform people's lives. I'm always discovering new aspects of myself because life is a process of learning and doing."

NETWORKING: THE SECRET TO A GREAT CAREER

If competence isn't the ultimate goal, what is? Colleen Johnston says the secret to a great career lies in one's people skills.

"Talent and smarts and drive are important, but it's people skills that set people apart," says Colleen. "My advice is to avoid what's called the Supercompetency Syndrome, in which you focus all your energies into getting the job done to the best of your ability and thus exclude other opportunities. For example, opportunities like joining one of your organization's social committees, or taking on a certain special assignment, or perhaps making a presentation at a big meeting. All these may take you out of your comfort zone, but you have to take that risk and feel that discomfort—it will help you grow."

As a proven leader, what advice might Colleen give a younger woman who's ready to assume her own leadership role?

"Try to find a way to have a personal impact," Colleen advises. "Surround yourself with the right people, value your relationships, and develop and nurture them."

When you're piloting a CF-18 at over Mach 1, the only relationship that counts is between you and your plane. It doesn't matter whether you're a woman or a man when you're 30,000 feet in the air. All that matters is that you're competent, confident and in control. Major Dee Brasseur is all that and more.

"Talent and smarts and drive are important, but it's people skills that set people apart."
—COLLEEN JOHNSTON, CFO of TD Bank Financial Group

As you'll recall from Chapter 1, Brasseur is driven to live a life without limitations. When asked if she has any advice for younger women entering the air force, she responds: "Go for it! Learn to play the game of life. Your responsibility is to live it to the best of your ability."

Yet Brasseur knows that women struggle more than men with their careers. "It's that old-school attitudinal thinking. Women still do more of the home-based work because they still have lots of social and cultural conditioning." But that's not her world. "My world is nongender. I like to follow that old credo—think like a man, work like a horse and act like a woman."

GETTING CONNECTED

If you don't already have one now, I strongly suggest developing and cultivating a career network. You need to have a network of contacts who can provide information and job leads, in part because the vast majority of job openings are never advertised. The reason most people don't achieve their career goals is either a lack of resolve or a lack of a proper network. In other words, they either give up too early or they forget to think through exactly what is really the best fit for them.

I'd like to point out that your network should never be a one-sided affair, created solely for your edification or personal aggrandizement. Networks are two-way streets—there's give and take. If you make the effort to share information, advice, support and time with each other, the network benefits everyone. If you don't, it will soon dry up and you'll be left wondering what the heck happened.

Catalyst, a women's research group, has identified exclusion from informal networks as one of the top roadblocks to the advancement of women.

"To get ahead," says Sheila Wellington, career expert, author, and past President of Catalyst, "you have to learn the ropes, and to do that you need someone who is willing to clue you in."

If you're a Canadian executive, an organization worth connecting with is Women's Executive Network (WXN). WXN is Canada's leading organization dedicated to the advancement and recognition of executive-minded women in the workplace. WXNWisdom is a powerful new mentoring initiative designed for senior executive women who form a confidential group of eight to ten members, meeting eight times per year for three hours. The sessions are moderated by a trained facilitator throughout their duration, and provide a powerful networking vehicle for executive-level women seeking high-level advice and support, and wishing to expand their interpersonal skills. Participation in WXNWisdom is by application only, but full details are available on their website at www.wxnetwork.com.

Pamela Jeffery, the President of WXN, says that career women must see network and mentoring sessions as a natural part of keeping "career fit"—just like workout sessions are for your body.

"In order to thrive in today's work environment, I think it's important to start networking early in your career and to build as broad a network as you can," she advises. "I was fortunate to have a series of wonderful mentors in my life. My first was the former Clerk of the Privy Council, Gordon Osbaldeston. He was the top advisor to three Canadian prime ministers including Pierre Trudeau. He had just retired and came to the Ivey School of Business in the mid-1980s to teach when I arrived there to do my MBA. I knocked on his door and asked if he would be my faculty supervisor. I was thrilled when he said yes, as I

> "In order to thrive in today's work environment, I think it's important to start networking early in your career and to build as broad a network as you can."
> —PAMELA JEFFERY, CEO of Women's Executive Network

wanted to study business-government relations. Thanks to him, I confirmed that this is what I wanted to do professionally."

Having a mentor who likes and trusts your abilities can open doors you didn't even know existed. Pamela's mentor, Gordon Osbaldeston, had been contacted by an association of landlords in Nova Scotia who wanted to retain him for advice. Pamela recounts how events unfolded.

"He came up to me and said, 'I want you to do this job.' I looked at him in shock, recovered my wits and said 'What do I charge them?' He said, 'You're in school. You have expenses to cover. Add up your tuition, rent, books and so on, and go from there.' So I ended up advising these landlords on how to lobby the Nova Scotia government to end rent control. My fee? Five thousand dollars."

HOW TO NETWORK EFFECTIVELY

Without a network, your task is made so much more difficult. The word "networking" seems to have developed a bad name in certain circles. But it shouldn't. High-achieving individuals live and die by the quantity and quality of their personal and professional networks, because among other things, they can't afford a gap in their income if they change jobs or get laid off.

You'll increase your odds for success if you connect with people who are already successful. Keep a list of useful contacts and acquaintances to help when you need to network for information. Participate in the activities of professional associations in your field or industry. Do simple things like send Christmas cards to your business as well as personal contacts.

Another way is by joining networking organizations that specialize in their sector. For example, in June 2006, CATAAlliance (Canadian Advanced Technology Alliance), perhaps Canada's leading, most influential and entrepreneurial technology alliance, established CATA WIT (Women in Technology). On the CATA website (www.catawit.ca/home/default.asp), the organization's Vice President, Joanne Stanley, says, "The technology sector is an area where women can advance quickly, if we get together and share our strengths. Science and technology depends on brainpower, which is inherently equitable. Already in sectors like computers and communications, 26 percent of the management positions belong to women. This could offer a fast track to women who are qualified and determined."

Women need to network the same way men have done for years. In a September 21, 2005, *Wall Street Journal* article entitled, "Men Do Numbers, Women Do Strategy" by Ronald Alsop, Goldman Sachs' recruiting chief Edith Hunt said that despite generally superior interpersonal skills, many of the women MBAs at her firm don't use those skills to build networks inside the firm. According to Hunt, "Men have the edge over women in informally networking within the firm. Women tend to prefer to work through the formal network. But we tell them part of work is building relationships; they need to walk the floor and talk to people."

THE BENEFITS OF VOLUNTEERING

Volunteering is something recruiters and human resources experts look for. Volunteering broadens a person's skill set and adds to the value they bring to an organization. And if you're wondering whether employers *support* employees who volunteer, the answer is most definitely.

Statistics Canada reports that more than half of all employed volunteers received some form of non-monetary support from their employer, and a third were allowed to reduce or change their work schedules in order to volunteer. Twenty-one percent actually received *paid* time off to volunteer. What's motivating most of these employees to volunteer? The majority want to make a contribution to the community or are personally affected by the cause they are supporting. But a sizable number (nearly 50 percent) also said they volunteered in order to network.

STAYING CONNECTED

It takes effort to get connected, but once you've made the effort, it's important to stay connected. That means keeping visible, staying in touch if only to drop someone a quick note or e-mail to say hello and ask after them. Even the Internet is a good networking opportunity.

According to a report from Pew Internet and University of Toronto sociologists, the Internet is helping to cultivate social networks for people needing help on important matters in their lives. About 45 percent of Internet users surveyed said the Internet played an important role in dealing with a major life decision in the previous two years, up 33 percent from a similar survey in 2002. Wondering if this further cuts people off from traditional in-person interactions? The report highlights an interesting fact: e-mail is *supplementing* rather than replacing the communication people have with others in their network.

Are you having trouble getting motivated because you think it's too late in your career to network? Get over it. In case you think everyone you know has too big a head start on you, consider this: While 84 percent of business managers polled in a recent online study by ExecuNet believe a broad network of personal and business contacts is essential for success in business, far fewer believe their own networks are in good shape, according to a *Fortune* magazine article ("Five Months of Networking, Still No New Job"). When *Fortune* senior writer Anne Fisher interviewed Mark Anderson, President of ExecuNet, a career-services network for executives earning $100,000 a year or more, Anderson revealed this startling fact:

LESS THAN 20 PERCENT SAY THEIR OWN NETWORKS ARE IN "GOOD" OR "EXCELLENT" SHAPE

That's right. Most people have lousy networks, according to ExecuNet's poll. It clearly reveals a huge disconnect between what people consider the ideal personal network and their own. When's the best time to start building your own network? Right now.

When you've gotten clear about yourself and your goals, it's time to ask some key people in your life for advice to help focus you even further.

"I still make use of my network, even though I'm at the pinnacle of my career," says Sarah Raiss.

Broadcaster Ann Rohmer may be in the public eye, but she's a very private person. "I don't like to talk about myself," she says. "I'm never very comfortable being on this side of an interview. I really prefer to put the focus on others." She has an interesting and very altruistic slant on the mentoring process.

"I don't really think of myself as a mentor to the younger women who work with me at the station," she shares. "I see them as my equals. If they come to me with career questions, I will always try to help. I'm delighted if they think of me as a role model. I try to give them the same advice I follow in my own life: take your job seriously but don't take yourself seriously."

I like what Ann says because I have that philosophy myself. No matter how good you get at your job, if you start taking yourself too seriously, nothing good can happen. You'll alienate the people who work with you and you'll make it harder to "connect" with potential mentors as your career evolves or changes.

HOW TO GET A MENTOR TO LOVE YOU

If you really want to get ahead of the competition, it helps to have a mentor who's passionate about your career. And the best way for that to happen is to get them passionate about you! These tips come from several of my interviewees:

- Listen
- Be passionate
- Don't make excuses
- Be positive
- Learn to be self-aware
- Willingly accept constructive criticism

Most people aren't good listeners, as we discussed in Chapter 2. If you want to stand out from the crowd, be an active, empathetic listener.

DON'T FOCUS ON *ONE* MENTOR—FIND A GROUP

Once you have defined what you want from your mentor, ask yourself exactly what you're hoping to achieve by developing this relationship. Some people want to develop a strategic alliance. Others may seek someone who has connections or has content knowledge or has access to information they don't have. If you need a new skill set, the mentor should either have it or know others who do. But keep in mind, the perfect mentor doesn't exist. Mentors have different strengths—some are more strategically inclined, some are technically very competent and others are highly skill-specific.

That's why it's considered a good idea to seek out more than one mentor. Many experts suggest that you develop a group of mentors. Having more than one mentor has several advantages, the most notable being that you will get more than one perspective on the career issues and opportunities facing you.

HOW TO FIND A MENTOR

If you have successful people in your life who you admire, ask them if they'll consider being your mentor. Join a networking group or a trade association. Successful people are usually flattered when they are sought out. Remember that this is a two-way relationship, and a healthy mentoring relationship has "give and take" aspects to it. One other tip: Mentors appreciate having a protégé who recognizes and articulates their own successes. They've worked hard to get where they are and it's just human nature to enjoy being complimented.

For more information on mentoring, the Alberta Women Entrepreneurs (AWE) have an excellent website at www.awebusiness.com. While it is tailored to businesswomen, I think the tips are invaluable for women in many other careers.

Yes, finding good mentors is work. But your career is a vital part of your life, isn't it? If it isn't, then maybe it's time to skip ahead to a more relevant chapter.

SOCIAL SKILLS

There are many barriers to career growth, but lack of social skills shouldn't be one of them. Why? Because it's the one obstacle that's easily removable. We were not taught interpersonal skills at school (unless we were lucky enough to attend a finishing school). But that doesn't mean these skills can't be picked up, even if they don't come naturally to you. One way to pick them up is through a commitment to expand your awareness of how you interact with friends and family. Increase the number and length of your interactions and make them purposeful. Simple examples? Watch out for ways you can listen more actively, try to be more engaging by being more empathic; respect other people's time and opinions; learn patience; increase your eye contact while talking and listening. I have to work hard at doing that myself, even though I consider myself a people person.

By the way, if you don't know how much of a people person you are, you're not alone. Apparently, we seldom see ourselves the way others see us. According to management consultant Karl Albrecht, what may separate the career "winners" from the "losers" is where we fall on something he calls the social intelligence scale. Author of a recently published book called *Social Intelligence: The New Science of Success*, Albrecht posits that the lower our social intelligence, the greater the impediment to career success.

In a September 30, 2006, *Globe and Mail* article by Virginia Galt, entitled, "In a Job Rut? It May Be that You're Socially Clueless," Albrecht writes: "The biggest single cause of low social intelligence comes from simple lack of insight.... The best people to work with, and work for, have developed their social skills as well as their business skills." Unless we develop a better sense of self-awareness, we may never know why we've been passed over for a promotion—employers are reluctant to be open about issues like this. Low social intelligence can sometimes be rooted in a lack of self-confidence, and all of us suffer from confidence issues at one time or another.

Career coach Penelope Trunk says that social skills matter today more than ever.

"Many fields that used to be havens for loners, like programming, increasingly require exceptional people skills," she wrote in an article entitled, "Social Skills Matter More Than Ever," on her excellent blog, the Brazen Careerist, back on July 18, 2006. And as the need for social skills at work grows, the bar for good social skills gets higher. Most of us have to work at being likeable. Fortunately, research by Tiziana Casciaro, a professor at Harvard Business School, (who Trunk interviewed) shows that the biggest impediment to likeability is not caring. "If you just decide you want to do better, you probably will," she concludes.

SELF-CONFIDENCE

In Chapter 2, I said that in order to develop healthy relationships with others we have to develop a healthy relationship with ourselves. By doing the hard work of being honest with ourselves, peeling away the layers and seeing who we really are, over time we can truly begin to accept ourselves—warts and all. That's when a calming feeling of confidence begins to infuse into you.

Why is confidence so important to career success? It's critical to effective performance in the workplace because it is the major source of assertiveness. If you are assertive, you fully express your opinions and recommendations to others. Assertiveness is a major aspect of self-leadership.

If you can't manage yourself effectively, many experts would argue that you can't effectively manage others. How do some of our interviewees see self-confidence? Lesley Southwick-Trask, President and co-founder of Owl's Head Retreat, feels it's a bit of a slippery slope.

"For some, self-confidence feels elusive as if it is a treasure to be found," she says. "And then again, there are many others who translate self-confidence into arrogance. I believe the mastery of self-confidence has been reached when it is no longer visible—when it is embodied in humility. The confident individual is light and giving, flexible and knowing, humble and authentic."

Confidence can be fleeting at times, especially when we are under pressure or faced with unfamiliar situations. It doesn't happen overnight. Self-confidence is an ongoing process. It requires developing and reinforcing a positive but realistic belief in your abilities. If you're Dee Brasseur, confidence gives you the spark to realize your fantasies.

"In my career and life, confidence in myself has enabled me to achieve everything," says Brasseur. "It's the fuel which fires my curiosity to venture into the unknown. With self-confidence came the courage to attempt the impossible knowing that regardless of the outcome, I believed that I had the ability to handle the results of my efforts."

But confidence seldom grows in a straight line. Lesley Southwick-Trask knows that only too well.

> *"With self-confidence came the courage to attempt the impossible knowing that regardless of the outcome, I believed that I had the ability to handle the results of my efforts."*
>
> —DEE BRASSEUR, the world's first female fighter pilot

"I suffered from a lack of self-confidence in my early teens, only to turn that high school dynamic into my passion to prove myself," she says. "I never from that moment on lacked self-confidence. That was until I hit a huge wall. I am forever grateful for that wall, for without it I would never have appreciated that what I thought had been self-confidence had actually been bravado."

Many people mask low self-esteem through displays of arrogance and bravado—which is an unwarranted, insincere show of self-confidence. People can be arrogant and highly egotistical on the surface but have low self-esteem underneath. That's why self-confidence—the belief in your external abilities—is not the same as self-esteem—the belief in your inner worth.

Knowing ourselves and developing our interpersonal skills are the key steps to building a real sense of self-confidence and self-respect, as opposed to pride. Dee Brasseur explains how she handles life's challenges.

"I seldom have trouble finding self-confidence, but if I do, I merely go 'inside,'" she explains. "Whenever I am confronted with a challenging situation and am uncertain as to whether or not I have the required skills or abilities, I recall a memory of myself in similar situations in the past where I had the confidence to take action and the confidence to deal with the consequences of that action. What I've learned is that there is no such thing as failure, there's only feedback. I learn something valuable from every situation in life."

Real confidence is about feeling comfortable with uncertainty and not knowing what the outcome will be. Entrepreneurs and leaders fit into that category—at least when it comes to work. In their personal lives, the situation might be quite different because self-confidence does not necessarily pervade all aspects of a person's life. A person might feel confident about her work, for example, but not confident in her personal appearance or social relationships. Or vice versa.

HOW DO WE DEVELOP CONFIDENCE AT WORK?

We build confidence by solving our own problems, overcoming challenges and dealing with setbacks and failures—in other words, through hard work and perseverance. Self-confidence is cultivated through what I call an ongoing "success loop," in which we perform a task, get positive support and feedback for it, receive ongoing coaching and mentoring, and then repeat the process over and over.

"Invisible, authentic self-confidence means that I do not ever worry about what others are thinking of me," says Lesley. "They have the right to any opinion they have of me, but I stand in my own sense of self."

If I think back to my own working life, the progression was fairly straightforward. I developed a certain level of competence; I had a good attitude and a willingness to learn. I learned to appreciate myself as I developed and expanded my talents and began to experience my own "power." Power leads to confidence. I've had my ups and downs—don't get me wrong. But I always regained my focus and my self-confidence, grew from the experience and continued to stretch myself through a series of self-imposed challenges. And that got me to the stage where I am now, which is knowing that *the harder I apply my talents, the greater my potential for success.*

Self-confidence is essential to a successful career, but it's not about pride or false modesty. Self-confidence is an attitude with which individuals can develop and maintain a positive yet realistic view of themselves, their actions and reactions. Self-confident people *trust* their own abilities. They have a sense of control in their lives, and believe that they will be able to accomplish what they wish and plan for.

We all know people who lack self-confidence and underachieve, yet many of them have a great deal of ability. What's holding them back is "paralysis by analysis" and an inability to take calculated risks. How can you take a calculated risk if you don't know what the calculations are? These people are often trapped by their own unrealistically high expectations and standards. At the same time they can easily be swayed off course by what others think.

Self-belief leads to self-confidence. Studies have shown that self-confident people often succeed out of sheer determination. They feel convinced that they know what they're doing, even when they clearly do not.

Confidence can be cultivated by getting to know yourself and your abilities; by learning to focus; by seeking advice and support from people you trust; by listening well and with enthusiasm; and by developing your social skills. If you follow these steps (assuming that you're technically competent at your job), a feeling of greater self-confidence will begin to grow.

SELF-BELIEF LEADS TO SELF-CONFIDENCE

If you take the time to figure out who you are, what you like and what you value, the odds of finding your passion increase dramatically. But there's another reason to know yourself. It's about self-belief, another key factor that contributes significantly to career success. But how can you believe in yourself if you don't know yourself first? Dee Brasseur explains.

"Believing in your 'self' is absolutely critical to achievement," she says. "If you don't believe in yourself then who will? If someone else believes in you and you don't then so what? Belief in self cannot come from an external source. If you believe in yourself and no one else does, it doesn't matter, you can still achieve your goals. Belief in self is the rudder with which you steer your dream to success—hold tight to the tiller, ride out the storms en route, and achieve your self-determined destiny."

We all want to achieve our destiny. Let's see how we can do it.

PART II

ACTION

"It's important for us to go to places that scare us, to embrace change."
—Lesley Southwick-Trask, Co-founder of Owl's Head Retreat

TO HAVE THE CAREER WE WANT, we start by expanding our self-knowledge. But there is a critical next step. Step two is developing the power to act. How do we find a way to act on that knowledge and prepare ourselves for the unique opportunities that can make a difference to our lives and the lives of those around us?

Jennifer McNeill found a way. She did a lot of soul searching earlier in her career and came to realize she and her children had to leave her abusive husband—and the United States—to find a safe haven. They moved to Calgary, where her training as a computer systems analyst and marketing manager, and her solid work ethic, allowed her to hook up with a small software company called CipherSystems. After a number of great years there, she bought out the owners and now has a company of her own called CipherSoft Inc. With offices in Calgary and Las Vegas, Jennifer and CipherSoft are making a name for themselves with Fortune 500 companies as they convert old legacy systems to newer Java-based platforms.

Jennifer could have stayed where she was and lived a life of quiet desperation, but she chose to act. And when the Calgary establishment told her she could never run a software firm, it was like raising a red flag to a bull, and she never looked back. Is she leading a charmed life? Hardly. But she enjoys a very demanding, fulfilling, high-energy job. The secret to her success?

"I watch and listen to successful people," she says. "I admire resiliency and the passion to build something. Life as a CEO is highly rewarding, but it's no bed of roses. I have a private company, but the board is very demanding. Although there are no women on the board, a third of my twenty-five employees are women."

Have jobs changed very much in the last thirty years? Absolutely! We live in a Knowledge Economy driven by technological advances and our unending desire to become more productive. Have attitudes to jobs changed as fast? Probably not. If your job is failing to give you the right balance of psychic and/or monetary rewards, have you asked yourself some questions. For example, do you really know what you want out of a job? Do you really know what you want out of life? Those are the questions to ask *before* you ask the secondary questions:

1. Do I know how to get what I want?
2. Am I being honest with myself?

That last question is one of the toughest to answer, but it must be answered if you want to get real about your career. Ann Kaplan knows herself pretty well. She's the mother of six children, but she's also a CEO.

"Most people don't know what they don't know, if you follow me," says Ann. "They want to be honest with themselves, but they seldom pull it off because they lack enough self-awareness. I think that slows them down in the workplace. I've worked hard to get to a place where I truly know what I don't know. In my business, for example, I immediately pull in people to help me when I don't know the answers."

Publisher Sarah Thomson knows herself pretty well, too. Although she's been working full time since she was a teenager, work doesn't define her.

"No job and no amount of money is going to make you happy," says Sarah. "Happiness and self-worth come from within. I worry about women who haven't learned that yet. I see all kinds of people who are addicted to the paycheque and don't know why. I've been broke and happy, and I've been wealthy and unhappy. And I can tell you it's not about the money."

If we were able to enter H.G. Wells' time machine and switch back in time to a typical 1970s corporate office, we'd probably be bored out of our minds. Why? Because the Knowledge Economy has changed everything. It's changed the *pace* at which we work, *how* we work and the *content* of our work. Now whether that's a good thing or bad thing, I'll leave you to decide. But not only has the *way* we work changed, the type of career path we take has changed as well.

ZIG IT AND ZAG IT

The new career path is a zigzag, not a straight line. And that is a good thing. People today zigzag through their careers the way hikers scale switchbacks to reach the top of a mountain. Along the way, they gain competencies in different organizations and sometimes in different fields of work. Switching jobs every few years has become common because today's workers want to keep themselves marketable. They refuse to get "stuck" in jobs that prevent them from staying "current." No longer dependent on the whims and wishes of our employer, many of us prefer to see ourselves as free agents or independent contractors—whether we actually are or not is irrelevant. This has added yet another layer of complexity to the already complex relationship we have with our work.

The ultimate free agents are people like Trish Kmet. Although she's a dentist, she managed to refresh her career—and her practice— by watching and listening to her mentor.

"At the beginning of my career I was a sponge, absorbing as much information about the business as possible," she says. "Now, I challenge myself to take on more difficult cases. My mentor, Dr. Serota, influenced me to go high-tech with my practice. Refreshing the business like that has made a huge difference to the level of service I provide my clients. Dr. Serota gathers groups of people together to discuss issues. We had a dinner recently in which we talked about women and dentistry, which is still a male-dominated profession."

As you know by now, I'm a big believer in finding your passion and making it work for you. To me, passion can never be a cliché, because passion is heartfelt desire, and desire can never go out of style. Unlike some people, I do not believe in quick fixes. There's no "five-step method" to career success and if there was, wouldn't everyone be doing it?

Colleen Johnston didn't become CFO of the TD Bank Financial Group by accident. She was always a self-motivated person, even as a child.

"My dad was a chartered accountant, and he was a great role model for me," she says.

Colleen believes the key to career success is to focus on the vital few, to pay attention to things that are important, not just urgent, and to pace yourself.

"I've become more passionate about my career as the years have gone on," says Colleen. "Twelve years ago, when I was working at another major Canadian bank, I was appointed to my first senior role, as CFO of Domestic Banking. I was more than a little naive because I tried to lead and build a vision for my team and develop concrete measures of success. I put the focus on customers, on internal morale, on leadership and on people. It was very exciting. It lit my passion for leadership. But I'm the first to admit I took a risk when I decided to lead this vision. I was questioned in subtle ways, like, 'How do you have time to do your job?' But in the end the strategy paid off, both for the organization and for me."

"I didn't see it as reinventing myself so much as finding the core person who was always there."

—LINDA WHELER, Pastoral Minister

I would add something else to Colleen's success keys— drive and determination. She found her passion early in life, but clearly it didn't grow into a burning desire until many years down the road. I think her drive and determination helped keep the passion alive.

Finding your true passion can be a slow, drawn-out process. Why? Because for many of us, the process begins with a commitment to self-insight. As we learned earlier, Minister of Pastoral Care Linda Wheler found her calling the hard way—when she was pregnant with her third child.

"The decision to leave accounting and become a minister was daunting at first," she admits. "But I knew it was the right choice after talking to my mentors and then going through a thorough self-assessment. I didn't see it as reinventing myself so much as finding the core person who was always there."

In my view, no one can advise you which way to turn unless you're already on the road. And Linda had been travelling that road for a while.

If Part I of "Get Real about Your Career" was about rethinking and refocusing, Part II is about making some kind of *change*, whether it involves incremental baby steps within your current job or jump-starting a brand new career. It's about developing the power to act. I'd like to highlight two distinct choices facing you if you want to get real about your career.

STAND STILL AND YOU'LL GET LEFT BEHIND

"My job's all right," you say. "It could be better, but I'm making an okay living. And if something better comes along, I'll grab it." But guess what? If you stand still, you'll get left behind, because the twenty-first century workplace is changing too fast.

I think there are two ways to transform your career.

The first, and probably the easiest, is to find a way to *refresh* your current job situation. If you decide to refresh your career, you're making a decision to *love what you do*. A lot of people never think about this route, seeking instead to make radical and potentially perilous career change instead. There's really no need to change careers if your current job is in an organization where other job opportunities are plentiful, or if there are opportunities to expand the scope and challenge of your current job. If for financial or other reasons you simply will not or cannot switch careers, then a career refresh could be in order.

For publicist Danielle Iversen, taking a career coaching course helped revive her career and her life.

"The self-knowledge I gained helped me end an unhealthy relationship," she says. "I got out of my comfort zone and refocused. I made the changes I had to make to grow, not just as a consultant but as a person."

The second way to transform your career is to find your *true vocation*. In other words, *do what you love*. If current job opportunities are extremely limited, or you are truly unhappy and performing poorly in your job, then a major career switch could be in order. However, embarking on a brand new career usually requires a sizable financial adjustment. Depending on your age and financial situation, switching careers can be painful or it can be liberating.

When Akela Peoples left her job in the school system to start her own company, Women in Motion (later to become Youth in Motion), it took courage and vision.

"I had no formal business training," she admits. "Fortunately, I have a lot of great role models and mentors in my life. One of them is my father, and another is Russ White, who hired me out of university. He helped me grow and develop my skills, and when I started this program, he helped me understand the business side of things. Russ is now my business partner at Youth in Motion."

If you're young and don't have a mortgage or family to support, the process is much easier than if you're a boomer with a mortgage and other responsibilities. You have to assess the potential sacrifices involved and make your decision accordingly.

But as I mentioned in Chapter 1, finding your passion is one of the greatest joys anyone can experience. It doesn't mean you can't find it later in life, or that there isn't more than one passion bottled up inside of you just aching to break out. The process of following your passion or finding a new career passion doesn't happen overnight. But the

"I got out of my comfort zone and refocused. I made the changes I had to make to grow, not just as a consultant but as a person."
—DANIELLE IVERSEN, President of That PR Thing

rewards, especially the psychic reward, can be enormous. The women you are meeting in this book have done both. They have refreshed their careers and reinvented themselves.

REFRESH YOUR CAREER—*"LOVE WHAT YOU DO"*

I want you to think hard about something before you decide on any radical changes to your own career. Do you have the right *attitude*? That's right. What's your mindset right now? Okay, you're in a rut, we know that. But if you're in a rut, be honest with yourself. Is it someone else's fault, or is it really your own? Try and be realistic in assessing the internal factors—not just the external ones—that are preventing you from enjoying your work. After all, the last thing you want to do is change direction, find another opportunity, and then discover you've put yourself in another rut.

START BY CHANGING YOUR ATTITUDE

A joint initiative between Statistics Canada and the Canadian Council on Learning, entitled "Survey of Canadian Attitudes towards Learning, 2006: Early Childhood Learning," found that Canadians think early childhood learning should focus on *attitudes*—such as fostering a positive attitude toward learning—rather than on school readiness. On the Canadian Council on Learning website (www.ccl-cca.ca/CCL/Reports/SCAL/SCAL2006ECL.htm) there is an excellent summary of the report, which covers a lot of issues and provides some interesting responses from Canadian mothers versus fathers. For example, while the mothers polled felt that "informal activities, such as reading and playing, are *more* important than more formal academic activities, such as organized classes," the fathers responded that "reading, playing and formal academic activities, such as organized classes, are all *equally* important."

"IT'S NOT LIKE I HAVE A LUCKY CHARM."

What's a corporate lawyer with three young children to do for a living if she doesn't have any mentors to guide her? Aimée Israel found the answer through her social network.

"I used to be a Bay Street lawyer," she says. "Now I'm an entrepreneur mom with a thriving national business. Many of my friends say that everything always works out for me. But I think a lot of it is due to my planning and focus. It's not like I have a lucky charm or anything!"

Maybe not a lucky charm—but lots of *personal* charm. After talking with her at length, I realized it's no coincidence that people like Aimée do well in life. She's very focused, and she radiates positive energy. People like to help people who know where they're going in life, and are poised, professional and fun to be around. It's as simple as that.

A POSITIVE OUTLOOK ALWAYS BEATS A NEGATIVE ONE

When you're in a negative state, focusing on your weaknesses or fears, your blood pressure and your breathing increases. Your facial muscles tighten and you prepare for "fight or flight." Your body literally shuts down. Being positive allows you to open yourself to new possibilities. Being negative closes off those possibilities.

As I mentioned earlier, the vast majority of the high-achieving women I interviewed consider themselves to be positive people. It's no coincidence. They see the glass as half full, not half empty, and if they had to choose between option (a) "life is difficult" and option (b) "life is fulfilling," most would choose (b). This is not mere semantics or idle speculation. Their answers are very much linked to their success in life because the answers they choose reflect their world view. And world view colours our choices, our interactions with others and everything we say and do. I'm sure you've heard the expression, "Thoughts become things." It's a cliché because it's true.

"My coaches believed in me, and that gave me confidence and extra motivation. I also had a 'mental coach' named Terry Orlick. He is still with the team. In fact, he was a very important part of my success and the team's success. I'm an optimistic realist—if I've done my preparation, I just naturally believe in an optimistic outcome. I've always been this way."

Who am I quoting? Olympic gold medallist Kerrin Lee-Gartner.

Think something negative often enough and long enough, and over time it becomes ingrained into your world view and eventually into a negative attitude. Think something positive often enough and long enough, and over time it becomes ingrained into a positive outcome—like perhaps a gold medal! If negative thought patterns about work have been ingrained into your world view, they can be very damaging to your career progress. Happily, negative thought patterns can be changed. Your world view can be changed with a little determination.

When it comes to making an adjustment to a belief, or a change to any long-held habit, practice makes perfect. Attitudinal change doesn't happen overnight, but when it does the payoff can be remarkable.

"If I've done my preparation, I just naturally believe in an optimistic outcome. I've always been this way."
—KERRIN LEE-GARTNER, Olympic gold medallist

Hopefully, you've started the process by rethinking your attitude to your job and to work in general. You may even have made a commitment to upgrade or change your attitude. What's next? It's time to revisit your strengths, desires, skills and inner motivations. You need to make sure you know who you are so you can map out some rough idea of where you want to go.

HOW NETWORKING CAN CHANGE YOUR PERSPECTIVE

When things have started to come into focus, I would strongly suggest contacting your network and using them as a sounding board for any ideas and thoughts you have. Why? Because a change of perspective is just as important as an attitude adjustment. And that's what your network and your mentors are for. Just remember, you must do some deep thinking first or you'll waste their time—and yours.

The only person who can ever truly recognize what general career path is best for you is *you*. Some women are lucky enough to recognize their path early in life. Pamela Jeffery, CEO of the Women's Executive Network, is one of those.

"My mother and father never pressured me to be something," Pamela says. "I figured it out for myself when I was a business student at the University of Western Ontario. I then figured it out again in 1997 when I decided to create the Women's Executive Network, while continuing to run a public affairs strategy consulting and search firm."

For the majority of women who haven't been lucky enough to see their career path as clearly, a very important next step is to regroup and refocus. Why? Because rethinking your job or career is going to feel uncomfortable at first. To refocus effectively, think about how you can be more open to the process, and begin to push yourself to think outside the box. Thinking outside the box means becoming more positive, adaptive, flexible and creative in your approach to your current career path. It will allow you to "see" things you haven't seen before, to quickly dismantle internal barriers you may have inadvertently set up for yourself.

The idea here is to come at things from a different angle. You need to be willing to stretch your thinking—and yourself—in novel ways. The goal is to see ways to increase the challenge and scope of the tasks in your current job, even if they are outside the job description you were given when you began.

RETHINK YOUR JOB

Don't forget to get back to basics. Remember what aspects of the job come easily to you or challenge you in a positive way, and then focus on expanding the scope of those activities. Study the internal job listings and look for new teams and opportunities sprouting up within your organization. Read the relevant trade journals and find out the latest trends and developments affecting your organization. Visualize yourself providing solutions in one or more of these areas. Find a way to insert yourself into the vanguard of these developments by, if appropriate, talking to your boss or network or mentor about some of these ideas and get his or her feedback.

But don't stop there. Life is a process of growth—and growth means constant learning, whether formally, through courses, or by doing some outside research. The Internet is one great source for ideas. You need to stay up on the latest issues and trends.

If you're wondering whether CEOs are too busy to read and learn, just ask Jennifer McNeill at CipherSoft.

"I read technical journals constantly, magazines like *ComputerWorld* and *Information Week*," she says. "I do Internet research to check out new technology and software. It's a never-ending process."

Get re-engaged with your job. Learn to do what high achievers have trained themselves to do and fully engage.

ACCEPTING CHANGE

Do you remember the classic Peggy Lee song, "Is That All There Is?" I think those words aptly sum up the malaise people feel when they're stuck in the wrong job. But it doesn't have to be that way. Don't get me wrong. You don't necessarily need to change your *job* to break out of the doldrums. Sometimes it can be as simple—and as complex—as changing your attitude, because research has proven that attitude has a huge impact on happiness and productivity.

If we want to make a lasting change in our lives, we have to overcome initial feelings of inertia and then the fear of the unknown. But when you face your fears head on, there's a freeing sense of relief that will enable you to enter the next phase of your transformation: rethinking your job. Again, this is where thinking outside the box comes into play. How can you make your job more fulfilling without incurring your boss's wrath? Ask him or her!

Specifically, ask how you can add more value to the job you already do. You're unlikely to get a negative response. Depending on the exact answer you get, ask if there are internal training programs or courses that will allow you to upgrade your skills and education to create that added value. And so goes the upward cycle.

KEEP ON LEARNING

How important is constant learning to your career? A survey jointly developed by the Council of Learning and Statistics Canada found that almost 69 percent of adults take courses to perform more effectively in their current jobs. This is according to the first-ever "Survey of Canadian Attitudes toward Learning: Canada's Barometer of Opinions, Perceptions and Beliefs about Lifelong Learning." In a purely coincidental yet related press release, the Council of Learning reported on October 10, 2006, that the majority (two-thirds) of parents say they can't help their children with homework. I think the latter point is the most important one.

REINVENT YOUR CAREER

Making a mid-life career change often means changing your lifestyle because your income is no longer as high, stable or secure as it once was. But, like all change, it also holds the opportunity for tremendous fulfillment and personal satisfaction. Do your research—know what you bring to the table, and what skills you'll need to pick up. Be emotionally prepared for what "starting at the bottom" means to you and your family after you've held a more senior job in your old occupation. Prepare a detailed budget and allow for unexpected expenses. Use professional career counselling services if you need help.

The first step to reinventing yourself and your career is *wanting* to make it happen. Sometimes, we discover a hidden talent or passion, or it is discovered for us. Sometimes, a life-changing experience will force us to re-examine our lives, as was the case with Pamela Jeffery and Natalie Bean-Sole.

In 1997, Pamela and her partner ran a public affairs strategy consulting firm called Burstyn Jeffery. She was there four days a week and arranged flex time with her partner so she could take her then 3-year-old son to medical appointments. One day each week she would take him to a pediatric rehab hospital to help him recover from a bout with deadly bacterial meningitis when he was seven weeks old.

The business was going well and they had fifteen to twenty clients when her partner left to join a competing firm that had wanted to buy the company.

"The company was raided by my competitor, who my former partner joined forces with," she says. "It was a devastating experience. I was left with all but a handful of clients (they, at least, were loyal to me), virtually no staff and a $250,000 lease. Fear is a great motivator. I changed the name to The Jeffery Group and worked day and night to be a good mother and to rebuild the business. Back in 1995, GM was a client and they wanted to bring a diverse group of women opinion leaders together. It turned out there wasn't such a group in existence, so we brought them together ourselves for the first time at a breakfast meeting."

Pamela's former partner had not been interested in "the women's business," but Pamela was. Late in 1997, Pamela began to hire staff as she rebuilt the firm and launched the Women's Executive Network. Pamela and her group eventually organized a half-dozen breakfast meetings until in the spring of 1998 they launched the Women's Executive Network (WXN).

"I trademarked the name, and we now work with a who's who of corporate Canada as clients," she says proudly. "We provide them with learning and development opportunities for their female managers and executives, as well as providing them with valuable marketing opportunities to connect with this important target market of affluent women opinion leaders. WXN now has over 10,000 members across the country who are invited to attend thirty-four breakfasts each year, receive professional development in our Women's Executive Forum program and obtain peer mentoring in our WXNWisdom program. In 2003, I decided there wasn't enough being done in Canada to recognize our female leaders and so we created and launched the annual Canada's Most Powerful Women: Top 100™ Awards and Summit."

Nutritionist Natalie Bean-Sole had a big weight problem until she turned 16 and decided she'd had enough. She wanted to feel good about herself for a change, so she worked to pay for a personal trainer and gradually lost the weight.

> *"Fear is a great motivator."*
> —PAMELA JEFFERY, CEO of Women's Executive Network

"I graduated and then studied social work, focusing on women and eating disorders," she says. "It became a passion. If anyone wanted to know anything about how many calories there were in anything, I had the answer! I went to work for Jenny Craig and gained the practical nutritional experience I'd need to eventually start my own business at 27."

FACING YOUR FEARS

Fear of change is a very real phenomenon, but it is also a debilitating one. All of us have self-limiting beliefs. It's part of being human. And when it comes to careers, there are two really big ones: fear of failure, and fear of change.

Fear of change is a reality—I certainly know what it feels like. When I changed my first job, I was terrified I'd made an irreversible mistake. It takes hard work to change. Real change requires commitment and a willingness to exit your comfort zone for an extended period of time. This is probably why people rarely make fundamental transformations of this kind. Not because the transformation is not possible, but because we lack the commitment required.

Lesley Southwick-Trask has an interesting take on the fear of change.

"A client manager approached me and said, 'I see exactly what you're talking about, all these organizations learning from one another. This is Corporate Culture Anonymous for Managers.' I laughed, but I think he hit the nail on the head. We're all addicted to maintaining control, to avoiding failure, to doing things the way we always have. We can't help it. And we need one another to break the habit," she says.

If you're serious about changing, you must accept that hard work and discipline lie ahead. But the rewards are worth the effort. As this change develops, you will begin to internalize the new feeling and develop confidence in your new direction. Confidence is derived from repetition because repetition fosters familiarity.

OUR FEAR OF FAILURE

We're "addicted" to work for a slew of very practical reasons, including money and habit. Habit might be a tougher addiction to shake than a big salary, but not by much. In our society it's usually considered a failure if someone leaves a job with a big paycheque for one with a smaller salary.

Failure is a very subjective word. Most of the women interviewed in this book say that failure is a necessary learning experience. And that should apply to organizations as well as individuals. But unfortunately, that's not always the case. Why does good news always travel upward so much faster than bad news? Some of that is fear of "killing the messenger." It's interesting that the former head of Enron, Jeffrey Skilling, was notorious for telling his executives that he didn't want to hear *any* bad news. He was clearly an executive in denial.

Denial comes from fear. Fear of change and fear of failure are almost interchangeable. Even thinking about new situations and challenges makes some of us doubt our abilities, our intelligence or our capacity to overcome obstacles that may arise. However, if our self-worth is strong, fears may still exist, but they no longer have the power to permanently cripple us. Failure is just a temporary setback or a learning experience.

Fear of success is the flip side of fear of failure. Fear of the unknown creates anxiety. You may wonder if you can live up to the demands and expectations of others. If you are a private person, you may not want the spotlight. You may believe you don't deserve to be financially successful or think it's selfish or sinful to achieve wealth. Some may wonder whether they deserve to be happy, or whether happiness now will result in tragedy later on. We may worry about negative reactions from bitter or envious friends and family.

There are many reasons people are fearful, but there is only one thing that will get rid of them: face your fears head on. And the quickest way to overcome fear of failure is to take a risk. Not a "bet the farm" risk but a smaller one and preferably a calculated one. What's the downside? If you fail, you'll realize it's not such a big deal. And if you succeed, you'll feel a genuine sense of accomplishment and, if you let it, your confidence will begin to grow.

WHAT WOULD YOU DO IF FAILURE WASN'T POSSIBLE?

"If you knew you couldn't fail, what would you do?" Dee Brasseur said to me when I asked her about failure and how debilitating it can be for many people.

Imagine that there was no such thing as failure, just success in everything you did. How would that change your mindset about your job? Failure is the thing most of us spend the greatest amount of energy trying to avoid. If failure wasn't possible.... Hmmm, yes. A nice thought.

You'd probably visualize a different picture, reframe your thoughts, start freeing yourself from fear. But how? Fear is reduced by knowledge. The better you know yourself, the lower your fear levels, and the lower your risk. The more you know and accept yourself, and focus on the positives, the less you worry about what your peers think, the more likely you are to see yourself as an independent free agent who has choices and takes action.

Procrastination is another big obstacle to change. We're only human, and making tough decisions isn't always easy. It's much simpler to take the easy way out rather than deal with something that's difficult, boring or unpleasant.

It's clear to me from talking to my interviewees that a lot of people are living their lives without passion, and many are slaving away at jobs they hate. As you can probably tell by now, I truly believe your work should either be your passion or it should become your passion. At the very least, it should be a source of satisfaction or recognition. If it isn't any of these, why the heck do it? Life is too short to spend forty, fifty, sixty or more hours every week doing something you dislike, no matter how much money they give you.

But it's much easier to stay stuck, isn't it? The status quo may not be great, but it doesn't hurt *that* much. People are quite logical, intelligent beings: "My life doesn't hurt that much right now, why go out and change everything? Hey, if and when things get too painful, I'll do something about it." Fine, I understand the logic.

But there's just one BIG problem, as we know. Logic has nothing to do with change. Change is all about an emotion called fear. Failure is really only feedback. Failure means that we tried something and it didn't work. Human beings learn by trial and error, by understanding what doesn't work, and by continuing to adjust their strategies until they find out what does. People never fail if they never try to accomplish anything with their lives. And they never succeed either. We can't grow unless we take risks. Taking risks is about finding the courage to say yes.

FINDING THE COURAGE

We humans seem to be pretty adaptable species. We bounce back to our "normal" state of happiness after critical injury, natural disasters or even winning the lottery.

But ask virtually anyone you know and if they're honest about it they'll tell you: the effects of a job loss linger long after they've returned to the work force. Is it any wonder we are sometimes afraid to get off the spinning carousel? The carousel? What's that?

Think of your job or career path like a carousel at an amusement park. You get on it early, when it's barely moving. At first, that's fine because all you're doing is feeling your way around. But as you progress at your job, you generate energy and competence and comfort, and the carousel begins to spin imperceptibly faster. The more experience you get, the faster the carousel goes, until one day you wake up and realize it's spinning pretty fast even though you don't want to be there, and you start to think about jumping off. But maybe you don't make the leap because you figure you'll wait until the opportunity is right. You know, when deadlines slow down, you'll get off. That sort of thing.

But the carousel doesn't slow down, you don't make a decision, and things keep going faster and faster. And the faster the carousel goes, the harder it is to jump off without really hurting yourself, until you reach the point where you say, "Hey! How do I get off this thing?" There's no response, so you start to shout. "Help...! Help...!" But no one hears you because of the din—thousands of like-minded souls are screaming all at once.

THE FASTER YOU SPIN, THE DIZZIER YOU GET

It's easy to get stuck on the job carousel. The faster you spin, the dizzier you get, until you lose perspective of the outside world. Why do so many intelligent people jump on this carousel in the first place? According to my interviewees, there are at least a couple of reasons.

When children are young, especially children from professional or well-to-do families, friends and family continually reinforce and emphasize certain values and attitudes. Youngsters are impressionable and they learn a lot of unwritten rules. For example, they learn that certain lifestyles and future career-tracks are deemed "appropriate," while others are discouraged. As a result, when some of these kids become adults, their career or lifestyle views have gotten so internalized they go unquestioned.

Children in other families might grow up anxious about money because their parents were always that way. Or they might learn to value material things to the exclusion of personal fulfillment. If anxiety trumps creativity, or if money needs triumph over inner needs, they may grow up to choose dull jobs that pay a steady salary, or they may choose careers that have loads of status but offer little in the way of personal growth or creativity.

The satisfaction of a secure job; the thrill of moneymaking; these things always wear off. But by the time they do, the carousel is usually spinning too fast.

UPGRADING YOUR SKILLS/EDUCATION

If you've decided to follow your passion, you're going to reinvent yourself and create a new career path. You'll likely need to upgrade your skills and probably go back to school, either part-time or full-time. But first you need to identify any transferable skills, abilities and experience developed through previous work and education. Skills such as the ability to negotiate, analyze, create, write, communicate and persuade are always in demand. Make sure you include any volunteer and community work. If you're serious about making the move, read the key trade publications and literature in the industry to which you're moving.

FOLLOW YOUR PASSION

Saskatchewan girl Joan Kelley-Weisshaar came to Toronto to find herself and make a career. She started as a waitress and a model, but worked hard and took the risks needed to develop a highly creative and rewarding career. She's proud to have made a difference in the lives of the people she's met through the years. A mother, TV producer and owner of a production company, Joan now sits on boards, and performs charity work. Yet she maintains her prairie values—being kind, doing what you say you're going to do, enjoying life and treating others with respect. "I've found my passion. But it's funny, in my high school yearbook, under my photo where it says 'Ambition?' I wrote, 'To find one.'"

"I think there should to be passion in everything you do. And that means being true to yourself and being realistic about your true desires, not about status or prestige."
—JOAN KELLEY-WEISSHAAR, TV Producer and Director, Founder of Hero Media

Joan's philosophy is to always give people the benefit of the doubt because, "I always look for the good in people. I feel people are naturally good, but I'm not naive. I realize that conditioning and socialization can sometimes change that."

"I think there should be passion in everything you do," she continues. "And that means being true to yourself and being realistic about your true desires, not about status or prestige. If you don't have a passion for something as an adult, I think it slowly eats away at you. You really need to work at it, to explore all your options. It's horrible when people are afraid to try."

Joan knows how to keep an even keel when it comes to career issues. "From the very beginning I felt I wanted to focus on and establish my career, to accomplish something before having a family. I wanted choice! And I'm fortunate to say that I now have it."

PERSIST

Perhaps the biggest factor separating successful career women from unsuccessful ones is persistence. Yes, it's an old-fashioned word, but it's as valid today as it ever was.

A great example of persistence is Ann Kaplan's story. She has built Medicard into Canada's leading medical finance company, but it certainly didn't come easily.

Ann wouldn't take no for an answer in 1996 when she went looking for financing for her medical finance start-up business. She remembers the sheer will it took to keep going.

"I knocked on what seemed like hundreds of investment doors without success," she explains. "But I continued to believe in myself and my idea, and I always made sure I left every meeting with a referral. Then one day, I met Stuart Belkin of Belcourt Industries. He liked my idea, but most important, he liked the passion and commitment to the business that was behind it."

Belkin agreed to give her the initial financing she needed and her dream took off. Medicard was an idea no longer. She was now able to offer financing to persons seeking elective medical procedures. At the time there was a growing demand for reconstructive surgery, laser eye treatments, skin resurfacing, cosmetic dentistry and other procedures not covered by the public health care system.

> *"I continued to believe in myself and my idea, and I always made sure I left every meeting with a referral."*
>
> —ANN KAPLAN, CEO of Medicard

But the hard work had just begun. To make her business a major player and a long-term survivor, she needed a second round of financing. Not long after, she went to the Bank of Montreal and secured a line of credit for $5 million—an unprecedented amount for a woman entrepreneur at that time. But her personal struggles were equally challenging.

"My first marriage ended shortly before Medicard really took shape," she says. "I was left with two young children to raise and I was in a precarious position financially. I worked full-time as an interior designer and put a portion of each cheque back into the business. I rented out rooms in the house to foreign exchange students."

Ann's goal was to make Medicard "Canada's medical finance and information company." With a driver and a map she also canvassed physicians and clinics in all the major cities across Canada to present the concept, seeing as many as thirty-five physicians in one day, and making appearances at trade shows.

"The business grew," she says. "It took thirteen months to book the first million dollars in loans. It took a month to book the second million. I'm proud to say Medicard is now the largest medical finance company in Canada, and we've expanded to offer medical equipment leasing and third-party collections for dentists and physicians."

Now that's what I call persistence!

WHY WOMEN BUSINESS OWNERS SUCCEED

More women than ever are leaving the corporate world to start their own businesses. Women are increasingly abandoning the corporate world for entrepreneurship in search of better control of their time, their futures and their financial destinies. Between 1989 and 2004, the number of self-employed Canadian women increased by 50 percent. Self-employed women currently make up approximately one-third of the total number of self-employed Canadians.

Anecdotal evidence shows that a large percentage of successful businesswomen had a supportive father. This was confirmed in my interviews with business owners such as Ann Kaplan, Sarah Raiss, Jennifer McNeill and Sarah Thomson. They all considered their fathers to be their biggest supporters.

THE GLASS CEILING

Are there invisible barriers to career growth for women—the so-called "glass ceiling"? It depends on who you ask, and what sector you're talking about. But a good indication comes from third-party research. *CFO Magazine* surveyed a group of finance executives on the topic (June 1, 2006, "What Women Want: In Finance, the Operative Words Are Opportunity, Flexibility, and Balance" by Alix Nyberg Stuart). This was their major finding: while an overwhelming 83 percent of the male executives *don't* believe the glass ceiling exists, only 44 percent of the women executives agreed with them. Although virtually no one thinks women lack the skills or talent to be a CFO, perception and reality do not always mesh.

I'm a believer that there may be subtle barriers, but there is a fool-proof way for women to overcome these hurdles. It's called persistence. Colleen Johnston is CFO of the TD Bank Financial Group, a multi-billion-dollar organization.

> *"Criticism never deterred me."*
> —COLLEEN JOHNSTON, CFO of TD Bank Financial Group

"Criticism never deterred me," she says. "My experiences just make me more determined to go on with the road I've chosen."

AGENTS OF CHANGE

It's interesting that many of the women I interviewed referred to themselves as "change agents." I see myself that way, too, because I'm trying to make a positive impact on the lives of the women I meet at financial seminars and financial forums. Money issues play a huge role in the quality of our lives, and the more financially literate we become, the happier and more independent we will be.

As an Executive Vice President at TransCanada Corporation, Sarah Raiss has a slightly different perspective.

"I see myself as a change agent because I'm in a position to help people grow while I help my organization grow as well," she says. "From a very young age, that was my mission. I initially wanted to be a teacher, then decided to get into the business world. I received degrees in applied math instead of an electrical engineering degree so that I could take psychology and sociology courses, then went back to school to get my MBA starting part-time and finishing up full-time when I was 30."

With this kind of background, Sarah was clearly arming herself for a uniquely powerful career. But there's more to career success than just technical competence, and for Sarah it was reflected in her choice of role models—first, her parents, and now, her sister.

> "I know who I am and I'm not afraid to take risks."
> —SARAH RAISS, Executive Vice President at TransCanada Corporation

"My father was a businessman who gave back to the community," she explains. "He was a very logical thinker, very focused on his career, and a very intense communicator. My mother was a very creative person. She was the leader of tons of non-profit organizations and her motto was, 'one person *can* make a difference.' Everyone loved her and respected her. But now, my biggest role model is my sister. She got a B.Sc. in electrical engineering, taught at university, and went on to get her master's in Divinity. She met and married the love of her life— another minister—and now she teaches at a bible college. She's truly an authentic being."

Sarah says one of the keys to career success is being willing to volunteer for special projects. Some people may think they're time-wasters or career-killers, but not Sarah.

"[Volunteering for special projects] offers you visibility, creativity and a welcome element of control." Sarah's formula for success is pretty simple. "I know who I am and I'm not afraid to take risks. I've always challenged myself and I've never allowed myself to get bogged down in the politics."

In contrast, Lesley Southwick-Trask's job is to consult on and implement change, as President and co-founder of Owl's Head Retreat. Her company is known across Canada for its innovative thinking and change implementation expertise. Lesley attributes a good part of her success to being able to "get out of her own way."

"In the past I might have constricted my value to others because I wrapped myself up in so-called 'proven' paradigms for change," she explains. "Then, about ten years ago, I stopped deluding myself that change is mechanistic. Because I now see change as an organic process, it must be carefully cultivated or it will wither away."

Lesley is intimately acquainted with personal transformation. Earlier in her career she was VP of Human Resources for an oil and gas company and later CEO of a company with two hundred employees. Lesley estimates she has "reinvented" herself five times. She's gone from management consultant to entrepreneur to strategy consultant to CEO to her current position as a transformational strategist.

Lesley is paid by people and organizations to reshape their futures. But there is a much deeper issue for her. Her ultimate mission is to optimize human performance at a time when a sea of change is taking place in the workplace and society as a whole.

"It's important for us to go to places that scare us," she says, "to embrace change, because we're so much more capable than that for which we give ourselves credit."

One of her keys to success is focus.

"Focus is absolutely mandatory for me," she explains. "I deliver on every commitment by continually sticking to my priorities no matter the distractions. I'm a bit of a workaholic, partly because I love my work and partly because I don't know how to say 'no' very easily. But I'm learning."

> "It's important for us to go to places that scare us, to embrace change, because we're so much more capable than that for which we give ourselves credit."
> —LESLEY SOUTHWICK-TRASK, Co-founder of Owl's Head Retreat

A key turning point in Lesley's life occurred when she was in her twenties. She was accepted as an apprentice for CBC Radio but chose to go back to what she calls the "faster track business world." There's no question, her early role models helped forge her world view and passion for life.

"My father was a brilliant consultant and speaker," she says. "I used to sit in the back of the room while my father told stories. He was a workaholic, and so I learned from the best. The qualities I most admired in him were his optimism, his ability to debate and his futuristic approach to life. He was one of the founders of Medicare, and I believe the source of many of his innovative ideas came from a wonderful ability to never accept the status quo. I'm grateful he's passed that along to me."

As a Vice President and Director at TD Securities Inc., Jacqui Szeto might not define herself as a change agent. But now that she's also become President of Women in Capital Markets (WCM), a voluntary networking, education and advocacy group, she's having an impact on the "old boys" culture that still defines the capital markets workplace. WCM members are women involved in the issuing, buying, selling or trading of securities, currencies and derivatives. Jacqui says there are nearly six hundred members, and she's working on increasing the number to seven hundred by the end of 2007.

"The culture is changing slowly, not quickly," she says. "Women working in the capital markets arena feel they have to act like a man, be like a man. Then later on, they get tired of it. A lot of them leave. Not because they can't handle the workload so much as the culture or, in some cases, the need to have a family. This creates a whole new issue—work/life balance. The problem isn't attracting skilled women to capital markets, it's retaining them."

Jacqui quotes a 2001 WCM study, which found that more than two-thirds of women believe the "commitment to personal and family responsibilities" is the biggest barrier to advancement in capital markets.

Jacqui Szeto isn't worried that being the President of Women in Capital Markets will hurt her career. She's been a risk-taker all her life, although she doesn't necessarily agree with that assessment.

"People see me as a risk-taker, but I feel I'm quite a cautious person in most ways," she says. "When I'm driving, for example, I never overtake people on the road. Growing up in Hong Kong, I guess I was a bit of a black sheep, I avoided conforming. The

"You do need to find the right time to shine, so pick your spots wisely."
—JACQUI SZETO, Vice President and Director at TD Securities Inc. and President of Women in Capital Markets

biggest risk I ever took? Marrying my husband just seven days after meeting him! And to top it off, my mother nearly disowned me for marrying a non-Chinese person!"

Jacqui has worked hard—and still works hard—to build an outstanding reputation in Canada's bond markets. Her institutional clients depend on her for up-to-the-minute market information. But they depend on her honesty and tenacity even more. Ironically, women who take career risks are usually extremely passionate about their jobs, although their passion sometimes takes a while to take root. Jacqui explains what happened during her own career.

"I have a real passion for my work, I'm good at it, and if I didn't like it, I know the *quality* of my work would be tremendously affected," she says. "I work in institutional sales in a heavily male-dominated area: capital markets. Capital markets include mutual fund management, investment banking, sales and trading, financial planning and corporate finance. I had a pretty difficult time when I entered capital markets. I didn't get a lot of support and direction, and what I did get wasn't always that clear. The experience made me stronger and I gained some valuable insight as well."

And what's her advice to up-and-comers in her area?

"If you want success in capital markets—or in any financial services arena—my advice is to keep learning about different products, always think outside the box, keep adapting to the changing environment," she offers. "The Internet has accelerated everything. I do masses of internal research but I also read *Bloomberg, Barron's,* and I do a lot of self-learning by downloading business books on my iPod. Be diligent, always be willing to learn, have a good work ethic, and don't be a prima donna, be a team player. You do need to find the right time to shine, so pick your spots wisely."

LEARNING TO TAKE CALCULATED RISKS

Younger Canadians seem to be more risk-tolerant when it comes to careers. What about our high-achieving women? You guessed correctly if you said they were risk-takers, no matter what their age. In fact, the majority of the women I interviewed said that their willingness to take calculated risks was a key reason behind their career success.

Sarah Raiss took a risk early in her career when she worked at Michigan Bell.

"There was a staff meeting of about 350 people on a difficult topic," she explains. "I don't exactly know what happened, but I put my hand up and volunteered to do a presentation on this difficult topic. I realized I wanted to stand out from the crowd and be visible. I was extremely nervous before the presentation, and I spilled tea onto my business suit and blouse. That sure broke the ice and helped to make it a success!"

Why is risk-taking so important? Writer and career coach Penelope Trunk had an interesting take on this issue in the May 7, 2005, edition of her blog, the Brazen Careerist. In an article entitled "Career Change Is Inevitable, So Plan for It" she says: "One look at the Amazon.com business books bestsellers' list reveals the biggest career problem, at least for people who buy business books, [is] fear of changing careers."

TODAY'S EMPLOYEES HAVE TO BECOME "OWNERS"

Today's career female could be characterized this way: *Flexible. Entrepreneurial. Accommodating. Focused.* I think these might be the key attributes of *all* modern employees and their twenty-first-century employers. The world of work is changing rapidly, and the pace of acceleration can only quicken. In this environment, we keep learning or we fall behind. We have to be entrepreneurial because jobs are no longer guaranteed to us. And we have to be flexible so we can take advantage of the right opportunities when they arise. Today's employees have become "owners." To succeed, we must take ownership of our careers.

Today's employers must allow employees to become creative, self-directed "entrepreneurs" within the organization. We all want to work harder and smarter, but time and energy and lack of confidence and focus are our greatest opponents. If we *don't* know what we want, how can we possibly get it? And if we *know* what we want and have the ability to get it, why don't we just go out there and grab it?

CONFIDENCE

Self-confidence means (literally) "faith in yourself." Lack of inner confidence is a key reason people don't have the career they could have. Confidence isn't about being able to speak to people without being shy. That's really about being an introvert or extrovert. Confidence is about having a feeling of certainty and self-belief—an absence of doubt.

AN ANTIDOTE FOR THE GLASS CEILING

Many of my interviewees say the glass ceiling is not an issue. But not all. "The ceiling may have been shattered," says Jacqui Szeto, "but some of the pieces have been glued back together."

Just what is the biggest obstacle to developing a great career? Is it lack of education? Lack of experience? Poor bosses? Uncooperative co-workers? Lack of interpersonal skills?

It's none of the above, according to Catalyst, a not-for-profit women's research organization with offices in Toronto, New York, San Jose and Zug. The glass ceiling seems to be alive and well in the corporate world. In a 2005 study, "Women Take Care, Men Take Charge: Stereotyping of U.S. Business Leaders Exposed," Catalyst surveyed 296 corporate leaders (128 men and 168 women), of whom 34 percent were CEOs, 41 percent were one reporting level from the CEO, and 10 percent were two reporting levels from the top.

The study's top finding—and one I find most surprising—was that men consider women to be less skilled at problem-solving, which is one of the top qualities of effective leadership. The second big finding is equally shocking: women are not considered "take-charge" people. To quote the report: "Both women and men considered significantly more men superior to women at 'take charge' behaviours such as delegating and influencing upward."

What's disappointing is not so much that men have this view, but that women see themselves as not being take-charge types as well. Do I believe these findings? Of course. However, I think these studies may be looking more at the symptoms than the root cause.

Yes, I believe there is gender stereotyping in the workplace. But I believe it's a barrier that both men and women must help bring down. The good news is, I think it is happening as a new, younger, more forward-thinking generation rises up the executive ranks.

What can women do—on their own—to break down the barriers to career success? In other words, what is under their own control? The wonderful women I've been interviewing for the book may have the answer. Besides the glass ceiling, there's another equally big career obstacle for many women—a problem that is more difficult to explore, and that in some ways is a much more powerful barrier than the glass ceiling. And it's a much more common problem than people think.

It was hinted at in the Catalyst research report above. The biggest career obstacle women face could be their own self-limiting *belief* system.

NEGOTIATING YOUR WORTH

Many competent women wonder if they have what it takes to be successful at the top jobs. This feeling occurs less frequently with men than with women. Why? In general, women have been conditioned to play along, to be nurturing and supportive team players, rather than achievement-oriented agents of their own destiny.

Want evidence that women undervalue themselves? One clear example is during performance appraisals. As I discussed earlier, women often fail to push for a pay raise or promotion, no matter how deserved.

What it all comes down to is choice. *Our* choice. But we have to make things happen, not let them happen. Publisher Sarah Thomson believes traditionalist thinking is made more prevalent by the media.

"Most media companies don't understand that women's interests have changed since the fifties," says Sarah. "They continue to produce beauty, fashion, health and gardening magazines that in general attract very young women and very old women, but do not capture the largest, most powerful segment of the female market. Women want intimacy, emotion and context. Give them ideas and information, but give it to them in an intimate format, one they can relate to in a voice that carries emotion."

Your career can be a source of pride or it can be a source of frustration. It can be a lifelong adrenalin rush or a source of anxiety and heartache. It's your choice. I do not mean to oversimplify such a complex issue, but how your career affects you is always, in the final analysis, up to you. It's very difficult to create major changes for yourself without reaching out. Some say don't even try.

FIND A GOOD CAREER COACH

If you're looking to make a big change in your life, I recommend talking to a reputable life coach or executive coach first. There are many good ones. Do some checking, and start with a list of Canadian coaching associations.

Focus, self-awareness, confidence, a support network, interpersonal skills, courage and tenacity are all key factors, whether you are looking to refresh your career or reinvent it. However, I don't believe you need to change your career unless you truly are the proverbial round peg in a square hole, because reinventing yourself and your career can be a pretty drastic financial and emotional move. You either need to be young or have lots of financial support. But it's entirely possible to *refresh* your job or career without bending yourself into a pretzel, as you've witnessed with my own career at the TD Bank Financial Group.

Money plays a big role in our choice of careers. But maybe that role is overplayed. As we'll see in the next chapter, there are four ways you can become wealthy: Win it. Earn it. Inherit it. Invest it.

Personal finance is of rising interest to women as they strive for full financial independence. Most of us need to educate ourselves more fully, which is why financial education is an area I've dedicated my life to. Now I'd like to share with you a few secrets to making your hard-earned money work harder for you. Are you ready to get real about your money? Then let's go!

FOUR

GET REAL ABOUT YOUR MONEY

WHY DO WE GET SO DARN emotional about money? Why does making it, spending it, losing it, borrowing it, lending it, handling it, gambling it and sometimes just thinking about it, hit every jittery, jumpy nerve in our body?

Money touches virtually every primal emotion inside us. It inspires fear, greed, anger, love, envy and frustration. Money flirts with us, loves us, leaves us and returns to us as if it had never been away. Money is the most self-absorbed, unappreciative, two-timing lover we're ever likely to meet. Money couldn't care less about our feelings but is always willing to be adored. Money gives us not a whit of love or affection, yet we always come back for more. Why?

Because money is a mirror. It reflects back our energy, and our financial focus. If we stare at it, it just stares back at us. If we put it under the mattress, it won't sleep like a baby, it will just stagnate. But, if we put energy and discipline and creativity into our money, it will reflect that back and grow. I don't see money as a friend or a lover or a pet. If I were to compare it to a living thing, I'd say it was an ever-green that needs watering and the right location to flourish year after year. If you look around, you'll see a lot of evergreens in need of some tender loving care.

Money is a kind of living organism without a brain. We are supposed to supply the brain. But instead of treating money simply and in a straightforward way, we invest our hopes and dreams into it, we rely on it for emotional support and we even restructure our lives around it. Money is the ultimate example of unrequited love. We can love it all we want but it's never going to love us back.

MONEY TIP: *Canadian women live 4.8 years longer than their male counterparts. At some stage in your life, you could be entirely responsible for your financial future. The time to take charge of your money is now.*

TURNING NEGATIVE INTO POSITIVE

Whether we want to admit it or not, the power of money comes from the mind—*our* mind, and nobody else's. And we simply don't want to admit it. Money conjures up so many illusions. We sometimes believe it will set us free at last and make us young again and turn the world into a magical place.

Am I saying money issues are all in our mind? Of course not. Money is very real and very necessary. We all need a *base* amount of money to survive and to live a decent life. What I'm talking about for most of you is the *extra* money you think you need to be happy. I'm talking about the money you think you need to get off your own financial treadmill.

I don't for a moment buy into the stereotype that women are emotional about money and men are not. We're *all* emotional about money, if in highly different ways. Women often associate money with anxiety and loss of love. I think a lot of this is the residue of female social conditioning around *protection* issues. Men's feelings around money often focus on power and prestige. Men are raised to believe they'll be good at dealing with money—yet they seldom get schooling in how to do it. I think a lot of this is the residue of male social conditioning around *status* issues.

If anyone should know about money issues, it has to be Colleen Johnston, Chief Financial Officer of the TD Bank Financial Group.

And the role she plays with respect to the bank's money is supported by her years of professional experience and training. "For me, there's no emotion attached to that aspect of the job. I've been trained in the art of corporate money management most of my life. But for many people, how they deal with their personal finances really reflects their values and, perhaps, control issues," she says. What's Colleen's approach to personal money management?

"My husband and I have always worked hard," she tells me. "We both had great parents who made sure we were well educated—but after that we made every dollar ourselves; nothing has ever been given to us. My husband was more frugal than me at first, but we're a team. We've always lived within our means, and that reduces stress and emotion. Having said that, we don't use a detailed budget. We take the view that you have to decide how you want to spend your money over- all, because it's important to enjoy the money you earn."

Jacqui Szeto agrees. She and her husband work hard because they love their work, and they see money for what it is—a great instrument for a lifestyle of freedom and independence.

"Friends ask me why I work when my husband is a bond trader and makes plenty of money. 'Why not?' I say. I love my work and I want to make a difference," she states emphatically. "Money should not be the most important factor, but society measures a lot of our success by how much we make. I want to be valued and independent. My husband and I think it's important to manage the money we earn. We're both in the capital markets arena, and we use Quicken every day to man- age our finances. We know to the cent what our net worth is. It's all electronic."

> "You have to decide how you want to spend your money overall, because it's important to enjoy the money you earn."
> —COLLEEN JOHNSTON, CFO of TD Bank Financial Group

Jacqui's not a hoarder, however. She loves to shop, she loves to do charity work and she's a new mother, having adopted a beautiful baby girl.

Does money really buy happiness? We know the obvious answer: "no." The clever answer is "yes." But the true answer prob- ably lies somewhere in between. We all know money is important, and we know it's a sensitive subject. We usually know more about our friends' love lives than we do about their money situation. Thanks to the media and the most recent boom and bust cycle in the stock market, we know more about money than ever before. At the same time, we seem to be more fearful about it than ever before. What many of us don't seem willing to acknowledge is how deeply money infiltrates the smallest fragments of our daily lives. Money seeps insidiously into every nook and cranny of our existence, sometimes helping, and sometimes spoiling things like spilled red wine on a cream-coloured sofa.

When I started to ask questions about money, the answers that came from the women in this book made me realize something. There were a ton of contradictions. As I said before, many women tend to see money as a source of security and protection. They have a much more egalitarian, almost dependent view of it, and recent research backs that up. But today's woman doesn't want to be dependent any more, and so money contradictions arise. I've learned that the best way to cure money anxiety is through *knowledge*. That's why the women who come to my seminars are way ahead of the game financially. They may not have decided on a course of action, but they've decided to take charge of their money in some way. All they need is some guidance. In my experience, women have carried around too many myths about their money, but as recent polls suggest, they are becoming more financially literate. That's not only helping improve their future retirement plans, it's helping their *current* lifestyle as well.

SWEEP AWAY THE DUSTBALLS

Money can't rob us of our power unless we let it. The key word here is "*unless*." How do we contain that evil desire that lies within us all—the need to keep up with the Joneses? There's a simple starting point, and we discussed it in Chapter 1. And Chapter 2. And Chapter 3. It's called *knowledge*—more specifically, *self-knowledge*. And the first key element in developing self-knowledge is a change of attitude. And that happens when we clear the negative myths out of our financial closet. These myths are what I call our "financial dustballs." The high-achieving women I interviewed for this book have very different money behaviours, but two constants were these: They had a decidedly *positive* attitude to money, and they cleared away many of their financial dustballs.

The attitude adjustment process starts with a good financial housecleaning. Get rid of the myths you carry around by thoroughly sweeping away all your financial dustballs, starting with the biggest one of all:

Dustball #1: *Self-worth equals net worth.*
Get rid of the notion that your self-worth has anything to do with your net worth. It doesn't. How much money you earn, and how many assets you possess has nothing to do with who you are as a person, how valuable you are to your friends and family or how much of a contribution you have yet to make to the world. As proof, I asked my interviewees the following question: Would earning a fabulous income improve your net worth even more than your self-worth?

The huge majority of the interviewees said no, and most also pointed out that the two had little to do with each other.

Dustball #2: *A little debt never hurt anyone.*
I wish it were true, but for many of us, a little debt has a habit of growing into big debt over time. In January 2007, TD Economics reported that total household debt in Canada was equal to 122 percent of personal disposable income. A generation ago, families saved 20 percent of their after-tax income. The Vanier Institute of the Family in its 2006 annual report on family finances reported debt per household has now surpassed $75,000 and keeps on rising. Our collective debt load is up by 42 percent since 1990, while real earnings have only increased 4.8 percent. That's a lot of debt—and it's just getting worse.

Let's say you have a $3,000 balance on your credit card at 19.8 percent interest, and make only the minimum payments without making any new purchases. It will take you just over seventeen years to pay off the debt and cost you more than $3,300 in interest. Figures are based on minimum monthly payments of 3 percent or $10, whichever is greater.

Dustball #3: *I need at least $1 million to retire.*
Not true, unless you plan to live it up big time during retirement. A lot of people come up with the million dollar number because if you

invest the million at the bank and receive a very modest 5 percent return, you and your partner could retire and live on $50,000 a year. Not bad. But what you may not realize is that when you and your partner eventually pass away (even if you are both 100), you will take that same $1 million to the grave with you. In other words, you have lived off the interest income and have not touched your capital at all. That's why most of us need a lot less than one million dollars to retire. Oh, and did I forget to mention that inflation-adjusted Canada Pension Plan and Old Age Security payments can add up to another $16,000 per year to your retirement income?

Dustball #4: *I need to be a math major.*
Many women think that the only people who are financially literate are math majors. And we all know how many women—and men—feel about math. Investing isn't rocket science. Guess what? I never majored in math. And if you recall, I never even went to university. So please, get over this male-versus-female math issue. Learn a few basic investment concepts. You'll be surprised to find it's not very math-intensive, and the added knowledge will give you a lifetime of investment confidence.

Dustball #5: *I don't have enough money to start investing.*
You can open a mutual fund account with as little as $25 per month. Starting as soon as you can is the key. If you continue to put in your $25 over time, the magic of compound interest will let your contributions grow into a nice little investment portfolio. How much?

At a modest 6.6 percent annual return, after thirty-five years your little contributions would grow into $40,958. You only had to contribute $10,500—the rest is compounding.

Dustball #6: *It's too late for me to start building a nest egg.*
It's never too late, no matter how little you have. Think about dustball #5. Let's say you're 50 years old, earning $75,000 a year and wish to retire at 75. If you save 10 percent of your income (in other words, $7,500 per year) at 6.6 percent for twenty-five years, you'll have accumulated $448,000. That is one tidy little nest egg.

Dustball #7: *Personal financial planning is about investing.*
Financial planning is much more than minimizing investment risk and maximizing your investment returns. It's about learning how to manage and control your money and your savings and expenditures. It's about creating a financial plan that will instill confidence, focus and direction. It's about harnessing your precious financial resources and making them work together, so you can achieve your short- and long-term goals. Financial planning covers the whole gamut, from investment and retirement planning to tax minimization strategies to insurance opportunities and will and estate planning needs.

Dustball #8: *I can do it alone.*
Yes, you can. But if you're a beginner investor, I don't recommend it. Depending on the size of your portfolio, managing your money and investments can be a time-consuming process. You must be knowledgeable about the financial markets or be willing to educate yourself—and keep up to date with the shifting trends in the market. That's why some of you might need a planner, while some might not. You should have a good handle on the enormous number of financial products out there, and if that's all too much to put on your plate, a good financial advisor can be worth his or her weight in gold.

MANAGING YOUR MONEY

How well do Canadians handle their own financial dustballs? Canadians' savings rate today is a minuscule 1.5 percent as debt loads continue to grow at an astonishing rate. Current debt is at the highest levels in years. Do you want to be part of these statistics? If you don't, you have to start developing a better money mindset. And you have to start doing it today, not tomorrow. You have to take *action*. And that means you have to become financially literate. Colleen Johnston echoes the thoughts of many of the high-achieving women in this book when she says that we should assess where we spend our money, and never carry credit on a credit card.

"My husband and I are both CAs," Colleen tells me, "so we're financially literate people. We split the money management issues up this way: I control our day-to-day finances, and he manages our investments. It's important to have a plan, to set goals and to monitor against those goals. I must admit, when it comes to money, I don't understand why there are gender differences. Everyone, whether male or female, should make the time and effort to become financially knowledgeable and responsible."

LEARN MORE TO EARN MORE

There's an old saying: "Give a man a fish, and you feed him for a day; teach a man to fish, and you feed him for a lifetime." The same philosophy applies to money. Give someone money and you feed them for a day; teach someone about money and you feed them for a lifetime.

If we learn to become financially literate, we're doing ourselves a lifelong favour. But as we now know, our relationship to money is very complicated. I'd like to spin around Al Pacino's famous quote in *The Godfather*: "It's not business. It's strictly personal." Our relationship to money *is* emotional, at times neurotic and always very personal. Hey, maybe that's why they call it *personal* finance.

MAKE YOUR DREAMS COME TRUE

Becoming financially literate is a lifelong process. The economy, the stock markets and the investment vehicles that drive them are constantly changing.

How financially knowledgeable are you? I asked this question in my book on retirement planning, *Live Well, Retire Well*. It's worth revisiting here because studies show your money anxiety level is clearly connected to your financial IQ.

CHECK OUT YOUR FINANCIAL IQ

The following simple quiz will help determine where you fit on the "Financial Expertise Scale."

	Always	Usually	Sometimes	Never
I balance my chequebook every month.				
I understand the financial jargon in the newspapers and on television.				

	Always	Usually	Sometimes	Never
I know what types of insurance I need.				
I pay off my credit card balance monthly.				
I know the value of what I own (property, savings, investments).				
I have money saved for the unexpected and I save regularly for my vacation.				
I am able to cope financially with life's changes.				
I feel I will be able to retire when I want.				
I take the time to consider what my financial needs will be in the future.				
I feel that my financial affairs will be in order when I pass on.				
Source: Financial Planners Standards Council (FPSC). Used with permission.				

The left hand column ("Always") counts for 4 points. The next column ("Usually") counts for 3 points. The next column ("Sometimes") counts for 2 points. The right column ("Never") counts for 1 point. Total your answer scores to each question. Out of a possible total of 30 points, if you scored 26 or more.... Congratulations! You are definitely on the right financial track. If you scored between 20 and 25, not bad, not great; you may need to rethink your finances as well as your investment strategy. If you scored less than 19, you need to be very careful about your finances.

> "The best thing any woman can do is to develop a financial plan, and to start saving when you're young and there's no peer pressure."
> —KAREN RADFORD, Executive Vice President and President of TELUS Quebec and TELUS Partner Solutions

If you want to get up to speed on the basics, a good starting point is the TD Waterhouse Canada Inc. website (www.tdwaterhouse.ca) or the Investor Education Fund website (www.InvestorEd.ca). There are many excellent articles to be found on both sites.

Through family, Karen Radford and Jacqui Szeto each learned the importance of money at an early age.

"I started saving when I took my first job, as a teenager," says Karen. "I had no choice. My dad took 75 percent of my paycheque and invested it in RRSPs and education. I've been maximizing my RRSP since I was 16, and it's made me realize that the best thing any woman can do is to develop a financial plan, and to start saving when you're young and there's no peer pressure."

"My father died when I was very young," says Jacqui. "For a long time, I wondered how my mother would cope. I shouldn't have. She became a currency trader despite having no formal training! She was very focused, very driven and she read copiously. To her, currency trading was all common sense. All the money she made went to provide for us kids. Private school, tutors—the whole gamut. Today, we always budget on my income, so we save a lot through RRSPs and RESPs, and we do it a year ahead of time. The key is financial knowledge. The reason so many lottery winners lose all their money is they have no money training—they don't know what to do with their winnings so they spend it all."

THE SIX MONEY HABITS OF THE WEALTHY

There's a lot more to being wealthy than you might think, which is why wealthy people have a lot of things in common besides money. They've developed good money habits, and that's the most critical part of financial success. Why? Because it's a lot easier to spend money than it is to make it, and as I've noted before, it doesn't matter how much money you make—if you're spending out of control, you'll never be rich. What habits keep the wealthy from getting into trouble? Here are the big six.

The six money habits of the wealthy
    1. **The Mindset Habit**
          Attitude, knowledge, goals, discipline

2. **The Spending Habit**
   Live below your means
3. **The Savings Habit**
   Pay yourself first
4. **The Investing Habit**
   Learn more to earn more
5. **The Compounding Habit**
   Magnify your earnings
6. **The Collaboration Habit**
   Make an advisor part of your team

If you commit to these six habits, I'm positive you'll increase your financial success. Best of all, you'll start to feel in control of your finances for perhaps the first time in your life. Let's lead off our discussion about the six top money habits by discussing the biggest impediment to financial success: our money *mindset*.

I. THE MINDSET HABIT

The women whose stories you're reading have succeeded in simplifying many of the puzzles that surround their lives, but does that extend to their money issues? We'll soon find out.

To develop a positive money mindset, you have to begin with a change of attitude. Most women have a high level of anxiety about money; they don't feel in control of their money and they are often paralyzed by the thought of investing because it seems such a complex subject.

One of the first money questions I asked the women I interviewed was, "Does money drive us more than we're willing to admit?" Few people will openly admit they're materialistic, even though we live in a decidedly materialistic culture. It's considered the height of boorishness to say we like money. And most of the women I interviewed were reluctant to say "yes" to the question. Even fewer wanted to admit that their—or their friends'—spending patterns are out of control. Yet everywhere we look, we see and hear advertising and promotion encouraging us to spend, spend, spend.

As I said, this book is not just about money. It is about our lifestyles! Money is just one aspect of our life, but it drives so many of our life decisions that if we're not careful, it can overwhelm us. Lots of financial writers talk about how we all have different money personalities—hoarders, spenders, planners and so on. But few bother to explain that a person's money personality is a symptom, not a cause. And one of the root causes of our attitudes to money is a latent insecurity about our position in society and our self-perceived value to our family and circle of friends.

Developing your money mind

This isn't a book about self-esteem. It's a book about choices, and finding the courage to make those choices. Through the choices we make—and our interviewees have made—we get to control who we are. Yes, money choices can be difficult. But when you tackle them head on instead of shoving them into a drawer, you'll discover that life is suddenly not about money any more. That's because money just frees you up to do the things that give your life more balance and meaning. When you have your finances in order, you have freedom of choice, and that is a great feeling.

Money can be a driving force but I guarantee you it is not a motivator—at least not to me. But then I've spent my life studying personal financial habits of people from all walks of life across this great nation of ours, and I'm particularly aware of how women deal with their finances. Like it or not, women approach financial decision-making quite differently than men. According to an October 2005 study by Ipsos-Reid, "Women respondents are less confident about their financial situation, less comfortable carrying debt but are more likely to be more impulsive spenders than men." Conversely, men are relatively more risk tolerant when it comes to their investments.

The study, which surveyed 2,000 people, goes on to say that men were more likely to disagree than women when asked their degree of agreement with the statement: "I don't like to invest in the stock market because it is too risky." Men were also considerably more likely to agree with the statement: "I find banking and personal finance interesting and know quite a lot about it." Clearly, women lag behind men in this regard, but I'm happy to say that the money mindset is one that more and more women are adopting.

Goals

It's been my experience that both younger women and more mature women are more actively engaged in financial planning than those in their middle years. Perhaps this is because of lack of time rather than lack of interest. This is also the case with many of the middle-aged women I interviewed for the book. Many were excellent savers and had a financial plan, although fewer had a clearly articulated retirement plan. Here are some examples.

"I save a certain amount each year. I have investment return targets each year that run around a 10 percent real rate of return. I only have step-children who are older, but I contribute to RESPs for my nephews and so on. I'm a 'buy and holder' but I have that luxury because I started early. By the way, starting early is invaluable savings advice to younger women."
—SARAH RAISS, Executive Vice President of TransCanada Corporation

"I have an annual plan. I maximize my RRSPs and other investments, and don't spend my money on frivolous things. I invest a large percentage of my salary each month."
—DR. PATRICIA KMET, Dentist

"My husband, Greg, crafted a financial plan, with some support from our advisors. The goal is for me to retire early—earlier than I want to! My retirement plan has a dollar number attached. The idea is for me to write more (at home) and travel less (on business). I can read financial statements, so I guess you could call me aware but not enthusiastic about personal finances."
—LESLEY SOUTHWICK-TRASK, Co-founder of Owl's Head Retreat

Discipline

Discipline is a word that doesn't get used enough today. But it's one of the keys to financial success. Many of my interviewees know the word intimately.

"I started putting money away when I was under 40. I maxed out my RRSPs and I've always been an infamous bargain shopper. I learned

my lesson with my first husband. He didn't pay his bills and we lost our car."
—JENNIFER MCNEILL, CEO of CipherSoft Inc.

"I don't have a concrete financial plan. I do have RRSPs and RESPs. I go through a budget process each year, but I'm still trying to get a feel for our household expenses."
—AIMÉE ISRAEL, Co-founder and CEO of LifeSpeak

"I've been careful to separate my fixed and variable expenses. I'm trying to trim my variable expenses more and more so I can go beyond maximizing my RRSP contribution."
—JACQUELINE CARROLL, Visual Artist and Author

2. THE SPENDING HABIT

Comedian George Carlin once joked that we've got so much stuff, we have to get bigger and bigger places to keep it all. It's not such a joke anymore because it works both ways. Every time we move house, we usually move to a bigger place, which means we need to purchase more "stuff" to fill the extra space. According to the overview report from Statistics Canada's 2004 summary tables on home construction (www41.statcan.ca/2162/ceb2162_000_e.htm), "Houses are also becoming larger. In 2001, the average home had 6.3 rooms, excluding bathrooms, hallways and rooms used for home business, which is up from 5.3 rooms in 1961. Interestingly, this trend toward larger homes has coincided with a drop in the average household size, from 3.9 people per house in 1961 to 2.6 people in 2001."

Our need for stuff to fill those enlarged houses, along with confidence that our houses will continue to earn us extra "money" through appreciation has helped lead us into a negative savings trend. Negative savings simply means that for every dollar we earn, we spend at least a penny more.

Our unwavering need for plastic

Ah, yes. How we love to use plastic to buy stuff so we can keep up with those elusive and infuriating Joneses.

Research indicates that consumers tend to dramatically underestimate how much credit card debt they carry. Most card users owe more than *twice* what they think they owe. Credit cards may not be the cause of excessive spending, but they sure don't help you stop! I'm not going to suggest you cut up all your credit cards, but I recommend you do some-

MONEY TIP: *Take out your shopping money from the bank machine, stuff it in your purse, go shopping and spend until you run out of cash. Forget the credit cards. Running out of cash is your signal it's time to go home.*

thing far less radical but just as effective. It's a form of budgeting without all the effort and pain and paperwork. I want you to reacquaint yourself with the feeling of having a wad of cold hard cash in your hands. If you're going shopping, estimate how much you plan to spend. Then take out all the cash you think you'll need. Let's say it comes to $200. That's a fair amount of money—a nice big bundle of twenties.

Ditch your cards and feel the cash
Both men and women can be shopaholics, but it's an especially thorny problem for women. Shopping is an emotional experience, tied to feelings of pleasure, power, guilt and entitlement. And credit cards make it worse.

If you never actually hear the cold, hard-sucking sound of hard-earned cash slipping out of your wallet, it's easy to spend more than you planned. Publicist Danielle Iversen agrees: "I'm in my thirties. I live below my means by living on a budget. The key for me is to avoid frittering away my hard-earned money. I put it back into the business—that's my nest egg."

The experts say some of us shop out of loneliness, others do it for the rush, others shop to seek greater self-esteem or battle depression. Even a couple of my interviewees told me they were shopaholics. Luckily, both of them make a pretty good income, so their habit won't be sending them to the bread line anytime soon. But excessive spending can create a real problem for the rest of us if it creates debt that cannot be supported by our income—in other words, if it creates negative saving.

Having said that, I'm not opposed to spending. In fact, I encourage it because it's good to have some kind of financial balance in your life. Creating good money habits is never about hoarding. I actually *want* you to spend—even borrow—but only if it's for the good stuff.

Good debt versus bad debt

"Good" debt is used to make long-term investments, like a loan to purchase an RRSP, or pay for skills training or educational courses, or to take out a mortgage on your principal residence. These are clearly investments in the future. High credit card balances or lines of credit or loans incurred to buy fancy powerboats and vacations and flat-screen TVs and clothes are clearly "bad" debt. No matter how you may try to rationalize them, they're simply not investments, so you should never even think about borrowing to purchase them. Society recognizes that forced savings are good—that's why RRSPs and mortgages will never go out of fashion.

Eliminating the "compulsive spending" mindset

There's an old saying about money: "Either you control it, or it will control you." In some ways money is like picking up a stray Pit Bull from the pound. Just as you need to train the dog early before it develops any fearsomely bad habits, you need to train your money mind before it can develop some equally alarming behaviour. Training involves effort. It requires discipline and patience. If you don't bother making the effort, your money "dog" will grow up to train *you* and dominate your life in nightmarish ways. If overspending is the biggest money "dog" of all, how do we get the darn mongrel "fixed?" It starts with an assessment of your spending habits.

My husband and I share a disciplined money management ritual. We have one chequing account, with full disclosure on what's coming in and what's going out. Every week we know exactly where we stand financially. We set a threshold on spending, and anything over and above this limit we discuss and reach consensus on. If we go overboard, we shut it down. We shut down the spending, and that means all the discretionary things you think you really need to have.

Once a year we do a joint net worth statement, so we can track our financial progress and establish realistic short- and long-term goals—with benchmarks for our money.

What happens if there's an emergency? This happens to all of us, and there's only one sure-fire way to deal with it. Plan ahead. If your car breaks down, or your basement floods, you could suddenly be in a cash squeeze. Put three to six months of your salary into a liquid investment, such as a money market fund, a savings account or a guaranteed investment. I'd recommend having a line of credit or credit card—but only for emergency use.

Curb your enthusiasm

The following are some big and little expenses many of us have. I believe you can eliminate them altogether without feeling deprived. You can start slow by eliminating the easiest one first, then move on to the next.

- Credit card debt
- Car detailing
- Kitchen upgrades
- Impulse shopping
- Spa and massage services
- Cleaning lady
- Extra cellphone
- Premium cable TV
- Premium Internet service
- Club dues
- Magazine subscriptions
- Eating out
- Landscaping

It's a shame that while schools teach us all about reading, writing and arithmetic, they don't bother explaining the basic concepts of budgeting and personal finance. The unfettered need to spend when we're children is controlled by our parents and guardians. As adults, however, we have no obstacles except bankruptcy and common sense. If you're a money worrier, replacing poor spending habits with self-discipline and training will go a long way to easing your money worries.

We all know good spending habits help us save. But unless you were lucky enough to have parents who instilled money consciousness into you from an early age, the ability to *consistently* save is not all that common. So don't beat yourself up about it, take positive action. One of the absolute best ways to save is to pay yourself first.

3. THE SAVINGS HABIT

The wealthy say that the secret to being wealthy and staying wealthy is to live *below* your means. Research has proven it. Being prudent—saving your money and investing it wisely—may seem obvious, but hardly anyone does it! Part of the reason is, it's harder to save when you're earning less than other people. The rich save tons of money because they have tons to begin with. What about us? We can still take a page out of the lives of the rich and not so famous, as long as they live prudently. Even the unpretentious über-rich do not often appear in newspaper headlines. Why? Because their lives and financial habits just aren't that newsworthy.

The absolute best way to save is to pay yourself first. You may have heard this before, but it's amazing how many people just pay lip service to the concept. Every time you get paid, immediately siphon off a set amount—between 5 percent and 10 percent, or more if you can, into a long-term investment account. And, if you leave this money alone, you'll be surprised at how fast your money begins to grow—that's the power of time and compounding.

Pamela Jeffery, CEO of Women's Executive Network, agrees. She says, "A long time ago I made a decision to pay myself first. I've been putting away 8 percent of my earnings since I was 26. I'm now 45. I don't have a financial plan or even a retirement plan but I have a very healthy RRSP and I keep track of my finances."

So, why is it more of us don't take this approach? The problem for many is, it's hard to stay committed to doing it. Forced savings through a mortgage is a lot easier to keep up than voluntary savings through an RRSP. That's why few of us ever actually maximize our RRSP contributions. How many of us in this day and age want to deprive ourselves of additional disposable income when there are iPods and laptops and vacations and gifts and clothes to buy? "Once those purchases are made, then I'll save," you say. But I can tell you from personal experience, if you want to save money, you have to make it a priority. You have to make a firm commitment to it, then stick to that commitment through thick and thin. You're going to have to forget about re-upholstering that sofa or taking that "cheap" Vegas-weekend vacation. At least for a while.

But what if you're a saver and your partner is a spender? I suggest separate bank accounts, then set up a common account that both partners contribute to for paying household expenses and anything else there's a contractual obligation to pay for, such as the mortgage, the cellphone or gym memberships. Whether you do it together or do it independently, it still comes down to sharing and jointly aligning yourself to goals. Julie Toskan-Casale and her husband are a good financial team. "I always consult him prior to a big purchase, but I don't want someone controlling me," she says. "We have a joint chequing and savings account, and I'll cut back on my spending if needed."

> MONEY TIP: *When you get your next raise, instead of adjusting your lifestyle expectations upward, tuck the additional income away as retirement savings. Plan ahead or you'll just end up using your raise to raise your cost of living.*

But that doesn't work for everyone, nor should it. Joan Kelley-Weisshaar takes a different approach: "I do all of my own credit cards and bills. We have separate accounts, and my husband does all the household accounts. Having said that, we have an asset summary—sort of a net worth statement—which Don and I go through every few months. It's not my favourite thing to do; in fact it's kind of boring. But it makes sense to do it and I'm glad we do, so we're on the same page."

Do you want to know what kind of saver you are? Try filling out the online savings quiz available at the New Brunswick Securities Commission website (www.nbsc-cvmnb.ca).

Now let's talk about the flip side of the saving habit—making your investments work for you.

4. THE INVESTING HABIT

At my seminars and financial forums, the most interesting questions I get surround the concept of "risk." Women often focus on how hard they worked for their money and therefore want it exposed to as little risk as possible. They do want growth, however, and very often want to be involved in the decision-making process. They don't want to abdicate responsibility and often make it very clear it's their money and their financial future. Having said that, *women are more conservative investors than men.*

How hands-on are the women I interviewed when it comes to investing? For the most part, they leave the investing side of things to others—usually to professional advisors but sometimes to their husbands. Former entrepreneur Julie Toskan-Casale is married to a financier, and he does all the finances for the household.

"It's his skill set, so naturally I rely on him," she says. "I do a little bit of investing on my own, and I'm a bit of a risk-taker, unlike my husband. I've learned over time that the key to my investment success is to stay out of it altogether! I have an accountant, investment advisor and a private banker, but when it comes to financial planning, Vic takes care of everything."

Youth in Motion CEO Akela Peoples has a different view.

"As a single female who supports herself, I'm quite hands-on about investing," she reveals. "It's my money and I want to do it myself. My advisor makes recommendations for me, and I check these recommendations with people I respect. I'm happy with my investment strategy. I'm a low-risk investor, and I believe diversification is the key to investment success. My predominant investments are in real estate. I enjoy being in control, and my guiding principle has always been to live below my means."

Jennifer McNeill runs a thriving business and is happy to leave her investments to the experts.

"I'm not hands-on at all," she admits. "I have a wealth management advisor who helps me put together my investment strategies and retirement planning. In my experience, it's really not about how much you earn; it's about how much you spend. I know people who spend every penny, and they're no longer rich."

Isn't it comforting to know that even the rich have to watch their pennies or they'll get into financial trouble? Perhaps some of our money attitudes have to do with the "bag lady" syndrome. That's a fear many women share—that their financial security could disappear in the blink of an eye, leaving them homeless and penniless. WXN President Pamela Jeffery believes the potential to lose it all and be out of money drives women's behaviour far more than they let on.

"In my experience, women place a very high value on financial independence," Pamela says. "And it's getting higher. Marital strife and uncertainty play a big role, as does the fact that women are making unprecedented levels of income, and that's new territory for them."

It's common knowledge that Oprah Winfrey has $50 million in "mad money" stashed away, just in case things go wrong. How rational is that? Apparently, she's not the only celebrity bag lady out there. Lily Tomlin, Gloria Steinem, Shirley MacLaine and Katie Couric are all said to be prone to bag lady anxiety. So it's not surprising that women view investing as a key to financial independence. According to a 2006 TD Waterhouse Female Investor poll, independence was second only to retirement security as a goal of investing. In fact, of the women who have personal responsibility for managing their household's investments, 60 percent say that achieving financial independence was the reason they became interested in investing. This is a significant increase, because only 50 percent cited this reason the year before.

> "In my experience, women place a very high value on financial independence."
> —PAMELA JEFFERY, CEO of Women's Executive Network

Money deeply affects our choices in life. Money affects the choice of careers we make, the places we live, the lifestyle we choose, even the mates we attract. And if we look back over the course of our life-time, we may discover it has significantly altered our long-term dreams and goals.

Trish Kmet agrees with Pamela Jeffery. Money is vastly under-rated in importance in women's lives.

"Whether we have children or not, women need to make sure their future is stable and secure," Trish says. "And money is a vital component in that vision. Women value stability and security very highly, much more so than men."

Not everyone shares this view completely, however. Artist Jackie Carroll says that, "Everybody wants to have a sense of financial security, but it is also important to realize that money does not buy happiness."

Investing isn't rocket science, and I don't want to bedazzle you with charts and graphs. But if you have any anxieties about investing in the stock market, I want you to know that over the past *one hundred years*, the market has provided investors with better than a 6 percent real rate of return. That's *after* taking inflation into account.

MONEY TIP: *When you think about investing, think in terms of a marathon, not a 100-meter sprint.*

And if you're worried about inflation, the central banks of the world have made fighting inflation their number one priority. Today, if the Bank of Canada or the U.S. Federal Reserve smell even a whiff of inflation, they go into interest-rate-raising mode. And that's good for all of us in the long run.

I offer this warning, however: Reward always brings risk. Meaning that if you expect to get this kind of return without incurring the ups and downs of the traditionally volatile stock market, forget it, it won't happen. You have to develop a long-term investor's mindset.

Colleen Johnston, CFO of TD Bank Financial Group, agrees: "I'm a value investor because I'm a long-term investor. For the most part, I buy and hold. And that takes discipline."

The long-term investor is aware that there have been many occasions when the market returned substantially *more* than 6 percent, and there were many periods when the market delivered much *less* than 6 percent. You have to ride out the storms. And that, as Warren Buffet likes to say, means taking the emotion out of investing. What you replace emotion with is discipline, commitment and focus.

Learn more to earn more

The more you learn about investing, the better off you'll be. Whether you plan to work with an advisor all your life or want to be a do-it-yourself investor, it pays to know the field. What return do you really need over the long haul? How do you minimize risk, yet still meet your financial goals? How much do you need to diversify your portfolio? These are important questions, and the answers can be found on many financial websites, including at www.tdwaterhouse.ca. Knowledge is priceless; otherwise we make mistakes. And mistakes compound and thus get costlier every year.

Jacqui Szeto, President of Women in Capital Markets and Vice President and Director at TD Securities Inc., offers this sage advice: "Don't look for the overnight hot stock. Rumours and speculation are not good drivers of investment decision-making. To me, consistency is the key. You've got to know the products and know the tax implications, and understand the power of compound interest."

A big mistake many investors make is falling into the low-interest trap. If you put most of your annual retirement savings into low-interest money market funds and GICs, you're going to get burned. Not by risk, however, but by lack of return. Let's use a simple example of why you should avoid the low-interest trap. Let's say you're 40 years old and have $50,000 saved. You decide to put all of it in a 3 percent interest-bearing money market fund. If you don't contribute another dime until you retire, how much do you think you'll have saved by the time you retire at 65? Answer: $104,690 (before tax). But hold on. This scenario does NOT include inflation, which currently runs at about 2 percent. Your real (inflation-adjusted) return is actually only 1 percent. At a 1 percent real rate of return, you would actually have only $64,000 at retirement. That's the low-interest trap at work.

Asset allocation

Without diving into great detail about the subject, you should get to know about something called asset allocation. People are often confused about the difference between "asset allocation" and "diversification." Asset allocation is just a fancy way of referring to the best mix of cash, fixed income and equity to have in your portfolio based on your age, retirement time horizon and risk tolerance. The purpose of asset allocation is to minimize risk and maximize return.

Diversify—please!

Diversification is simply the next step in the process. It means spreading your money among different investments *within* the desired mix of cash, fixed income and equity you have in your portfolio. Alone, each one can reduce your portfolio risk, but most experts agree that asset allocation and diversification work best together.

Satish Rai's top ten investing tips

Satish Rai is Vice Chair and Portfolio Manager with TD Asset Management, and the following are his ten ways to become a better investor.

1. **Err on the side of caution**
   Take on less risk than you think you can tolerate. People only realize their true comfort zone when stocks or funds are going down.

2. **Have a long-term view**
   Many people have far too short of an investment time horizon. Block out the hype from investment brokers and the media. Many investors get bored and for excitement gravitate to the higher volatility investments over more sensible investments. Avoid this as it will punish your portfolio.

3. **Avoid over-confidence**
   People who have investing success early tend to have an inflated view of their investment skills. Time in the markets builds skill.

4. **Appreciate the power of compounding**
   What may seem like a small annual return can add up over time. For example, a 10 percent annual return results in a doubling of an investment's value in 7.2 years; 12 percent doubles the value in just six years.

5. **Taxes should be secondary to your investment strategy**
   Dividends, interest and capital gains all add to your wealth, even if they are taxed differently. The more tax you pay, the more money you've made, which is a good thing.

6. **Use margin sparingly**
   Margin can allow you to take advantage of special opportunities, but should be used with high-quality stocks, and never after a lengthy market rise. High margin levels accentuate the fear/greed emotions, move your focus shorter term, and margin calls actually force selling low after buying high. At the very least it's always preferable that investment income exceeds interest expense.

7. **Know where you're going**
    If you don't have a plan, or you don't stick to it, you likely won't get there. Having a well-laid-out plan can help you avoid chasing winners or selling out of investments too early.

8. **Diversify**
    Particularly important for Canadian investors at this point in time. The Canadian market is so concentrated in energy, materials and banks. So look outside Canada; get exposure to a variety of sectors.

9. **Know what you're doing**
    Make investments based on facts, not rumours or gossip or tips. Always appreciate the risk you're taking. Discipline gives you the edge.

10. **Do it now**

5. THE COMPOUNDING HABIT

By now you know something about the power of compounding. Compounding works to magnify your success over time. But compounding only works if you *leave your investments alone to compound in peace and quiet.* There is a simple rule called the Rule of 72. Whatever rate or return you're making, if you divide it into seventy-two, you'll discover the number of years it will take to double your money. For example, if your portfolio is making a 10 percent annual return, you'll double its value in 7.2 years.

As I said earlier, investing requires discipline, commitment and focus. If you start buying and selling when market volatility sets in, you'll attract unnecessary capital gains taxes and probably see your portfolio's value swing wildly up and down. Volatility isn't good if you want to take advantage of compounding. Below is an example of the power of compounding for a 40 year-old wanting to save $1 million. I've adapted TD Canada Trust's easy to use Savings Tool (available at www.tdcanadatrust.com) to determine the exact monthly contributions needed.

How to save $1 million
What you told us:

*"I'm 40 years old and I want to have $1 million when I retire at 70.
I have $50,000 in savings right now.
How much will I need to save each month?"*

Your savings goal: $1,000,000.00
Amount to be saved (after-tax):
Your savings goal will reflect inflation rate of: 2%
Number of years to save: 30
Your current annual income: $ 100,000.00
Annual Rate of Return: 8.3%
(before inflation, compounded monthly).

At a marginal tax rate of 50%, you'll
need to save: **$1,300.55/mo.**

Compounding gets eaten away by three things: inflation, taxes and portfolio churning (turnover). You can't control inflation. What you can control are the other two.

6. THE COLLABORATION HABIT

Choosing a financial advisor is a very important part of getting real about your money. This is a relationship that should last for years, so make sure he or she has the necessary qualifications and experience. Ask for referrals from friends, family or work associates, but never assume that who's right for them is right for you, so screen potential candidates over the telephone.

Make a shortlist, conduct in-person interviews and speak to references. Always ask two important questions when interviewing: What are their credentials? How they are compensated? Also find out if he or she is a Certified Financial Planner. To earn the CFP designation, the advisor will have to pass rigorous testing, agree to adhere to high ethical standards and engage in annual continuing education. Find out if they are paid a salary or charge a flat fee, or do they earn a commission? Commissions could influence the financial products they recommend.

What do some of our high-achieving interviewees have to say about using financial advisors?

"I probably don't use advisors as much as I should. An investment advisor helps me with my portfolio and my accountant does my taxes."
—AKELA PEOPLES, CEO of Youth in Motion

"I have an accountant and a financial advisor who do my planning, give me advice and complete my tax returns."
—AIMÉE ISRAEL, Co-founder and CEO of LifeSpeak

"I employ professional investment advisors and tax advisors because we have family trusts. It takes a lot of effort and responsibility to make sure we give our children a proper inheritance. For the most part, my husband and I believe advisors do a great job but they're not infallible. There are so many products out there. We use our trust advisors to filter out and narrow down the selection for us."
—LESLEY SOUTHWICK-TRASK, Co-founder of Owl's Head Retreat

Money is a very personal thing, so make sure the advisor is someone you feel comfortable with. If you feel you can't afford a financial advisor, let me say this: Financial advice doesn't have to be expensive. If you go it alone, you increase your risk of making mistakes, then compounding those errors over time.

Take your time in choosing, and trust your judgment. Don't be afraid, however, to make a change if it becomes clear your first choice was not the right one or your needs change as your finances evolve over time.

Five common investing mistakes

1. **Not diversifying:** *The biggest mistake of all.*
2. **Forgetting about asset allocation:** *Consult an advisor for the best returns. If you're a do-it-yourself investor, financial institutions have*

asset allocation tools on their websites to help you determine your optimal mix.

3. **Playing it too safe:** *Be risk aware, not risk averse (the low-interest trap comes into play).*

4. **Taking on too much risk:** *The flip side of the above. An investor with an average risk tolerance might consider 50 percent stocks, 40 percent bonds and 10 percent cash, for example. Accept more risk than your risk tolerance and you risk sleepless nights.*

5. **Trying to "read" the market:** *Pick quality investments, stick with them long-term and let your money make money through compounding.*

Retirement

How important is planning for the future to women? More than three-quarters of the respondents to a 2006 TD Waterhouse poll said that "saving for retirement" was the issue that first got them interested in investing. The study also shows that women carry fewer stocks in their investment portfolios than men do. Women should consider moving up the risk curve, because overcaution carries its own risks.

MONEY TIP: *When it comes to your retirement, there's a number you should be thinking about. In other words, do you know the size of your nest egg? Most Canadians don't.*

If you'll recall, dentist Trish Kmet saves a large percentage of her income each month and puts it into investments.

"I hope to retire at 55 with a retirement income that should be able to sustain my lifestyle comfortably," she says. "I believe in diversification, and have been very happy with the return on my investments over the years."

Not everyone is as lucky as Trish, but we can retire well by developing a solid plan, and then sticking to it.

Are you *sure* you want to be rich?

I've never been rich and I doubt I ever will be, but I'm not in the least bit upset about it. To me, true wealth comes from happiness, and happiness comes from within. So please skip this section if you're happy with your work and the money you're making and the people in your life and the journey you're on. But keep this in mind: Most of us would like to be rich, but few realize how much it will change their lives, and even fewer know how much sacrifice it requires.

Key money traits of our interviewees
1. They are responsible about their money.
2. They're not wasteful spenders.
3. They prefer to put their energy into their work, not their money.
4. Generally, they're not very hands-on when it comes to investing. Though sophisticated people with high levels of education, they're not necessarily sophisticated in the area of personal finance.

This last point is not surprising. If we don't get formal training in something, we're not likely to become sophisticated at it.

Take charge of your finances
I hope I've been able to impart some knowledge and some common sense about your money. For a more in-depth discussion of your retirement options, consider reading my latest personal finance book, *Live Well, Retire Well*. It covers all the strategic and executional steps you'll need to save and protect your money so you can retire comfortably.

Whether you need to get real about the money you earn, save, spend or invest, there's one thing you should always know. It's *your* life and *your* money, and ultimately what you do with your money is no one's choice but *yours*.

But it's not really money you need. It's knowledge. Money managers and advisors play a key role in my financial life, and I believe they should in yours. But they can never give me—or you—the confidence I've gained through developing my own "money mindset." For most of us, possession of even a modicum of financial self-knowledge will improve our money-confidence. Equally important, it enables you to ask better questions of yourself and your financial advisors. Good financial advisors are there to *help* you make the right choices, not make the choices for you.

Become your own CFO

Don't abdicate your decision-making responsibility. Instead, make your advisor part of your financial support team. I've said this before and I'm sure I'll say it a bunch more times before I retire: It's critical that you take control of your financial objectives. Take charge of your future by being realistic, committed and disciplined. I recommend that you set short-, medium- and long-term goals, then tweak the plan as required. Remember, building wealth isn't a sprint. It's a marathon and one of your biggest challenges is staying motivated and on track. That means establishing mileposts and monitoring your progress. You're only going to get excited about saving your money if it's for something of importance to you.

It is often said that a goal is a dream with a deadline. How do you create a deadline for yourself? By becoming your own Chief Financial Officer. Start treating your finances the same way a CFO would when running a business. That means getting your debt under control by cutting down on expenses, and doing it *now*—not tomorrow. There's an old saying, or maybe I've just been saying it a long time: Hard work hurts, but procrastination kills.

Lack of action will kill your finances faster than anything else, because good intentions don't translate into results. Remember, creating wealth isn't about how much you earn, it's about how much you spend. The rich tend to live below their means.

It's all relative

If after reading this chapter, money issues still worry you, know this: everybody struggles with money issues from time to time.

It's unfortunate that money has become such a taboo topic in our society. Money often creates envy, shame and other negative emotions, and none of us wants to admit that it does. But if we come to understand ourselves better and learn what truly makes us happy, we'll stop pursuing money for its own sake. We'll stop seeing rich as some Holy Grail, and realize money is just a means to an end of our own choosing. Being positive about money gets back to being comfortable in our own skin, making the right choices, taking the time to sweep the dustballs out of our financial closets, and remembering that believing there's a link between self-worth and net worth is the biggest dustball of all.

FIVE

GET REAL ABOUT YOUR LIFESTYLE

I WAS LISTENING TO THE LOCAL all-news radio station today and I heard some disturbing news. According to the Heart and Stroke Foundation of Canada, a whopping 52 percent of Canadians are inactive and yet 80 percent of us still think we'll enjoy a longer life than previous generations. Follow-up research unearthed its source: The Heart and Stroke Foundation's 2006 Report Card on Health, entitled "Is 60 the New 70?" The report says that 58 percent of boomers think their weight has little or no effect on their heart health.

There's a whole lot of denial going on out there.

Oh, in case you were wondering, "overweight" is defined as roughly 10 to 30 pounds over a healthy weight. "Obese" is defined as 30 or more pounds over a healthy weight. Body mass index, or BMI, which is discussed later in this chapter, is often used to define weight issues. However, BMI is not used to measure athletes, children, pregnant women and the elderly.

Okay, so you want to lead a healthier life, and become fit and slim, and eat well and feel great. Why not make *all* these goals your goals?

And best of all, why not plan on achieving all these goals over a very short period, let's say over the next month or so?

You know my answer by now, don't you?

Get *REAL*!

I'm not being negative. You can do it—just not all together and not over a wickedly short time span.

I'm just being realistic. What the diet gurus and fitness buffs tell you is often plainly *un*realistic. It takes time to make these kinds of changes. If you try to do it all at once, you'll most likely fail because you're putting way too much pressure on yourself. Your expectations are going to go through the roof, setting up the potential for a sudden drop-off at the first obstacle.

Major lifestyle changes should best be done incrementally, especially if you have a job and other responsibilities. If you can take the time off, then sure, go crazy, fitness-wise and diet-wise. But most of us don't have that luxury, and few of us have the dedication to keep up a "crazy" pace for long. If you already lead a fairly active and healthy life, congratulations. Despite hectic schedules, most of my interviewees lead healthy lives as well. Publicist Danielle Iversen says she always tries to eat well and exercises two to three times a week.

"Exercise reduces my stress levels and makes me feel better," she says. "My eating habits are pretty good, especially given the lifestyle I lead. I go to tons of parties and functions, and the temptation to eat and drink too much is constant. I eat lots of fresh veggies, drink lots of water and I eat raisins if I need a bit of a sugar kick. As far as diets go, I create my own. But I have help from a naturopathic doctor I've been working with for years. He helps me with a detox program that cleanses my system."

HEALTHY HABITS

I'm a big proponent of working healthy habits into my life. I call them rituals, because I think rituals are easier to follow and in some ways more fun than habits. I have fitness rituals, nutrition rituals and relationship rituals—even financial rituals. And I stick with them no matter what, until they become so ingrained in me that it's as natural as breathing.

Lauren Jawno, a Registered Nutritionist, Certified Personal Trainer and Life Coach, has a similar view. She expresses her process this way: "I create the habits (and we can definitely create them) and then I create a lifestyle around those habits. At first it will be an effort—you will have to think about it and be conscious of it—but if you keep doing it, eventually it just happens and you honestly can not imagine not doing it."

What kinds of habits? Lauren believes besides keeping fit and eating well, personal growth habits are key.

"I think exercise and physical activity are extremely important, but you don't always have to participate in a structured workout, especially if you are emotionally not up to it," she says. "You can do activities that will allow you to be active but also recharge your emotions, like going for a walk in the park and appreciating the beauty and quietness around you. I take time each day for myself, for personal growth. This could be reading an inspiring book, journaling, sharing something with someone I trust or helping someone else develop and grow. I believe it's important to mentor others, not because they ask you but because of how it will impact both their life and your own."

A MIND-BASED APPROACH TO LIFESTYLE CHANGE

Many women are capable of creating their own diets and sticking to them for the long-term. But just as many aren't. New research is beginning to show that eating and lifestyle habits are intertwined with career issues, money issues, relationship issues and even childhood issues. Here's a quick glimpse into the lifestyles of two interviewees.

"I eat vegetables and fruit and healthy protein. I have software that tracks my caloric intake. Every day I input the total calories I consume. In the past, I've tried South Beach, Weight Watchers, NutriSystem. I now have a nutritionist who comes to see me every couple of weeks. I think the detox systems work until you get off them, and then everything reverts back to the mean. I don't feel any

cravings because I think a lot of that is in your mind, those feelings of being 'deprived' or that 'I deserve to eat well.'"
—JENNIFER MCNEILL, CEO of CipherSoft Inc.

"I just rejoined Weight Watchers. I tend to go on and off track. I've tried other diets such as Dr. Bernstein's and L.A. Weight Loss. It's difficult for me, especially eating out at lunch. The portions are often big, so I end up having two big meals a day instead of one. You asked me how a person eats healthy without feeling constant cravings. My answer is: I don't know. I guess that's why I fall off track so often, and then my self-critical side kicks in."
—LINDA WHELER, Pastoral Care Minister

Lauren Jawno says going on any typical diet is not sustainable. It doesn't teach a long-term, lifestyle approach to nutrition. She says people need to learn how to make the best choices for their unique situation.

"We live in the real world, and we eat in the real world," Lauren says. "It's as much about eating to improve one's quality of life as it is weight loss—although this is often a great side-effect. That's why we need to provide people with lifestyle strategies, not just information."

THE PSYCHOLOGY OF WEIGHT GAIN

People allow environmental cues to dominate their eating choices, rather than actual biological feelings of hunger and fullness, according to a December 14, 2005, article in the University of Toronto newsletter News@UofT, entitled, "Anxious about Holiday Weight Gain? Don't Look to Others for Social Clues, Study Shows." In the article, Elizabeth Monier-Williams quotes U. of T. psychology professors Peter Herman and Janet Polivy, whose study found that peer pressure (the food intake of fellow eaters) was a powerful influence on a person's food consumption.

"People are often rudderless in eating situations," she quotes Professor Herman, "And they look to the activity of others, their own previous behaviour or other social cues to guide them."

Professor Polivy adds that current medical research is not focused on this issue.

"No one seems to be aware of the power that social influence has on eating," she says.

What may help is the emergence of a new breed of health-care professional in this country. They're called Health Service Providers in Psychology (HSPPs), and they're specifically trained to promote emotional and physical health in individuals, families, groups and organizations. HSPPs fill a need for a more psychological approach to lifestyle and wellness issues. They have special expertise in assessment and diagnosis, prevention and treatment techniques. The Canadian Register of Health Service Providers in Psychology (CRHSPP) is a national credentialing body, and approximately 3,200 credentialed psychologists have been admitted to date. For more information, go to their website at www.crhspp.ca.

SUPERSIZE ME

I'm a positive person, but as you know I'm also a realist. And from where I sit, the state of our health and our lifestyles looks a little bleak. Statistics Canada's Canadian Community Health Survey (*The Daily*, June 15, 2004) reported that in 2003, 14.9 percent of adult Canadians were considered obese and 33.3 percent were considered overweight! Obesity you'll remember, is defined as being 30 or more pounds over a healthy weight. Why is this important? Because obesity is a risk factor for an array of diseases and illnesses including heart disease, stroke, type 2 diabetes, fatty liver, gallbladder disease, cancer and hypertension.

Wow. I don't know about you, but this is scary stuff. But maybe not scary enough for a lot of people, or we would all be doing something about it. *Wouldn't we?*

The fact is, we're not. Why? Unfortunately, one reason is that facts like those above breed fear, and studies have shown that fear is a fickle motivator at best. I happened upon a fascinating article entitled "Marketing Self Care" by Professor Laurette Dubé in the April 19, 2001, edition of the *McGill Reporter*. Dubé, a former nutritionist and now Professor of Marketing at McGill University, says most health-care professionals are convinced people will change their lifestyle if they're provided with the right information. But, she says, they're dead wrong. You can't ask people to change their lives by preaching.

You can tell people what's right for them until the cows come home, but people will still give up. Dubé thinks there's a better solution to the massive issue of lifestyle change.

"You start by understanding that many people are stressed to death and just cannot make the change," she says. "We should give less advice and more help dealing with their emotions."

Emotions. Hmmm...that's an interesting approach. If we sit down and think hard about our own experience, we'll soon come to the realization that making a lifestyle change is very difficult emotional work. The process always begins with an honest self-assessment of our current problems and issues, and hey! Who wants to dwell on our dark side? That's why the prospect of major change too often causes us to go into denial. Denial is our way of protecting ourselves from facts that are too painful to accept as truth. And when it comes to making healthy lifestyle choices, our denial can sometimes go through the roof. Examples abound. Just look how hard it is for smokers to quit smoking and binge eaters to stop binging.

CHANGE IS A VERY EMOTIONAL PROCESS

Why don't people change their lifestyle when they know what bad habits do to their hearts and bodies? Toronto wellness expert Lauren Jawno says there are a variety of reasons.

"For many people it's just not a priority—they're too busy focusing on work, family and other things," she explains. "Many people are in denial about their particular situation or haven't taken the time to really understand themselves and so they don't know what's feeding the negative behaviour."

Lauren says that as a society we're used to instant gratification—e-mail, online shopping, online banking, medications that produce instant results, fast food. We live in an indulgent, throwaway society. Our need for most things can be met easily and immediately. We're not used to waiting any more, and since most things are easily accessible at any time, this reinforces that mindset. We also tend to get too negative.

"Most of us focus on the obstacles and challenges of making a lifestyle change—so that is what we attract," she tells me. "We need to change our thinking. We need to see and feel the benefits of a lifestyle change: more energy, better health and improved confidence. However, this is not enough—we have to know and understand why we are making the changes and truly believe in the benefits that will come."

In other words, if you really want to make a change, you need to truly appreciate the benefits involved. You'll feel better, have more energy, look better and be healthier.

Could we want anything more than that? Of course not. But healthy lifestyle habits have to become an integral part of everyone's daily lives, no matter how old or young we may be. New habits take effort and time, but once they're incorporated into our daily lives, they soon become rituals that self-reinforce and compensate us with sizable quality-of-life rewards.

NEW HABITS DON'T TAKE ROOT OVERNIGHT

Like so many things in life, lifestyle is all about attitude. Attitude is our tendency to evaluate some symbol, object or aspect of our world in a favourable or unfavourable manner. Attitudes become beliefs which become behaviour, and while we can be influenced to change our behaviour, change can happen only if we overcome our natural barriers to change.

Lauren says negative attitudes to lifestyle change surface very often.

"Many people look at a lifestyle change as deprivation," she explains. "They're likely to be the same people who look at all the obstacles in a situation instead of focusing on the positive. For example, if you decided to climb a mountain and three-quarters of the way up there was a fallen tree blocking the path, it is unlikely you would just turn around to go back. Unfortunately, many of us don't look for alternate routes in life. We either stay where we are (allowing circumstance to control our lives) or we turn back (give up)."

A CHANGE IN CORE VALUES

We can choose to be positive, of course, but a positive attitude is far more than just a simple decision. It's a commitment to a "style" of thinking, and it needs to be nurtured every day if it's going to flourish. It all begins when we rediscover our inner discipline, which is a lifestyle choice all on its own. We've all experienced pivotal moments in our lives where we decide we need to make a change. The process always starts with some kind of commitment to ourselves that often involves a change in core values—only then do we begin to express that change outwardly to the world.

In a July 15, 2005, article written for the Canadian Health Network, writer Kristin Jenkins interviewed two Canadian experts on stress, Dr. Richard Earle, Managing Director of the world-renowned Canadian Institute of Stress and the Hans Selye Foundation, and life skills coach Jan Hill, Ph.D. According to Dr. Earle, "In every spoken language around the world, the ratio of pessimistic adjectives to positive adjectives is three to one." The implication is clear: we're conditioned to focus on what could go wrong rather than what could go right. "We lose motivation to change before we really get started," he says. "People choose to make a change when they can no longer stand it," confirms Jan Hill. "They tolerate and tolerate until the situation becomes too uncomfortable."

Lauren says pessimism isn't the only countervailing force to making a change. Sometimes it's plain old-fashioned inertia. "Laziness? Yes, that's definitely true for some people. It's just easier for them to stay the way they are than make the effort to change."

WELCOME TO THE GOOD LIFE

By now, you know that I'm a big believer in common sense. How we live our lives and relate to others is more than a function of choice and self-awareness. The quality of our life is not about how much money we make but about how we eat, drink, exercise, love, socialize and handle stress. Common sense comes from knowledge, and as we discussed in Chapter 1 and Chapter 2 and Chapter 3 and Chapter 4, knowledge always begins and ends with self-knowledge. So having said that, are you surprised when I tell you that the women I interviewed are making healthy choices? For the most part, these women are anything but lifestyle experts, yet despite their hectic schedules, they find the time to watch what they eat and live a healthy life.

But what really is a healthy life? I adapted a pretty good definition from the World Health Organization (WHO): "A healthy life is not merely the absence of disease or infirmity but one in which we are in a state of complete physical, mental and social well-being."

The WHO says that healthy living is not just about our physical state but our mental and social well being as well. This is not new— the definition adapted above was established by the WHO back in 1946.

If you want to learn a little more about your mental well-being, it may help to go back and read Chapter 1, which is all about finding your passion. To reassess your social "health," go back and read Chapter 2, which is about relationships. And to understand your *physical* well-being, read on, as it is the main subject of this chapter.

IT'S NOT ABOUT LIVING LONGER, IT'S ABOUT LIVING BETTER

"Why bother exercising and eating right?" people say. "Who wants to live longer anyway?" The best answer I can give is, it's not about living longer, it's about living better. I want to level with you about my own lifestyle. Although I exercise as much as I can, and I eat well, I could do better. A lot better. As we get older, the number one issue confronting us is our health. I don't want to live to be 110, but I *do* want the years I have on this planet to be as pleasant and issue-free as possible. Don't we all?

Not according to world health experts. Most of us are doing very little to enhance the quality of our lives as we get older. And a lot of that is pure laziness. We allow bad habits into our lives and, as they grow, we do little or nothing about them. And perhaps the worst routines involve our eating habits.

GET REAL ABOUT YOUR DIET

Nutritionist Natalie Bean-Sole told us back in Chapter 2 that she was a "fat little latch-key kid," an emotional eater who didn't much like herself. But then in her late teens, she finally did something about it. She lost 70 pounds and never put them back on. Today she's a successful professional nutritionist with a varied client base that includes some movie stars. And developing good nutrition habits is hard work.

Baby steps are the way to developing any good habits, she says, and this goes double when it comes to good nutrition. Natalie argues that the initial goal of any good nutritional program should be to ensure people: Do not become overwhelmed.

"If you subject your body to too much change all at once, it—and you—will react badly," she says. "It's easy to get discouraged that way. I encourage my clients to start slow and pace themselves. 'Get into your comfort zone,' I tell them. I'm 100 percent realistic with these women because while anyone can lose weight, far fewer manage to keep it off. In my view, a diet isn't a diet, it's a lifestyle change."

What's Natalie's own lifestyle like? She tells me that it's all about balance, which means building easy-to-follow habits into her life. Here are the main healthy habits she practices and preaches.

Natalie's nutrition habit #1:
"I eat every two to three hours—mini meals, I call them. It keeps the metabolism going, which is critical to fat-burning. And it keeps my sugar levels down, which is also a good thing. I must have breakfast or I'll binge at lunch. The biggest meal of any-one's day should be lunch, never dinner, because we don't have enough time to burn dinner off like we do with lunch."

Natalie's nutrition habit #2:
"I drink lots of water. At least 2 litres a day to keep the body hydrated. Contrary to popular opinion, drinking water doesn't help by flushing out fat from your body; it regulates your appetite, which of course reduces the amount of food you con-sume each day."

Natalie's nutrition habit #3:
"I take an appropriate amount of supplements, but I don't take them instead of food! I take calcium and magnesium and multi-vitamins. I also take flaxseed oil, which helps prevent breast cancer and helps maintain healthy looking hair and skin."

Natalie's been a registered nutritionist for nearly ten years. She says there's a lot of misinformation out there.

"Contrary to popular opinion, 90 percent of significantly over-weight women (50 pounds or more) are *not* happy," she says. "And obesity is *not* genetic. People who are overweight feel powerless. That's why they seldom make the changes they need to make."

Lauren Jawno believes in a highly disciplined approach.

"Before I even see a client, I ask them to complete a food and exercise journal," she tells me. "I need to know what they are currently eating so I can adjust and balance their diet gradually and systematically. Most diets are unbalanced, which is a problem, both physiologically and psychologically. I create a balanced nutritional plan that is directly customized to their lifestyle and preferences. And then there is also the emotional factor to deal with, and this is critical because we eat for so many reasons other than true hunger."

"A diet isn't a diet, it's a lifestyle change." —NATALIE BEAN-SOLE, President of NutritionForeverInc.com

What kinds of foods go into her diets, exactly?

"I recommend organic foods when possible," she says. "Our regular food supply is low in nutritional value and filled with hormones, antibiotics and chemicals."

Natalie says she went through an extensive period of trial and error before finding her own solution.

"I tried every book, every gimmick, every trick, any amount of money and I'd try it. They worked temporarily, but I didn't know they wouldn't work long-term. I wanted to diet and still *live!* Through trial and error I developed my own formula which came out before the South Beach Diet. Ironically, my diet has many similarities to it."

I asked her if she would give me the "big picture" description of her own nutritional approach.

"First of all, I disagree with the idea that you should never mix carbs and meat," she says. "The best way to eat right is by using common sense and making sure you get the right support. I would start by simply eating smaller portions. Any feelings of emptiness go away in a few days as your stomach shrinks. Pretty soon your pants get looser, which is always a positive motivator. I eat red meat once a week to get iron and I eat good carbs—whole grain, oatmeal, whole wheat pasta. I stay away from white flours—they raise blood sugars and actually make you hungrier. There's nothing wrong with a little red wine."

That's all well and good. But how does a person eat healthy without feeling constant cravings?

"It's all about the mind," she says. "Mind over matter, mind over the body. And if your mind tells you what you're doing is making you feel good, that will become your reality."

Lauren says our minds are so powerful, we can will ourselves to do anything. But if we deprive our body of essential nutrients (for example, nutritious carbohydrates) for too long, not even the strongest willpower will help because our body will demand we get those carbohydrates by—among other things—causing us to crave sugar.

"Our attitude and outlook on life also influence our eating habits," she says. "When we feel good about ourselves we tend to eat better, and when we eat well we feel better. The way we do one thing is the way we do everything."

THE QUICK FIX

We all want to eat right, get plenty of exercise and rest, but it takes time and effort and it means changing our routine. And most of us simply don't want to hear that. We prefer the quick fix. That's why crash diets are so popular. Atkins Diet, Jenny Craig, Fit for Life, Bob Greene, NutriSystem, Dr. Phil, Scarsdale Diet, Slim-Fast, South Beach Diet, Sugar Busters, Weight Watchers, The Zone—the list goes on and on. Diets offer us an instant, one-size-fits-all magic bullet, and what could be a better fit for our fast-paced, 24/7, image-conscious lifestyle than that?

The trouble is they're doing nothing to stop obesity in its tracks. As I mentioned earlier, one in four Canadian adults is obese. Here are the BMI measurements that define our weight category (in case you were wondering). A detailed calculation of your own BMI can be created using the formula on Health Canada's website at www.hc-sc.gc.ca. Click on the "Nutrition & Healthy Eating" tab, go to the "Healthy Weights" topic (right side of the page). In simplistic terms, the formula is BMI = weight (kg) / height $(m)^2$. But again, it's worth noting that BMI does not take into consideration the true percentage of body fat, and that is what really contributes to health issues.

Health and fitness expert Lauren Jawno says comparing yourself to others is the wrong way to motivate yourself.

Health Risk Classification According to Body Mass Index (BMI)		
Classification	BMI Category (kg/m^2)	Risk of developing health problems
Underweight	< 18.5	Increased
Normal Weight	**18.5–24.9**	**Least**
Overweight	25.0–29.9	Increased
Obese class I	30.0–34.9	High
Obese class II	35.0–39.9	Very high
Obese class III	> = 40.0	Extremely high

Note: *For persons 65 years and older the "normal" range may begin slightly above BMI 18.5 and extend into the "overweight" range.* Source: Health Canada, Food and Nutrition, 2003. Used with permission.

"Many people compare themselves to others and end up feeling they can never match up or reach that point," she says. "But really they should only be looking at themselves and trying to be the best that they can be. Every individual has their own unique goals and values, so trying to look like someone else who may have a totally different body type and lifestyle is going to be nearly impossible to achieve and sustain."

DIET-CRAZED

The diet craze will never end as long as people are looking for the quick fix instead of a long-term lifestyle change that will restore their body's health. Low-carb, low-fat, low-calorie diets are all unbalanced. Following a low-carb diet leaches calcium from our bones because of the acidic environment it creates. In the long term this can affect bone strength and density. Following a high-protein diet for a few weeks might not have much effect on bone strength and density, but doing it for a long time very likely could.

By now, most of us realize that carbohydrates from white bread, white rice, sugar, fat, pastries and other highly processed foods are not good for your physique. Registered Nutritional Consultant Tara Postnikoff says that most fad diet plans are unbalanced. While they work in the short term, she says they're detrimental to your body in the long term.

"Many of these diets have way too much saturated fat," she says, "especially if you continue to overload by eating a lot of meat. I believe it's important to try and eat more plant proteins to limit your intake of saturated animal fat. The one good thing about some of these low-carb diets is they get a lot of people off refined carbohydrates like bagels, muffins, danishes and so on. If people just eliminated those from their diet, they'd be ahead! Additionally, some of these diet plans' branded bread products are so refined and adulterated that they're toxic to the body in other ways."

NUTRITION MYTHS

Nutrition experts have differing views on some aspects of diet, but they do agree on one thing: There are many misconceptions out there. Here are a few:

Myth #1: Lean protein diets are the way to lose fat.
"Not true. Although we do want our protein to come from lean sources, an excess for your body will be converted into adipose fat—loose connective tissue that stores energy and also cushions and insulates the body. In fact, an excess of any kind of food eventually turns into fat."
—LAUREN JAWNO, Speaker, Coach, Trainer, Consultant and President of Personal Health

Myth #2: Metabolism levels are the same for everyone.
"Not true. Each person is metabolically different in terms of the efficiency/inefficiency of their metabolism."
—LAUREN JAWNO, Speaker, Coach, Trainer, Consultant and President of Personal Health

Myth #3: Dr. Bernstein and others have it right: radically drop your caloric intake and your weight issues will quickly go away.
"Not true. If you follow diets like Dr. Bernstein's and put only 700 calories a day into your body, you'll lose weight but you won't be living a life! And that increases the odds you'll backslide."
—NATALIE BEAN-SOLE, President of NutritionForeverInc.com

Myth #4: Weight loss is easily measured by your bathroom scale.
"Not true. Just because you see a number on a scale doesn't mean you're losing weight. It could be you're losing water or muscle."
—NATALIE BEAN-SOLE, President of NutritionForeverInc.com

Myth #5: All you have to do to diet is eat less.
"The purpose of losing weight is to lose body fat and ultimately change body composition. Unbalanced diets will cause our bodies to lose muscle mass and this will result in a slower metabolism. That's not good. But remember, we all need a certain amount of essential body fat in order to be healthy. For active females, 18–20 percent is fantastic, and anything less than 24 percent is healthy."
—LAUREN JAWNO, Speaker, Coach, Trainer, Consultant and President of Personal Health

Myth #6: A calorie of ice cream is the same as a calorie of carrot.
"Not true. All calories are unfortunately not created equal. Different macronutrients require different amounts of energy to be digested and absorbed (the technical term is thermogenesis). Different foods also have different nutrient contents and qualities. All these factors will affect how many of the total calories consumed will be stored or used up by the body."
—LAUREN JAWNO, Speaker, Coach, Trainer, Consultant and President of Personal Health

Myth #7: Fast food salads are a healthy alternative to regular fast food.
Not necessarily. In January 2004, the British Nutrition Foundation checked the Interactive Nutrition Counter on McDonald's website, and found that a "Caesar salad with Chicken Premiere" contains 18.4 grams of fat compared with 11.5 grams of fat in a standard cheeseburger.
—*Harper's Magazine Weekly Review*, March 16, 2004.

NUTRITION TRUTHS

The road to wellness begins with the basics. And a few tips never hurt along the way. Some tips I picked up from the experts include:

- Find a friend to diet with. It's much easier that way.
- It's probably not the fat in your diet that makes you fat, it's the sugar.
- Motivation has to come from within. Don't compare yourself to others; it will often discourage you.
- It's not a diet; it's a lifestyle. Make good nutrition a part of your everyday life.
- Live a life, not a diet!

Senior executive Sarah Raiss says she was extremely heavy as a child.

"I was a very likable, but extremely obese child," she tells me. "I loved sweets and snacks between meals. I struggled with my weight until I was about 30. Then I started making smarter choices."

What's Sarah's diet like today?

"I eat healthy foods, veggies, fruit, fish and chicken," she shares. "I'm pretty good about portion sizes. I did the Scarsdale Diet when I was young, Weight Watchers, doctor-supervised diet. But then I started educating myself about nutrition. I began to check the labels and ingredients. That doesn't mean I've become a dieter's role model. My husband and I are chocoholics! However, I do know about blood sugar issues and that knowledge has reduced my cravings. I'll reach for an apple instead of a cookie, for example."

An apple a day keeps the doctor away, is still pretty good advice.

DIETS: THE GOOD, THE BAD AND THE UGLY

Health and fitness expert Lauren Jawno doesn't even recommend diets. She says a diet implies going on something, depriving oneself—and this usually means coming off the diet, and eating the deprived foods.

"Diets don't teach lifestyle change, coping with real situations in the world or how to deal with all the foods we're exposed to," she says. "Instead of a diet, I would recommend a portion-controlled, balanced intake of natural, whole foods specific to the person's lifestyle, personality, body type and ability to process carbohydrates. I definitely recommend keeping a food journal because it makes you accountable, helps you plan and identifies patterns or trends that may be problematic."

But aren't most of today's diet plans logical and based on sound medical principles? I mean, how can anyone argue against the old truism, "calories in" should be less than "calories out"?

"The theory of calories in and calories out is so outdated," Lauren says. "It's much more complicated than that. Most diets are low in calories and that's why people lose weight. *But they don't keep it off.* They also don't deal with the emotional issues that lead to the weight gain. And there's *always* something emotional behind it. The dieter just may not know what it is. That's why I believe personal growth is so important. It helps you really get to know yourself and what pushes your buttons."

I asked Lauren why people have so much trouble sticking to their diets. She says there could be any number of reasons.

"Frequently, the diet plan is not individualized, or it's sometimes too low in calories or it's not balanced," she explains. "Or it may not be not addressing the real problem. Often, there's a lack of proper monitoring, or the dieter is not doing it for the right reason. Typically, they're doing it to please someone else, but motivation has to come from within."

VITAMINS AND OTHER SUPPLEMENTS

The so-called "happy hormone," serotonin, is supposed to control appetite and cravings. If levels are low, cravings for carbohydrates become stronger, making it difficult to avoid unhealthy carbohydrate choices such as cookies, pastries or muffins. Chromium supplements supposedly increase serotonin production and thus reduce cravings. Whether this is true or not is unclear. And it doesn't address the underlying dietary imbalance. Due to food refinement and loss of topsoil through poor agriculture practices, there's a reduced level of chromium in foods today. Brewer's yeast, beef, liver, whole wheat, rye, fresh chillies, oysters, potatoes, wheat germ, green peppers, eggs, chicken, apples, butter, bananas and spinach are good sources of chromium. Chromium is essential because it is not made in the body and must be obtained in the diet.

Most of the women I interviewed take daily vitamins, and many nutritionists recommend them as well—not as a substitute for, but as a complement to a good diet. But you have to be more careful than you might think when choosing vitamins, says Registered Nutritional Consultant Tara Postnikoff.

"Standard store-brands are often laden with fillers including sugar, and usually contain synthetic, cheaper forms of the vitamins/minerals," she reveals. "Some don't even fully dissolve in your body. Do yourself a favour and spend a bit more, get a high-quality multivitamin/mineral complex and know that your body will actually get a chance to utilize these nutrients."

Lauren Jawno has a very different take on the use of isolated, fractionated vitamins. She says more and more research is showing that supplementing our diet with isolated, non-synergistic nutrients is potentially not as effective or even safe compared to the synergy of whole food.

"I rely on a whole-food nutritional supplements, specifically Juice Plus, to complement the lack of nutrition in our food supply," she offers. "The difference with Juice Plus is that it is whole food, with all its nutrients except the water, salt and sugar—this is truly food in a capsule that provides bioavailability. Research has proven its effectiveness."

IT'S ALL ABOUT BABY STEPS

Moderation is the key to so many of our lifestyle issues. Instead of making a major lifestyle change that may be doomed to fail, how about making a small change? Many of us try to do the impossible and change everything in one fell swoop. It's admirable to want to dive into a diet with gusto, but Lauren heartily recommends against it. Making too many changes at once isn't psychologically sustainable. Rather than fostering new habits it will, if anything, overwhelm you and become self-defeating. Lauren has some common sense advice for all of us would-be dieters.

"I believe starting with baby steps is the best approach," says Lauren. "If you slowly incorporate changes, they will gradually develop into habits. At the same time, we will start to see results and feel good about what we're doing simply because we are able to do it. Remember though, those 'baby steps' will be different for everyone depending on their personality and past history. That's why it's so critical to individualize your lifestyle program."

"It's critical to individualize your lifestyle program."

—LAUREN JAWNO, Speaker, Coach, Trainer, Consultant and President of Personal Health

HOW TO EAT "HEALTHY" WITHOUT GETTING CONSTANT CRAVINGS

How do I avoid cravings? This is a question a lot of us would like an answer to.

"But that's the interesting thing," Lauren says. "When you eat healthy you don't have cravings." She explains it this way:

"When you're giving your body the nutrients it needs, then it becomes nourished and satisfied. If you constantly eat processed, refined convenience foods, even though your body is getting calories it's not getting nutrients and therefore your body is always hungry. Your body is always going to want what you give it most, so if you eat a lot of simple carbs, that's what your body is going to want and crave. Conversely, if you eat nutritious, real food then that is what your body will want."

Registered Nutritional Consultant Tara Postnikoff says we need to learn to distinguish true hunger—which is our biological cue to eat—from appetite or craving, which is a construct created in our head. I have to admit, I never thought of my appetite that way before, but those beautifully photographed cookbooks seem to target our appetite for food rather than our hunger for it, don't they?

Want some quick tips to manage your hunger? Eat protein at every meal, eat smaller portions but eat more often (every two to three hours), include vegetables with all your meals, drink plenty of water and drink it often.

SUGAR, SALT, MARGARINE AND COOKING OILS

Sugar

Sugar alone doesn't cause diabetes or heart attacks, but an excess definitely contributes to an increased risk factor. Sugar is added to processed products, providing loads of empty calories but very few, if any, vitamins, minerals and enzymes. Lauren's biggest issue with sugar is our excessive consumption of it. "It's extremely difficult to buy anything that's not loaded with it. Did you know the average child eats 5 pounds of sugar a week? It's out of control." Research backs up her claim. According to U.S. Department of Agriculture surveys, at least 20 percent of the daily calories of nearly one-quarter of adult women come from added sugar. Ketchup, cereals, canned beans, breads and many things that aren't sweet still use sugar as cheap filler, which is one big reason why consumption of added sugar has risen 30 percent in the last two decades.

Salt

Salt is basically sodium and chloride, and we need a certain amount of sodium for our nerves and muscles to function properly. But we eat far too much of it—on average, nearly 60 percent more than we should. Salty food tastes good to many of us, which is why we eat so much of it. But Lauren says there's an excellent alternative.

"We all know that salt is high in most processed and prepackaged meals," she says. "I stay away from them, and recommend cooking with fresh ingredients, and using spices and herbs to flavour food. They do an excellent job and many have great health-promoting benefits."

Cutting down on salt should be a gradual process; otherwise it will be a shock to your system (and taste buds!) and you'll feel deprived and likely give up. I cut down my own intake of salt because research has shown that too much salt/sodium can raise blood pressure, high blood pressure leads to hypertension, and hypertension is a major risk factor in heart disease and stroke.

Margarine

For years we've known that butter contains fat—unfortunately, it happens to be of the saturated variety. But recent research has shown that most hard-stick margarines are hydrogenated, which means they're full of unhealthy trans fats. The more hydrogenated an oil is, the harder it will be at room temperature. Spreadable tubs of margarine may be less hydrogenated and have few or no trans fats, however, we have to beware of terms such as "modified and fractionated" as they also have negative effects on the body.

So what choice should we make? Butter or margarine? Lauren Jawno offers this perspective: "Margarine versus butter? Butter is my choice for sure—it's natural, and even though it's a saturated fat, our body can recognize it and metabolize it. It's also stable for cooking at high heat. Margarine is processed and full of chemicals, additives, colourants, et cetera, that our body cannot metabolize. I recommend using coconut oil for cooking at high and medium temperatures as it is stable and does not 'denature' easily. Butter is the same. I prefer using olive oil raw, not heated. Sunflower and canola oil are okay for cooking at medium temperatures but avoid vegetable oil—it is petroleum based."

WHAT DO OUR INTERVIEWEES SAY ABOUT THEIR OWN DIETS?

You might expect that high-achieving women have high-achieving diets. But that's not always the case. In some respects, they're very much like the "average" Canadian in that they do some things well and some things not so well. A surprisingly large percentage of them have taken up—and dropped—multiple diet plans. Here's what they have to say about their eating habits.

Brenda Eaton
"I've been a pesco-vegetarian for ten years. I'm a picky eater, but I have a terrible sweet tooth. I don't watch my portions. At home, my husband—who is retired—makes steamed veggies and maybe fish. At restaurants, I have fish. About three years ago, I tried a 'detox' fast. The first day I thought about nothing but food, and by day eight I was feeling a distinct lack of energy."

Jacqui Szeto
"I was overweight as a child, and I wasn't a high-energy person. Today I eat pretty much everything except processed food and I

watch my intake of fat and sodium. I remember eating at the local food court once—it made me sluggish, I noticed it quite clearly. As far as diets go, I've tried Scarsdale, South Beach and www.e-diets. Because of my history, I'm probably a little obsessed with my weight."

Ann Kaplan
"I'm lucky to have good genetics because I can still wear the same jeans I owned in my twenties. I watch my portion sizes, I don't like to feel full. I don't eat white flour or sugar or dairy. I'm a vegetarian—no chicken, fish, meat. I've done this for twenty-five years. I don't bother with diet books, I eat three meals a day, no snacking, and I eat at the same time each day."

Sarah Thomson
"I try to watch what I eat, no fast foods and so on, but I forget to eat lunch sometimes. My only craving is for a cup of coffee, sometimes I give in to the craving and sometimes I don't. I eat cereal or fruit or sometimes whole-wheat toast for breakfast, and I take vitamins B and C. One time I tried a rice diet but I only lasted one day!"

Dee Brasseur
"I don't avoid anything, but I do believe in eating smaller portions. Everything in moderation—I have pizza, donuts maybe once a week. Fish and meat whenever I want. I don't believe in diets—the first three letters in diet are 'die.' I think the unconscious mind takes over and says it doesn't want to die. Somehow it knows it's a fad or a trend and knows it's only going to do this for a few weeks. I believe in gradual reduction—little bits often. Instead of two scoops of ice cream, have just one so you don't feel deprived. Good eating habits are all about choice."

Akela Peoples
"For breakfast I have fruit or an egg-white omelette. Lunch is salad and/or protein. Dinner is vegetable and protein, no potatoes, bread, rice or pasta. I've tried to cut down on my carbs but

no diets for me, per se. I look at it as more of a lifestyle change. I love to cook but during the workweek I usually make a salad or something simple. I take vitamin C and multivitamins every day, just to ensure I get all the nutrients by body needs."

Joan Kelley-Weisshaar
"I have two coffees and none after 11:00 a.m. I don't drink pop, and junk food is a treat only. I try to be an example for my kids. All the food groups are on the plate at each meal. In the morning, we'll have toast, cereal, juice, bananas and fruit, plus organic versions of cereals. I buy organic when possible. And only whole grains and lean meat. I shop at Costco if we are having a large group at the cottage. Diets? I've tried them all at some point or other. I find it hard to stay on a diet but I think it's logical stuff. I take bits and pieces of information from each one, like South Beach and Dr. D'Adamo. On the connection between best foods for your blood type, I think a key is to eat a lot of little meals throughout the day. Listen to your body. Maybe a treat as a reward, periodically. We don't eat snacks when watching TV, and we go for smaller portions."

Julie Toskan-Casale
"Do I watch what I eat? Sure. I watch it just before I swallow it. I won't eat all day sometimes, and then I'll be famished in the evenings. I read the nutrition labels on the food I buy. I've tried every diet on earth, and I'm still looking. We eat fresh foods, not the packaged stuff. Chicken and fish and fresh vegetables. My husband and I both like to cook."

Aimée Israel
"We have a family history of heart disease, so I definitely watch what I eat. Stir-fries, whole-wheat pasta, sushi, that sort of thing. I did the Weight Watchers program to get back to my pre-pregnancy weight. It taught me a lot about portion control. I've never done anything extreme, like a low-carb diet, because I believe in moderation. I eat all kinds of things, just less of them. I don't deprive myself like many people do."

Lesley Southwick-Trask

"My husband is ill and we've established a cancer diet. We're much more vegetarian now. We avoid red meat; we have smaller portions, brown rice, fruit and veggies. We take four smaller meals instead of three big ones, that sort of thing."

HOW MANY CALORIES IS TOO MUCH?

Surprisingly, most of us don't know how many calories we should consume on a daily basis. Different factors affect your optimal caloric intake, such as gender, muscle mass, efficiency of your metabolism, age and so forth, which is why your family physician or, even better, a nutritionist, should be consulted for comprehensive evaluation of your calorie needs. By the way, physicians are not trained in nutrition. They tend to follow Canada's Food Guide, which many experts feel is outdated (even the newly revised version). Ultimately, one size does not fit all, especially when it comes to nutrition. Everyone has different needs.

Having said that, there is an optimal caloric range, according to your weight or weight goals. If you weigh (or want to weigh) between 130 and 140 pounds, for example, most experts say that your daily calorie intake should run between 1,700 and 2,380 calories, depending on your activity level. If you go onto the Internet, you will find many caloric tables. Diet Bites has a useful chart called "Caloric Needs Based on Weight" on their website at www.dietbites.com.

But dieting by itself is not enough. Exercise is the other half of the foundation for a healthy lifestyle.

GET REAL ABOUT YOUR FITNESS

I exercise as often as I can, but I don't exercise to look good. I do it to feel good and because I want to live a full and active life. Keeping fit is a very important part of my life. It's become a habit, a ritual. As a result, I don't have to put much effort into thinking about it or doing it. I'm an early riser. I tend to get up around 5:00 a.m. and work out for about an hour and half, usually five to six days a week. I watch TV when I work out, usually CNBC, Bloomberg Television or Business

News Network. It's multi-tasking but I enjoy it, and because of my job, I have to be aware of what has gone on in the overseas market.

Once I've finished working out, I'll check the wires to see what potentially will be moving the market that day. My leaving time is varied, and I'm often on the road speaking to internal and external clients. Rarely am I home Monday through Thursday, and if I'm in the office I tend to leave around 6:00 p.m. It's better for me to get going before I get delayed by an impromptu meeting.

Okay, so maybe you're saying to yourself, "I'm busy too, but I have to prioritize. Besides, there's no way I can get up at that hour!" Well, I've got a surprise for you. Most of the amazingly busy women I interviewed have found a way to fit fitness into their lives, and nearly all of them are home for dinner at a reasonable hour.

Take Ann Kaplan, for example. She's the CEO of a medical financing company, as well as a mother of six, but she allocates time every day to keeping fit. She jogs to work, boxes at her lunch hour and doesn't belong to a health club.

"I've got two young children, four teenagers and a business to run," she says. "I get up at 5:00 a.m. or 7:30 a.m., depending on my volunteer work schedule, rowing with the kids, and so on. Unless there's a special project, I'm home by 6:30 p.m., but sometimes I have to work through the night. So there's only so much time in the day for exercise. That's why I incorporate it directly into my work routine. I find that exercise not only keeps me younger looking, it increases my energy level so I can multi-task and put in long hours without feeling drained."

> "I find that exercise not only keeps me younger looking, it increases my energy level so I can multi-task and put in long hours without feeling drained."
>
> —ANN KAPLAN, CEO of Medicard

Is Ann's integrated exercise routine typical of the women I interviewed? No, they're all different in their own ways. Julie Toskan-Casale and Linda Wheler are a little more sporadic when it comes to fitness. Julie says she's "constantly on the go, so my fitness periods happen in phases. When they do, a trainer comes to the house." Linda says she'd like to exercise, "but it's not always a priority for me. I have too many other priorities with my congregation and in my personal life. Long walks with the dog are about it for fitness right now." On the other hand, Natalie Bean-Sole is devoted to exercise. "It's my stress relief. I feel it gives me better energy, makes me a better entrepreneur, and a better mother." What is Natalie's weekly exercise routine?

"I go to the club at 6:30 a.m., five to six days a week," Natalie explains. "I work out with a personal trainer for one hour on the free weights and weight machines. I also do thirty minutes of cardio and stretching and abdominal crunches by myself."

If someone asks Natalie how they can stay fit without spending a fortune, she says, "Do you have two legs? Then use them!" And then offers these excellent tips:

"Try and avoid driving everywhere," she recommends. "Park further away than you usually do. Do a morning, lunch and evening walk. Put exercise slots into your day timer and keep your appointments with yourself. Make the time to exercise—realize that there's no magic bullet. I was back at the gym four weeks after having my baby. I don't make the rules. I follow them just like everyone else. I'm not the Diet God that says, 'I pronounce you fit!'"

> *"Make the time to exercise—realize that there's no magic bullet."*
> —NATALIE BEAN-SOLE, President of NutritionForeverInc.com

A graduated approach to diet works far better than an all or nothing philosophy. And the same holds true for fitness. Let's say you haven't worked out very much if at all over the years, and now you've reached an age where you realize exercise can help you, esthetically or physiologically. What choice are you going to make?

Natalie recommends taking things slow, and building up one day at a time. Do you recall what she said earlier, that most overweight women feel powerless to make a change? Here's her solution to overcoming your feeling of helplessness.

"Start small, and build up a certain comfort level with small weights and limited cardio and stretching," she recommends. "Then you'll start to feel good about yourself. You'll have more energy, and as your natural 'endorphins' begin to kick in, you'll experience a sense of calm and well-being, even euphoria in some cases. As you begin to feel better both physically and mentally, your outcome begins to appear. Things start to come together, and you'll feel a sense of power you never had before."

However, the last thing you should do, according to many experts, is dive into a concentrated exercise program without preparation. Why? For the same reasons you don't want to dive right into a diet. It's too much of a shock to the system, it's often psychologically and physically overwhelming, and it increases the odds you'll start to feel bad about yourself and then backslide. Perhaps most important, an all-or-nothing approach sets us up to fail because it's too external and event-driven, rather than lifestyle-driven. Exercise is a habit that you want to build into your life. It shouldn't be seen as an event-driven activity, something that we only seem to do when we're on holiday for example, like swimming or table tennis!

What exercise routines do the other interviewees fit into their busy lives? Aimée Israel, Co-founder of LifeSpeak, runs three times a week. She, too, believes in doing things gradually. She says, "Small but 'stretchy' goals are better than big or unattainable goals, because they produce noticeable results, and achieving those results gives you staying power."

Dr. Nancy Baxter knows she has to be more consistent about her exercise regimen. "I wish I was more committed," she says. "There are periods of time when I am committed, and there are periods when I'm not." She likes running, especially outdoors, "because it's cheap and good for you. But I don't do marathons," she says. "I believe a lot of people who run marathons are making a mistake because of excessive wear and tear on the joints."

Lesley Southwick-Trask says she's "not a diet person. If I want to lose weight I start running, exercising and walking stairs. I like getting into a rhythm and I tone but I don't do heavy fitness. If I'm watching TV I'll often do sit-ups and crunches."

By contrast, oil executive Sarah Raiss keeps fit through low-impact exercise like walking, being outdoors and golfing. "I'm not a runner or a skier but I like aerobics and snowshoeing. Walking is a fabulous and inexpensive way to keep healthy, and there are lots of fun walking clubs you can join if you're a very social person."

"Small but 'stretchy' goals are better than big or unattainable goals, because they produce noticeable results and achieving those results gives you staying power."
—AIMÉE ISRAEL, Co-founder and CEO of LifeSpeak

Dentist Trish Kmet loves to run, swim and bike "because the feeling I have afterwards is really great." Artist Jackie Carroll feels the same way. "I get an endorphin rush when I exercise and a strong sense of well-being. I prefer the early morning and I do about forty-five minutes of cardio whenever possible. For me, the endorphins kick in after about twenty minutes of working out."

As you can see from all these different women, there is no one right way to exercise. Jackie agrees. "I think it depends on each person, and their personality and body type. If you want to begin a complete weight and cardio program, however, I'd recommend getting professional advice before starting. If money is an issue, then friends and the Internet can be a great help."

CANADIANS ARE FACING AN OBESITY EPIDEMIC

One study after another involving large groups of people and their exercise habits have all come to one inescapable conclusion: *An inactive lifestyle dramatically increases your chance of becoming overweight and developing any number of chronic and potentially fatal diseases.*

Dr. Beth Abramson, of St. Michael's Hospital in Toronto, comes to a more explicit conclusion. One of Canada's leading cardiologists, and spokesperson for the Heart and Stroke Foundation of Canada, Dr. Abramson says Canada's baby boomers are facing an impending health crisis. "This tidal wave of Canadian baby boomers could be the first generation to turn back the clock and experience a serious decline in quality of life. The evidence is truly disturbing."

According to the Canadian Community Health Survey of 2003–2004, 52 percent of baby boomers lead a sedentary lifestyle today, versus 43 percent a decade ago. It's important to underscore that Canadians who are overweight pose a risk, but if they are overweight *and* sedentary, they are at greatest risk for heart disease and stroke. "Fat is the new tobacco," says Dr. Abramson. "As a society we take the easy way out. We sit in front of computers and televisions and we drive to the convenience store. Lifestyle changes are not only necessary, they're long overdue." And by the way, it's not just boomers who are becoming obese. Most alarming of all, childhood obesity is on the rise as well.

SOMETIMES IT'S BETTER TO BE OLDER

When we get beyond middle age and into the "senior period" of our lives, the tendency is to think that exercise won't do as much good so it's not a priority. Well, guess what? Studies reveal that older people have a big advantage over the young with respect to exercise. "Older people, those who are out of shape or those with disabilities may get as much benefit from thirty minutes of slower walking or other exercise as younger, more fit people get from the same amount of more intense activity." In other words, if an exercise or physical activity feels hard, then it is probably doing your heart—and the rest of you—some good, even if it doesn't fall into the "moderate" category.

That warms the cockles of my heart, I can tell you. But even more importantly, it should warm my parents' hearts!

Natalie Bean-Sole, President of NutritionForeverInc.com, tells me that weight training burns off 50 percent more weight than cardio. That I didn't know. Perhaps it explains why many of the weights-focused guys in the gym have less fat than the more cardio-inclined girls. She also advises against doing a "zillion sit-ups" to get rid of stomach flab. If you don't diet along with your exercise, you'll never lose your gut. Instead, you'll have a powerful stomach hidden under a not-so-powerful layer of fat.

Natalie's lifestyle habit #1:
"I exercise regularly, three to four times a week, about thirty to forty-five minutes per session."

Natalie's lifestyle habit #2:
"I get a proper amount of sleep, which for me is seven to eight hours a night."

As you might expect, Lauren Jawno, a health and fitness expert, loves to exercise. Before she came to Canada from her native South Africa, she was a competitive swimmer and tennis player.

"I love exercise, love keeping fit and feeling strong," she says. "I also love running and weight training, do a lot of swimming and cycling in the summer and when I have extra time love to get to a yoga class. I try and work out first thing in the morning but that depends on my client schedule, otherwise in the later afternoon, or both depending on where my training is at."

She says she's been active her whole life except for a couple of odd periods here and there. One of those non-active periods, however, was *not* after a recent car accident.

"My car was rear-ended during the past summer," she explains. "I was lying on the sidewalk on a stretcher about to be taken to hospital, and all I could think about was that I had a swimming session planned that night and could not miss it—and I didn't."

Here are Lauren Jawno's three most important lifestyle habits:

Lauren's lifestyle habit #1:
"I spend time on personal growth and development EVERY DAY!"

Lauren's lifestyle habit #2:
"I schedule five to six workouts per week for myself."

Lauren's lifestyle habit #3:
"I drink plenty of water every day, I take a whole food based supplement and I take fish oil (omega 3)."

Are most of us as committed to fitness as Lauren? Probably not. Nor do we have to be. As long as we do something modest but eventful to keep ourselves active every day, we're on the right path. Jacqui Szeto has a high-stress job in institutional sales at TD Securities' trading desk. She also has a new baby and she works in the evening co-running her own online shopping service. How does she fit in time for exercise?

"I've made a commitment to myself," Jacqui says. "I walk the dog and the baby. I do the occasional Pilates class. At home I do spinning or elliptical training. I try to work out at 5:30 a.m. I only do five- or ten-minute sessions, but I do it every day."

MAKING EXERCISE A PART OF YOUR LIFE

Studies have shown over and over that physical inactivity makes your body age faster. In fact, The Public Health Agency of Canada says, "inactivity is as harmful to your health as smoking." Wow. That's a scary thought. Staying physically active will help you to keep moving, and stay strong. Inactivity leads to declines in bone strength; muscle strength; heart and lung fitness; and flexibility.

But your motivation to get active or keep active should be irresistible. And maybe it will be if you read this excerpt from an article in the *Canadian Medical Association Journal* (March 14, 2006) by Darren E.R. Warburton, Crystal Whitney Nicol and Shannon S.D. Bredin: "We confirm that there is irrefutable evidence of the effectiveness of regular physical activity in the primary and secondary prevention of several chronic diseases (e.g., cardiovascular disease, diabetes, cancer, hypertension, obesity, depression and osteoporosis) and premature death."

I'm not trying to scare you. I'm just hoping you'll appreciate what my active lifestyle interviewees already know—that exercise is hugely important to the quality of their lives. And then perhaps you'll decide to take a page out of their book, and get active.

MAKE THE TIME, BECAUSE YOU'LL SELDOM *FIND* IT

If finding the time to exercise is your biggest impediment to regular exercise, Akela Peoples, CEO of Youth in Motion, has some advice for you.

"If you can't find twenty minutes a day to exercise, then something is seriously wrong," she says. "Exercise absolutely has to become part of your routine so you don't even have to think about it. If I miss a workout, I feel out of sync. My routine is to get up at 5:30 a.m. and run on the treadmill and do arm weights. On weekends I run outdoors, so I end up exercising six times a week."

But doesn't travel time and changing at the gym eat a lot of time, I ask? She smiles calmly and gives me this response.

"About twelve years ago I bought a big industrial treadmill," she explains. "For me going to the gym is a huge time commitment—packing, driving, changing, showering are all time obstacles. The only obstacle I face now is commitment, but because fitness is an integral part of my daily routine, it's easy to maintain."

Akela is not the only one addicted to the treadmill. Joan Kelley-Weisshaar really enjoys it, "because I get to watch my favourite show (on tape) for an hour. I also push the kids in the stroller up and down the hills. That can be great exercise, as they weigh about 70 pounds."

Most surprising is that *exercise can have no effect at all on some people*. Researchers have discovered that there's enormous variation in how people respond to cardiovascular exercise, with some not responding at all. They do say, however, that there are health benefits with exercise, even if cardiovascular fitness and strength don't improve. I wonder how much of it relates to the variations in *intensity* of the workout.

STAYING FIT WITHOUT SPENDING A FORTUNE

Walking and running are the two cheapest ways to stay fit. But if neither one appeals to you, find something you enjoy doing and that's as convenient as possible to do. Lauren Jawno advises that you work with a trainer for a couple of sessions to get a program that is specific to your needs.

"You really don't need to spend a lot of money on equipment, but you need to be creative," she says. "Some items that are great to use and relatively inexpensive are skipping ropes, resistance bands, dumbbells, medicine balls, stability balls and balance boards. You can use things at home like the stairs. It's very possible to do a great workout in twenty to thirty minutes, although I do not necessarily feel that is enough on a daily basis."

GET REAL ABOUT STRESS

Most experts agree that some stress is inevitable and even needed in our lives. But how much stress is too much, and how do Canadian women and men feel about stress? The Heart and Stroke Foundation of Ontario put out a pamphlet on just this subject, and these are some of the results.

How Canadians feel about stress	
Percent of Canadians Who:	
1) **Frequently feel stressed:**	
by work	Men 27%, Women 33%
by family responsibilities	Men 21%, Women 29%
by family finances	Men 20%, Women 21%
any or all of the above	Men 41%, Women 45%
2) **Lack time for:**	
family	Men 28%, Women 26%
friends or partner	Men 23%, Women 22%
things would like to do	Men 38%, Women 36%
any or all of the above	Men 54%, Women 52%
3) **When under stress, would be very/somewhat likely to:**	
eat comfort foods	Men 31%, Women 49%
smoke a cigarette	Men 29%, Women 26%
have an alcoholic drink	Men 39%, Women 25%
watch more TV	Men 46%, Women 39%
any or all of the above	Men 75%, Women 73%

Source: "Heart and Stroke Foundation of Ontario, Just the Facts, 2002/2003." Used with permission.

The numbers above show how stress helps create bad habits like excessive food and alcohol intake. I have a simple philosophy when it comes to stress. I worry about the things I can control and don't give a second thought to things I can't change. A good example, especially for women, is the issue of aging. Aging is going to happen, like it or not, so I've just decided to be the best I can be at every age. I get seven and a half to eight hours of sleep a night because I know how important it is in battling stress. I'm sure you don't need me to tell you it's becoming a 24/7 world, so stress management is taking on increasing importance, both at home and in the workplace.

STRESS FOR SUCCESS

Experience and common sense tell us that certain life events are more stressful than others—the death of a partner, divorce, a major injury or illness, for example. What isn't on most psychologists' lists of most stressful events is the heavy stress that can come from excessive workloads or deadlines. How do you deal with that kind of stress? This is what I do: I go for a run. If an extended period of excessive stress builds up in my life—and believe me that happens more often that I care to admit—I pamper myself. I often go for a trip to the spa. Not everyone can afford that, I know, but there are other things you can do.

TIPS FOR MANAGING STRESS

- Go for a run: If the pressure has been building for days, go for a run in the morning or at night. That's what I do, and it's amazing what a difference the oxygen intake does to my body, not to mention my agitated mind.
- Nap, if you can: More and more research is beginning to suggest that napping—provided it is short and relatively early in the afternoon—can stave off stress.
- Lie down on the floor and stretch: Read a book or website that talks about proper stretching, and feel the difference in your back and neck muscles.
- Sit down and shut your eyes for fifteen minutes: This is doable by any employee at any time. If you're cubicle-bound, connect yourself to a pair of telephone headphones and no one will know.
- Meditate for fifteen minutes: Similar to the above, but meditation is a more active process. Jackie Carroll says it clears the mind and creates a sense of calmness and inner peace. We'll talk more about meditation in the next chapter.
- Learn to say "no": A lot of the women I interviewed have told me, "I'm learning how to say no more often so that I don't get so stressed." If you continue to take on more than you can handle, no one benefits. Delegate downward or upward.

THIRTY ROCKS

If you think your job is stressful, think about Linda Wheler's for a moment. As pastoral minister, she presides at marriages, baptisms and funerals.

"I handle stress pretty well," she says. "I acknowledge it when it comes, I pray, I go to a spiritual director, and sometimes I perform a symbolic ritual."

One of those times involved the ritual of the thirty rocks.

"At one point, I presided over thirty funerals in three months," she tells me. "It was an emotionally trying time, and the pressure just kept building up inside. So I decided to find thirty rocks, and I identified each rock with a person's story. Then I released each rock one by one. It helped me clear my mind and calm my soul."

GET REAL ABOUT YOUR BODY

We all know that movies, television, billboards and magazines bombard us with a land of fantasy and make-believe. The trouble is, they're very good at their job. The razor-thin women are impossibly beautiful, and somehow we start believing we should look like that as well.

In a world of ever-increasing hype and consumption, it's important that we stay real and not chase illusions, says Lauren Jawno, who counsels women every day on being healthier and fitter.

"We have to try and see past the makeup and air-brushing," she says, "and realize that our soul is who we really are, and our body is just the packaging. When we go grocery shopping, for example, do we look closely at the vegetables inside or do we just check what the package looks like? We look at the vegetables, the content! We need to do that with ourselves and everyone around us. No, it's not easy. But it can be done with a lot of positive self-talk and knowing your true priorities in life."

If only for a few moments or a few hours or a few days, marketers want us to believe what they're selling. And that's fine. We think what they're selling is content, but what they're really selling is image and style—lifestyle. It's up to us how positively or negatively we want to be influenced by their images.

Nutritionist Natalie Bean-Sole also appears on television to offer advice and education on nutritional matters. She says media images of "heroin chic" models inadvertently pressure women to try impossible diets.

> "We have to try and see past the makeup and air-brushing, and realize that our soul is who we really are, and our body is just the packaging."
> —LAUREN JAWNO, Speaker, Coach, Trainer, Consultant and President of Personal Health

"The stakes keep getting higher," she says. "Everything in the media is constantly changing, and it affects young girls and young women most of all. Parents are constantly dieting, and their children are affected by this. Today it seems everyone wants to be the best of the best. The movie stars are judged on an even higher level and they're almost neurotic about their weight and their looks. Their lives are straight-jacketed—they don't even have the choice to have one cheeseburger just once. Because of the media, it seems like the average person is developing an all-or-nothing attitude to looks and weight, and to me that's just wrong."

Most of us have seen the Dove ad campaign in which real women proudly display real—not idealized—bodies. In 2005, Dove commissioned a remarkable study to explore self-esteem and the impact of beauty ideals on the lives of women and girls. Dove tells us that a total of 3,300 women and girls were interviewed between the ages of 15 and 64 in Brazil, Canada, China, Germany, Italy, Japan, Mexico, Saudi Arabia, the United Kingdom and the United States (check out Dove's "Campaign for Real Beauty" website at www.campaignforrealbeauty. com). Among many other things, the survey found that 90 percent of all women (15–64) worldwide wanted to change at least one aspect of their physical appearance, with body weight ranking the highest.

THE MEDIA ARE NOT ALWAYS YOUR FRIEND

Recently, I was surfing the news on MSN when I happened to click on a health and fitness article headlined, "Build the Perfect Set of Abs." I immediately had a problem with the article, not because there was a picture of a good-looking couple with those virtually-impossible-to-achieve "six-pack" abs. No, that wasn't my issue. The problem for me was the subhead which came right out and said, "Steps to a six-pack that will get you noticed."

Get you *noticed*? So the purpose of the article wasn't fitness. It wasn't to motivate you to do those millions of crunches so you'd strengthen your back and stomach muscles and in the process get healthier. No, it was targeted squarely at our inner narcissism, our need to be looked at.

The point I'm trying to make is, if you want to get real about your fitness, and stay real about it, you've got to do it for the right reasons.

What's the point of having six-pack abs? Clearly, it's not about fitness because I don't see too many personal trainers who have six-pack abs, and they're paid to be in great shape. So it must be to impress others. And that means it's either to attract the opposite sex, or to make our own sex green with envy.

That's not being real. Is it?

Besides, I'm not sure anyone is going to find their soulmate if that person's attraction to you is your stomach muscles. And if you're trying to impress members of your own sex, what kind of insecurities are you inadvertently betraying for the world to see? You catch my drift? If you're not convinced, consider that Dove recently released a short film called "Evolution." Its ambitious goal is to do nothing less than "turn the traditional concept of female beauty on its head."

The film's message is that the so-called "effortless" beauty depicted in ads and fashion magazines isn't real. How does it tell us? By showing an ordinary woman who is transformed by a team of hair, makeup and lighting experts. Then her picture is digitally retouched, and then her now "perfect" face appears on a billboard. The film ends with the words, *"Every girl deserves to feel beautiful just the way she is."* To see the film, go to Dove's "Campaign for Real Beauty" website.

MAYBE THINGS ARE CHANGING

In 2006, Madrid's regional government decided to ban "overly thin" models at a top-level fashion show which it sponsors. Madrid's fashion week organizers justified the decision by saying they wanted to project an image of beauty and health rather than a waif-like/heroin chic look. The sponsors mandated that models have a BMI (body mass index) of at least 18, saying the fashion industry had a responsibility to portray healthy body images.

EIGHT WAYS TO A HEALTHY LIFE

Like it or not, our quick fix, fast food, 24/7 culture is going to stay with us for a while. It will keep on pricking at us when we try to make a permanent, long-term change in our life. But that's why we have to build cornerstone habits into our life, so that they become foundational and not incidental parts of our lives. Healthy lifestyles are all about making good *choices*. And good choices start with the right attitude, an awareness of our body and how it works, knowledge of the options available to us, and the ability to make moderate change, not through a radical and unsustainable reworking of our habits, but through baby steps.

Yes, this may require a new attitude, and a new way of thinking. But remember, fads are easy but temporary. Habits are harder but permanent. Do you remember how Billy Crystal used to sign off his Fernando Lamas impersonations on *Saturday Night Live*?

He'd always say, "It's better to look good, than to feel good. . . . And you look *mahvelous.*"

Over the years I've learned an amazing thing. A whole lot of us would secretly like to be perfect. Whether we want to have a perfect body or a perfect mind or an amazing career or an out of this world social life. This is not a good thing, just in case you were wondering. In fact, this view often leads to stress, disappointment, bad habits and poor health.

Dr. Beth Abramson says, "If we just make small lifestyle changes, they can have a remarkable impact. Most of us gain a pound or two each year, which means by middle age we'll be fifteen pounds overweight. If we just decided to *lose* a pound or two each year—via small changes in our eating or lifestyle habits—we'd be doing ourselves a huge favour that would pay off for the rest of our lives."

YOU DON'T HAVE TO BE PERFECT

If you start making some small changes in your life, you'll be doing better than 50 percent of Canadians. Too many of us have an all-or-nothing mentality when it comes to diet and exercise. We don't just want to go from obese to slightly overweight, we want to go from obese to lean and chiselled. But perfect is the enemy of good, and when it comes to diet and exercise, you don't even have to be *close* to perfect. If you just make an effort, any kind of effort, and keep at it—and remember to be the best *you* can be—you'll be half way to winning the battle.

SIX

GET REAL
ABOUT YOUR
LIFE

THERE ARE EVENTS IN OUR LIVES when time seems to stop. The first moment for me was when our youngest son was taken into intensive care with a full-blown asthma attack. The doctors at Sick Kids Hospital couldn't get it under control, and they couldn't even say with certainty that he was going to make it through the night. At that moment nothing else mattered, and my life stood still.

I've never had a "near-death experience," but I'm told that time is wholly and absolutely suspended. At least two of my interviewees have had near-death experiences, including visual artist Jackie Carroll, who had a number of premonitions that felt so real they caused her to react and try to protect herself.

"I have one goal in life: to reflect the beauty that is in others and in the world around us."
—JACQUELINE CARROLL, Visual Artist and Author

"I was in a bizarre car accident in the early nineties, during which I experienced time stopping and the sensation of being out of my body," she says. "Oddly enough, when the accident did take place I felt totally protected and safe and was relaxed about the outcome of the accident. A truck without a driver rolled sideways right onto the passing lane of the highway in front of my car. I was en route to meet an appointment deadline for a painting commission. Even though I tried to break and stop, I slammed right into the side of the truck. My attempt to avoid it was impossible. While this was taking place, time stopped for me. It was like a slide show and was very fragmented. Somehow I knew that I was protected and just wondered how much of my car was going to be crushed. I watched everything take place in slow motion. Believe me, it taught me to slow down, and I was grateful I had good karma. I walked out of the car with minor scratches, which affirmed my faith even more."

As an artist and teacher, Jackie helps people "see" the way an artist sees, to understand the process called creativity and the outcome called art.

"I have one goal in life: to reflect the beauty that is in others and in the world around us. That's why I love my work so much," she tells me.

Jacqui Szeto's near-death experience had a different kind of impact on her life.

"Two years ago, I got very sick," Jacqui says. "I was four months pregnant and suddenly I felt incredible pain. My colleagues suggested I go to hospital. The doctors examined me and said my baby's fine, but I stopped breathing. I had an embolism, my kidneys failed and I was in intensive care for a week. I was given blood thinners but none of the experts knew what was wrong, so they induced labour and aborted the child. Afterward, the medical staff thought I was in denial about everything, but I'd been in so much pain earlier that I was relieved. They told me I'd had a massive hormone surge. All I remember was going through a near-death experience. When I came out of it, I noticed that people were sending me all these flowers and gifts. I suddenly realized the human side of people, and I began to truly appreciate how precious life is. A few months later, my husband and I decided to adopt a little girl from mainland China."

Today, Jacqui is a proud mother who continues her high-powered job in capital markets. But if you ask her what she's most proud of, she'll say it's her ability to have a work/life balance.

"I've now got a lot of balls in the air, but I've found a way to juggle them all," she says.

Pamela Jeffery's mother died of cancer when she was only 47. Six years later, her son Sam almost died in the emergency room at Sick Kids.

"He spent a week in critical care fighting for his life after being diagnosed with meningitis," she reveals. "He and I spent nine years in rehab on a weekly basis. I believe that tragedy teaches you important life lessons which can ultimately help you achieve your own goals and aspirations. Life is hard, filled with good times and not-so-good times, but the key I think is to get out of bed every day and do your best, help others in your community and never, ever give up."

Although Jackie, Jacqui and Pamela struggled through life-transforming events, they're certainly not unique. Jennifer McNeill fought with a dark secret for many years.

"I worked when my kids were babies," Jennifer tells me. "There were lots of sacrifices. It was a struggle to juggle motherhood, work and other things. I tried to be all things to all people. I saw my babies' first steps, but then it was... 'gotta go to work.' I didn't have much of a social life, but a lot of that was choice. However, I was in a tough situation when I lived in Alabama. I had four young children and my husband was abusive. I knew I was going to have to make a decision."

Jennifer decided to move to Canada, and she took the kids with her.

"I started a new life in Calgary, and got work at a software company that I eventually bought," she says. "When you go from being an employee to being the boss, strange things can happen. My girlfriends at work are now my employees, and that can create conflict. For example, if they don't get a raise in pay because we had a poor quarter, hard feelings can arise. It's true what they say. It can be lonely at the top. But I've learned to prioritize, so overall I'm pretty good at balancing my life. I start work at 6:30 or 7:00 a.m., and take a break at about 10:00 p.m. to exercise. I get home about 6:00 or 7:00 p.m., cook dinner, and then work until 10:00 p.m. If one of my kids has a play on, I'll stay at home no matter how big a deal is on the table."

Three years ago, Lesley Southwick-Trask received some terrible news. Her husband's prostate cancer had metastasized to the bone.

"The oncologist told us Greg had between twelve and eighteen months," she says. "But I just couldn't accept that prognosis. Our entire family took on the research. Our daughter Nicole discovered immune augmentation therapy (IAT) operating out of the Bahamas. The clinic has proven to be the nexus of multiple therapies brought to it by patients from all over the world—yes patients, not physicians! Today we're doing everything we can to strengthen his body for the ongoing battle. I've witnessed how strong and tenacious he is, and we've become stronger as a couple, we've bonded even closer due to his illness. He never feels sorry for himself, not for a moment."

Is the treatment helping at all?

"Yes, it's working!" she says. "Its been nearly three years since that dreadful day, and although most of the medical community considers IAT to be 'alternative' cancer therapy at best, I believe in it with all my heart. Specialists take healthy blood from umbilical cords (which are normally thrown away), and use the specific proteins and tumour blockers that are missing in Greg's system. Greg's PSA count was an astronomical 919 when he was diagnosed." The prostate-specific antigen (PSA) blood test is one of the best ways to screen for prostate cancer. It measures a protein made by the prostate that is normally present in the blood, but at high levels— 20ng per ml and above—there is a significant likelihood of developing prostate cancer.

"It's now down to normal levels," Lesley says. "He fought the cancer for eight weeks in the Bahamas when hurricanes Francis and Jean wiped out power to the entire island. He goes back quarterly for treatment. The clinic environment is just incredible—all the doctors and patients are there for one reason and one reason only: to support life. I've spent a lot of time with clients in the health care sector, and I've noted over the years that patients who believe in their prognosis die much more quickly than those who refuse to believe it. When Greg was diagnosed, he saw it as a death sentence. I saw it as a wakeup call. I really believe the medical community needs help in phrasing their messages and language to critically ill patients. Doctors are skilled and their diagnoses are real, but I kept thinking, who is this individual to tell you how much time you have left? I think it's in your hands and in God's. My message to anyone is, if you become critically ill, let it be a decision point—*your* decision point. You have to assume responsibility for your life."

Stories like these remind us how precious our time on this earth really is. What we do with our time is up to us, but sometimes it's easy to lose perspective, especially when we get caught up in our career to the point that we lose sight of our other priorities.

Sarah Raiss knows this all too well.

"There was a period in my life when I worked ninety to a

"You have to assume responsibility for your life."

—LESLEY SOUTHWICK-TRASK, Co-founder of Owl's Head Retreat

hundred hours a week, but I wasn't giving anything back to my friends and family and country. I felt I'd failed," she says. "No one wants to feel like they fail, but it happens. You can learn a lot from failure. I grew endlessly when I changed. I started to have a happy life. And then, about seven years ago, I broke off a pretty good relationship to come up to Canada and start a new career at TransCanada Corporation. I fell in love with Calgary, met a man who's now my husband, and had an instant family because of his two children. I still work hard, I'm on a number of boards, but there's a real balance to my life."

Jacqui Szeto feels the same way. In addition to her role as a new mother, and her demanding job at the traders' desk, she's also president of Women in Capital Markets (WCM). WCM is a volunteer advocacy organization that seeks to educate, inform and boost the careers of women working in the capital markets arena. Jacqui also runs an online shopping service called www.Gone.Shopping.com, a web company with 850 clients. How does she do it all? I ask her about balancing what I call the five F's: Family, Friends, Finances, Fitness, and Focus (or, for some, Faith).

"I work extremely hard at keeping up with friends," she says. "Family becomes more difficult, especially when the family expands. I'm always on top of my finances, as I said before, although I've regretted a few bad investments from time to time. I exercise early most mornings, although I could do better. I'm totally focused on what I'm doing, so that's never an issue. I think you can have it all, if you plan it right. At work I have a lot of responsibility but I've learned to properly delegate work to the right people. My husband and I start work at 7:00 a.m. and usually finish at 5 o'clock. We pretty well go non-stop. After work, I read a lot. I download business books onto my iPod and make them speak faster while I'm walking the dog and the baby."

Now that's multi-tasking! What about cooking? Does she have a nanny, or is she supermom and cooks the meals as well?

"On weekdays, our nanny cooks every night. But on weekends, I do the cooking, and sometimes Brad," she says. "I'm very efficient when it comes to food shopping. One of my tricks is to phone the people at the market and order the food in advance. For instance, I've gotten to know the guys at Whitehouse Meats, and they'll vacuum pack various meats for me. Murray at the Organic vegetable stand prepares packages of veggies according to my instructions. So all I have to do is go down to the market, pick everything up and leave. It takes about five minutes. We only do takeout about three times a month because I like for us to eat good home-cooked meals, and since I actually took domestic science at school, I want to do it right."

> "I work extremely hard at keeping up with friends."
> —JACQUI SZETO, Vice President and Director at TD Securities Inc. and President of Women in Capital Markets

Jacqui's a bundle of energy for sure, but when she was a child she was overweight, had low energy and lacked confidence. She transformed herself when she came to Toronto, thanks in large part to the faculty at Branksome Hall, a diversity-friendly private girls' school. Despite being alone, an immigrant from Hong Kong with English as a second language, Jacqui learned to get along with people, and developed her leadership skills to the point where she became Outstanding New Girl for the Year. She was also named Debater of the Year.

Just like Jacqui, I love my job, but sometimes I can get a little frazzled with the workload and the constant travel. When that happens, if I can't go for a run, I walk. I need to move in order to think things through. When I have speaking engagements that I can drive to, I often go alone so I can have time to myself to reflect and recharge.

THE RISK NOT TAKEN

For many people, unfortunately, life is about the risk not taken: the job opportunity turned down because it seems too daunting; the chance to speak in public that becomes a chance to fail; the move to a wonderful city that would snap us out of our comfort zone. These negative kinds of thoughts seldom happen to my interviewees. To them, life is about embracing risk, not shying away from it.

A key change in Ann Rohmer's career—and life—occurred after a trip to one of her favourite places: Ste. Anne's Spa near Grafton, Ontario.

"A visit to Ste. Anne's makes me feel like I'm ready to take on the world in a very peaceful way," she says.

A number of years ago, she needed Ste. Anne's peace and quiet for a couple of very significant reasons.

"I journeyed there when I was troubled about my second marriage," she reveals. "I also wasn't sure I wanted to stay on at Citytv's *Breakfast Television*. I made two huge decisions: to leave my marriage and to say a fond farewell to the show after twelve years. I needed a new challenge and a new life. Fortunately, my boss, Steve Hurlbut, was very supportive. I made the move to CP24, and I've never been happier."

I can only imagine how difficult a period that was for Ann. What I do know is how much courage those decisions must have taken. From time to time, we all have to make changes or our lives will stagnate and ultimately waste away.

If you are in the corporate or organizational world, change is necessary just for survival.

"Life is short," says Brenda Eaton. "If you want to be successful, you have to stand out. To do that, bigger steps are better than baby steps. I find it kind of fun to stretch outside my comfort zone."

But what if you're like many and find that really hard to do, I ask?

"If you have a solid base, it's not as hard as you might think," she says. "This base comes from having developed some kind of a skill set, then overlaying a belief in your ability, in other words, confidence. How do you get confidence? By building on a series of personal successes, one success at a time. And you have to take the occasional risk. If you do the same thing day after day you're never going to stand out and be a leader in your field. And personally, I think it would be hard to feel satisfied."

Trish Kmet says risk is in the eye of the beholder.

"Taking calculated risks is a part of life. I mean, selecting a career is a risk, isn't it? If you go down one road, you have to abandon the other," says Trish.

Maybe that's the reason so many people get stuck. They can't choose which road to take so they take neither. They're afraid the grass might turn out to be greener on the other side. Trish never had that problem.

"If you feel in your gut that a decision is right, then you go for it," she recommends.

Pamela Jeffery agrees.

"You have to take calculated risks if you want to get that special promotion, or start a business or grow as a person. If you don't, you'll languish in a job or a marriage you don't like," Jeffery says.

For artists like Jackie Carroll, just being an artist is a risk, Andy Warhol's negative comments aside. (Warhol famously said that saying that artists are risk-takers is an insult to our brave soldiers. But in the same interview, Warhol went on to say it was an insult to baby-sitters, stepdaughters and hitchhikers, so go figure.) Few artists earn a passable income. The biggest risk the artist takes is to be different—the endless task of being original and (if they want to make a living at it) accessible to a wide enough audience.

"Taking calculated risks is a part of life."
—DR. PATRICIA KMET, Dentist

"The last couple of years I've learned to really enjoy the unfamiliar," says Carroll. "My comfort zone is being in the moment, which always means being in the unknown. I'm a risk-taker, sure, if you define risk as being willing to be real; to take the leap into being original. You have to put total faith and trust in the process."

Artists have always challenged and questioned conventional wisdom because they work outside the box. That's why they're so often censored by dictatorial political regimes.

Entrepreneur, philanthropist, wife and mother Julie Toskan-Casale calls herself a "safe" risk-taker.

"I'm cautious," Julie says. "I know that failure is a part of success, and it's only a mistake if you do it twice. But I still fear failure because I'm a high-achieving person and I don't like being wrong. Many people think they're risk-takers when they're not. I'm referring to risk in the personal and professional sense."

You won't ever hear me preaching for some kind of zen-like balance. I don't think inner balance is possible. Balance, in the sense of achieving a perfect symmetry of time and effort to complete the daily work/life ritual, isn't even necessary. What is necessary is a sense of contentment derived from feeling that your life makes sense and that it's under control (at least for the most part).

> *"Failure is a part of success, and it's only a mistake if you do it twice."*
> —JULIE TOSKAN-CASALE, Founder of M.A.C. Cosmetics

Whether it is or not is unimportant. The editor of *Chatelaine*, Sara Angel, offers this comment: "There's no easy equation to figure out life. And it's not balance. I say embrace the chaos."

I only partly agree with her. For some, especially so-called type A's, living a hard-charging, chaos-embracing lifestyle continually stokes their creative fire. But for others, this type of lifestyle would do nothing but send them to an early grave. As with other facets of a person's life, there simply isn't a one-size-fits-all when it comes to the concept of balance.

WHY CAN'T WE ALL BE FRIENDS?

We live in what Senator Anne Cools calls the post-feminist era.

"Women have stopped bashing men," she says. "And men have stopped excluding women."

Many women today, especially busy professional women, see themselves as part of a subtle but supportive sisterhood. But I'm not naive. I know of or have heard of many women who like to spend their time criticizing each other. An example from a popular online blog caught my eye recently. The blog is called "43 things," and it's really a kind of social networking community. Contributors to the site publicize and keep track of their goals—to-do lists of up to 43 items—for anyone to see. A woman wrote in who calls herself "the gangster of love," and although she's happily married, she shares these thoughts with us at www.43things.com:

"Why do we tear each other down instead of building each other up? Why do we fight over men who probably wouldn't do the same for us in return? Why do we gossip about one another? Accuse someone of sleeping their way to top? Hate another woman who we perceive as being 'prettier' or better in some way? Throughout life I've had many interesting encounters with women. And I don't understand why we're not more supportive of each other."

I certainly don't have an answer for her, because my relationships with women are not like this at all. And what's more important, neither are the relationships that my interviewees have. Authentic women are not petty or catty. Their lives are too busy for all that stuff. And perhaps the busiest lives of all belong to those of us who work and raise children. Those of us who have experienced the delicate balancing act that is working motherhood know that it's difficult to satisfy the balance between work demands and meeting our children's needs.

SISTERHOOD, MOTHERHOOD, SAINTHOOD

As Chair of the B.C. Housing Commission, Brenda Eaton mentors a lot of women. Many are working moms, although she herself is married without kids.

"I've had to make lots of tradeoffs over my career," she says, "but not this one, and I think this would be the toughest. The women I know who have handled this successfully—that is, achieving important things and having few regrets about how they managed the work-child balance—tell me that they survived by acknowledging to themselves that they can't do it all, to their preferred standards, all the time. Sometimes children must take priority for a period, sometimes work issues will take priority; and this will fluctuate over the years. They tell me survival means being 'fully in the moment' with wherever they are in that cycle—and not beating themselves up about it. Then they tell me it's *very* hard to do. I believe them."

Joan Kelley-Weisshaar is a working mom, and she says making it work takes a serious amount of planning and commitment.

"Life as a mother is a big juggling act," she says. "Then you add a career into the balls already in the air and it's a serious matter of balance. If the balance is off, everything in your life has to adjust, which affects you, your children, your primary relationship with your partner and your work. Balance takes careful and serious planning and commitment. Children grow quickly and it's a sad day when a mother realizes her kids are grown and she missed it. But it's also sad if the big career chance comes and goes and you miss it because you're too exhausted."

Is time management the key, then?

"All you have in life is your time," Joan offers. "It is finite. You need to control how your time is used. Nannies help to meet children's immediate needs so mothers can spend quality time with their kids. I'm fortunate that our household has enough money for a nanny. However, having a caregiver for your children is having another ball in the air. First of all you need to find the perfect person, and you cannot rush that or take it lightly. There needs to be management of that person and an open relationship with them. After all, children are precious and impressionable, and who you select to care for them will have an influence on them. You have to be constantly aware of the relationship between the caregiver and your children. I've been blessed to have found strong, trustworthy, dynamic women who I share a mutual respect with!"

> "Life as a mother is a big juggling act.... You need to control how your time is used."
>
> —JOAN KELLEY-WEISSHAAR, TV Producer and Director, Founder of Hero Media

Denise Bebenek lost her youngest child Meagan to a brain tumour at the age of 5. Today, Denise runs Meagan's Walk to raise awareness about pediatric brain tumours and raise funds for research into this devastating illness. Brain tumours are the number one cause of cancerous death in children.

Even as Meagan's deadly tumour was destroying her life, she never gave up hope. Denise recounts her final days.

"Before she passed away, Meagan said she wanted to give every-one a gift," she tells me. "I just thanked her during her last hours for how many people she had touched. Anytime I went into Sick Kids Hospital with her, I realized that these kids needed our help. They are our greatest teachers, our children. I never gave up with Meagan. But how does a parent have a funeral for a 5-year-old child? It's not sup-posed to happen."

THE ART OF BEING A PERFECTIONIST

If you were to ask them, many of our high-achieving women would say they used to be perfectionists. They were intensely motivated by the triple demands of work, family and living the "superwoman syn-drome." Some believed they could have it all, others believed that if they twisted themselves into pretzels everything that needed to get done would get done. That's not so much the case today. Many of these women have reached a point in their lives where the pinnacle of success is no longer a distant mountaintop. In fact, for many, they are now looking down from up top, yet are acutely conscious of the effort it took to climb up there.

"I worked long hours for years," says Brenda Eaton. "I still work hard, but now I take long holidays to rest and recharge. Life is too short not to have fun."

But with age comes wisdom, and the need for perfection begins to subside. Especially if you become a parent. Motherhood brings a special set of demands that only other mothers can understand. At 38, Jacqui Szeto has become a working mom for the first time, but she doesn't foresee any problems raising a child while working.

"I know my little girl will grow up to be a nice young woman," she says.

- **Jacqui Szeto on motherhood:** "There are certain sacrifices, yes. But you have to pick and choose your battles. For example, every working mom seems to be in a subtle battle with the stay-at-home moms. We're accused of being selfish. You just have to ignore it. But then I was criticized for taking seven weeks off for maternity leave. For me, being a good mom is about being prepared, well-researched and organized for my baby's future, school and so on. I may not be there for her all the time, but when it counts—for example, when she gets her shots—I'm always there for her."

- **Jackie Carroll on motherhood:** "There was a time when I was painting all day, writing late into the night, making sure there were meals on the table, and trying to attend all the extra-curricular activities of my two daughters. At this time, my children were still living at home and I was determined to be all things to all people. I was writing and creating paintings for my first book. I realized if you are following your twin passions—in my case being a mother and creating—you just do it. But you have to take time to nurture yourself."

- **Sarah Thomson on motherhood:** "I balance things pretty well, although I miss having the whole day with my children. It's part of life, and their lives, too."

- **Karen Radford on motherhood:** "My husband has his MBA and he was a consultant and senior manager at BearingPoint. He's now running the Radford/Grelowski household. He made a choice to stay home, and we couldn't be happier with the arrangement."

- **Aimée Israel on motherhood:** "It's really a question of paying attention to both the demands of work and the needs of your children. And it takes some creativity. It requires changing some beliefs. Most days at 3:30, I looked at my watch and wondered what the weather was like because my kids were walking home from school. My nanny would pick them up, but I 'heard' my mother's voice saying they shouldn't be walking home in the rain or snow. I know my husband would never worry about this, but a mother's guilt is hard to shake. I realized that either I'd have to pick them up in the car or I'd have to change my belief. Knowing that the kids wouldn't melt, get sick or drown walking home, I was able to change my belief and dump the guilt."

- **Colleen Johnston on motherhood:** "I'd always intended to be a working mother. My husband Brian and I agreed on this. We've always had an excellent, trusted nanny/housekeeper—our current one for twelve years. With both my daughters, I took a four-month maternity leave, and I was always invigorated to get back to the office after my leave. I spend as much time as I can with the kids in the evening and especially on weekends and holidays. Our life has been a somewhat untraditional one, but our kids see it as normal. There wasn't always the quality time I'd have liked with the kids (we were tired at the end of a ten-hour day), but I never apologized to the kids. I focused on the important things with my children."

- **Denise Bebenek on motherhood:** "There's a huge and delicate balancing act between work and family. If the 'trunk' (family/children/home/oneself) isn't nurtured, how can the other facets of one's life (the branches) grow? If we are to make a decision to have a child, I think their needs and the needs of the family must be taken care of first and foremost before we can make any kind of work commitment. One of the biggest risks we take as human beings is bringing a child into the world. I've taken that risk, and have lost my own. But can you imagine if I did not take that risk?"

- **Joan Kelley-Weisshaar on motherhood:** "When I was in my twenties, from a work point of view, I was more of a sprinter. But now that I have kids, I'm more of a marathoner. It's easy to lose balance. I used to work four jobs at the same time. Now I'm better at balance. It can be frustrating, but I'm managing. I think most people juggle family, friends, job and so on. It's a personal thing, of course. Many of us try to balance things in sequence, rather than trying to integrate them."

PRIORITY ONE: UNDERSTAND WHAT YOUR PRIORITIES ARE

Hard-driving executive Karen Radford says to have any kind of balance in your life, you have to understand what your personal priorities are.

"I wouldn't use the word balance," she says. "I prefer the word harmony. I think for me, harmony is about enjoying the moment, always. One day a friend of mine mentioned the word harmony and everything just seemed to click into place. I believe life is a mix of peaks and valleys—some personal, some professional. The trick is to manage across the peaks while maintaining your long-term priorities. My top priority is to love and be loved by my children and husband and family. As for the rest of the five F's, my commitment to fitness has kind of taken a back seat because of my recent move to Montreal. I guess you could say my harmony is a little off in that regard, but I plan to rectify it very soon."

Karen works hard and has accepted a lot of responsibility. But she has also accepted that she can't be perfect. "As a result, I long ago stopped beating myself up. Pressure concentrates the mind, but priorities concentrate the heart."

When my own children were young, I didn't work as hard as I'm working now. That's because to me, it's about establishing priorities that make sense for each stage of your life. As my life has evolved, so have my goals, but my values have always remained the same. For instance, I have zero tolerance for prejudice, I'm very family-oriented and I'll never compromise my relationship with my husband. I also consider myself resilient and fair. I want and need to make a difference, career-wise, but I'm fully engaged in whatever personal or professional activity I do. My husband says I'm fiercely independent and fiercely interdependent. I like that description.

Julie Toskan-Casale married very young. She was all of 21. But she co-founded M.A.C. Cosmetics even younger, at age 20. She had her first child at 25, another at 28, and one when she was 30.

"My older brother was a photographer, and he couldn't find the right products for his fashion shoots," she explains. "My future husband was a

> "Pressure concentrates the mind, but priorities concentrate the heart."
> —KAREN RADFORD, Executive Vice President and President of TELUS Quebec and TELUS Partner Solutions

chemist at the time. He and my brother started formulating a line of products that worked for professionals. Our parents were immigrants who had great ambitions for us. They became part of the business after we persuaded them to mortgage their home so we could start M.A.C. They were so supportive because they'd always wanted us to have a better life. They were hard-working people and so were we, so away we went. The business just happened, we were all too busy, too caught up, too excited, and learning too much to worry about how difficult it could be. Now that we've sold the business, I spend a lot of time with my family, because family is always my number one priority. But the other 'Fs,' as you call them, can shift depending on the circumstances."

"MY FATHER WAS A MANUAL LABOURER"

If I've learned anything about values from these inspiring women, it's that they usually originate through their family and from certain other role models. As young adults, some were fortunate to have mentors who helped shape their behaviour and their view of the world. But not all. When you help run a global business in your early twenties like Julie and her husband Vic did (joining her brother and his partner, the co-founders of M.A.C. Cosmetics), you know that ambition and passion must run in the family.

"I'm non-judgmental, honest, respectful and fair," says Julie. "I have a passionate approach to life, and I have a strong need to support and help the underprivileged. A lot of my values come from my family. I really admired my parents' work ethic and deeply appreciated the sacrifices they made for us. My father was a manual labourer and my mother was a cleaning lady. They had four kids, and had to overcome language issues. My older brother Frank was an entrepreneur and a passionate free spirit. I really admired him, as well as Frank Angelo, my brother's partner and a co-founder of M.A.C. He would always put me in situations where he knew I could succeed, and coached me in areas where I struggled. He was a musician, he didn't graduate high school, but he founded the Haircutting Place and it was a huge success. Both Franks had great business minds, and were very creative and innovative."

"I'm non-judgmental, honest, respectful and fair. I have a passionate approach to life, and I have a strong need to support and help the underprivileged."
—JULIE TOSKAN-CASALE, Founder of M.A.C. Cosmetics

Their values come out loud and clear in what they created and the way they did business. They created the first line of professional-quality products for consumers of all ages, sexes and ethnicities.

They popularized the matte finish lipsticks that stars like Madonna and Linda Evangelista went crazy over. M.A.C. was anti-advertising and anti-animal testing. It used the bare minimum of packaging and offered its customers recycling incentives. Later, they became one of the first commercial supporters of AIDS awareness, sponsoring charity events and donating the proceeds from certain products to AIDS foundations.

HARD-WORKING PEOPLE WITH SOUND VALUES

Dr. Nancy Baxter didn't have a lot of role models growing up in small-town Ontario. "I always wanted to help people, which is why I began medical school at 19. It's an awesome responsibility and a privilege to be a doctor. I think to be successful, you have to have integrity and loyalty. But I've also been willing to question authority."

Major Dee Brasseur thinks her parents were her best mentors.

"They were hard-working people with sound values," Dee says. "They taught me self-reliance. I remember one time when I built my own deck, the guys at the lumberyard asked me if I'd ever built a deck before and I said no. I'm a pretty self-confidant person."

Dee had a special hero when she was a teenager.

"Montreal Canadiens' captain Jean Béliveau came to visit our high school once," she tells me. "He was such a quiet leader and a good sportsman. I thought he was the best. It's funny how our lives intersected—I was inducted into the Order of Canada at the same time as Béliveau."

She admits a lot of her life was work, work, work.

"Being single, I could do that, but that doesn't mean I was all work, no play. I was engaged to be married twice," she says.

Dee has some words of inspiration for those of us who wonder if it's too late to achieve something while we're on this planet.

"Do you know what Shania Twain, *Harry Potter* author J.K. Rowling and Phyllis Diller have in common?" she asks. "They were all late bloomers."

I don't know about the Phyllis Diller example, but I do know it's never too late to achieve. I know quite a few people who found their passion late in life.

MAKING WORK/LIFE CHOICES

Making our lives work means making choices. And work/life choices are often harder for women than men. Why? Because our lives are complicated by being the primary caregivers, and because I think women feel more guilt about this particular sacrifice than men. In an August 6, 2006, *Observer* article entitled "The Guilty Party," Stephanie Merritt says that women tend to treat their hard-earned freedoms as a sin. "I think the guilt women feel comes from a deeply entrenched sense tattooed into our psyches from generations past," she is quoted as saying. "We are not supposed to be selfish. Women have traditionally been seen as carers, nurturers, givers, supporters of men and children and elderly parents—the revolutionary idea that we might want to take something for ourselves still sits uneasily for many women."

Aimée Israel sees things from a more empowering angle.

"Working moms often feel alone because they don't realize others are facing similar challenges," she says. "They're in an environment where they feel they can't make it work. There's often no sense of recognition from their employer, an understanding that they have a life, have kids." After practicing corporate law at one of Canada's most prestigious law firms, and then working as corporate counsel for Cadbury Canada on a part-time basis, Aimée pursued a passion and capitalized on her strengths to launch a new business. "I went from a world where I had to docket every minute of my day to a flexible schedule where I could start at 9:30 a.m. so that I can take my kids to school and end the day at 6:00, when my nanny leaves. I often work at night once my kids are in bed."

"Working moms often feel alone because they don't realize others are facing similar challenges."
—AIMÉE ISRAEL, Co-founder and CEO of LifeSpeak

If corporate law is traditionally a male enclave, the capital markets arena takes it a notch higher. It has a culture driven by results, competition and the adrenalin rush of non-stop pressure. As an institutional bond salesperson, Jacqui Szeto knows the culture first hand.

"The nature of the business is competitive, fast-moving and cut-throat," says Jacqui. "But it's important to manage a fine balance. If you work too hard and burn out, it's counterproductive and it will reflect in your work."

In a 2001 study by Women in Capital Markets, the top barriers to advancement for women were identified by both men and women as "Commitment to personal and family responsibilities" (68 percent of female respondents, 45 percent of male respondents). I happen to think these kinds of commitments don't apply to men the same way they do to women, because workaholic men don't feel the guilt that many workaholic women do.

None of the high-achieving women I interviewed work these kinds of hours, perhaps because they have additional priorities (like family) or perhaps because they've realized there's more to life than just work. Remember there's an old adage: "No one on their deathbed ever wished they'd spent more time at the office." This is what TELUS executive Karen Radford has to say: "I'm the oldest of four and a proud Atlantic-Canadian born in Moncton, New Brunswick. At the age of ten, I wanted to be a doctor. I took science in high school and university. I had a month in the summer to do something, so I volunteered at the hospital. I was there twelve hours a day, but I noticed the best doctors were there all the time! I realized that I wanted to have children sooner than later. If I was going to be a doctor, I knew I would end up specializing, which would keep me in school until I was at least 32. Family was and is important to me—I realized this would make it more difficult for me to marry and have children, while also establishing a financial base for myself. So I got my B.Sc. in biology, then did an MBA and went into the corporate world."

Karen is now the mother of two young boys. And while she works long hours as Executive Vice President and President of TELUS Quebec and TELUS Partner Solutions, she has a level of flexibility she might not have had as a doctor.

VACATION? WHAT VACATION?

When you go on vacation, do you wonder whether to take your Blackberry or not? Do you even take your allotted vacation time? Expedia.ca/Ipsos Reid's annual Vacation Deprivation Survey for 2006 found that one in four working Canadians don't take all the time off to which they are entitled. Vacations are supposed to give us time to rest and reflect. They're supposed to let us recharge and come back to work more productive. Not any more. For many, they're just an opportunity for guilt, anxiety—and more work. Does this make sense? Is it really making us more productive? Over a hundred years ago in Germany, Zeiss Optical did a study and found that reducing hours by more than 10 percent actually *increased* output. Shortly after, and following their lead, Henry Ford moved car production from a six-day to a five-day week. Surprise, surprise. Output increased and production costs decreased.

It may seem counterintuitive that the fewer hours we work, the more we output. But the reason is really quite obvious: People are not machines. Unlike machines, humans get tired, distracted and need social interaction. Skipping vacations has become so pervasive that companies are forcing employees to take time off, according to an August 19, 2006, article by Timothy Egan in the *New York Times* ("The Rise of the Shrinking-Vacation Syndrome"). The accounting firm PricewaterhouseCoopers now shuts down its entire national operation for ten days over Christmas, and five days around the Fourth of July. The official reason? So anxious employees won't worry about missing anything important.

Wow. This is scary stuff.

THE FIFTY-HOUR WEEK

If you're thinking we don't work long enough hours and therefore don't need the time away from work, there has been a 25 percent increase in the proportion of Canadian employees working more than fifty hours each week. So said Statistics Canada's Labour Force Historical Review in 1998.

And according to a November 2005 report prepared for the Canadian Federal Labour Standards Review, entitled "Control Over Time and Work-Life Balance: An Empirical Analysis," workers in the transportation and warehousing sector report long hours, with over one in five working fifty or more hours weekly.

Statistics Canada says the average Canadian workweek is 33.5 hours. The figures that Statistics Canada puts out are the average of all workers, including part-timers. There is no breakdown. And so many hours are hidden. Two examples are teachers and truckers.

A peer-reviewed article in an academic journal on teaching called *Radical Pedagogy* reports that teachers' hours in Saskatchewan are vastly underestimated. Researchers William Michelson and Andrew S. Harvey, in a Spring 2000 article entitled "Is Teachers' Work Never Done?" found that in the Saskatchewan school system (Saskatchewan Teachers' Federation), "adding weekend hours brought the total to over 47 hours per week. Both beginning teachers and teachers in their first teaching term [averaged] 66 hours per week."

Truck drivers routinely disguise their hours for financial reasons. A significant number of "off duty" hours are spent doing paperwork, inspections and other administrative chores. Why do they show much of their non-driving time as "off duty"? Because most long-haul drivers are paid by the distance driven. Is it any wonder a 1997 Statistics Canada Labour Force survey indicates that truck drivers find their jobs stressful?

If Statistics Canada reports that the average Canadian workweek is about thirty-three hours long, there's clearly a disconnect somewhere. Clearly, some people work too many hours, and some don't work enough. Granted, these numbers includes part-time and contract work and people who are semi-retired. But how many of those people would be working full-time if given the chance?

Why are we working longer hours? Part of the answer may be found in our real cost of living. A Human Resources and Social Development Canada research paper, entitled "Work, Family and Community: Key Issues and Directions for Future Research," says it took forty-five hours of work per week to sustain a Canadian household back in 1970. By contrast, in 1991 it took sixty-five to eighty hours per week.

TAKING A DIFFERENT DIRECTION

What do some of our interviewees have to say about the issue of work/life balance?

"Leading a balanced life is my number one priority right now," says Akela Peoples, CEO of Youth in Motion. "I'm cutting back on my hours, and I've decided to take my career one year at a time. My organization is now ten years old. I'm continually challenged and excited by it, but I've just turned 40, I've never been married and I'm open to the potential of what may lie ahead, both professionally and personally."

Although Akela has a significant other, she wonders if time is slipping away.

"I may experience a period of regret about not having children," she admits. "But I'm very comfortable with myself as a person, and I'm very proud that I've lived life on my terms."

Karen Radford also has this "balance" thing in perspective. Although she was instrumental in the massive TELUS restructuring back in 2004, three of her proudest moments are non-work related.

> *"I'm very comfortable with myself as a person, and I'm very proud that I've lived life on my terms."*
> —AKELA PEOPLES, CEO of Youth in Motion

"Four of us raised $300,000 and got 750 women networked together in a matter of months. And I had a 'pinky swear' with three close friends," Karen says. "If you've never had a pinky swear, I can tell you that making a lifelong promise to someone is a pivotal event for everyone involved. I'm deeply proud of my loving relationship with my husband and our two children. And on a professional level, I'm honoured to be an inspiration to women through the creation and execution of the Women's Leadership Forum, and through my role in corporate Canada."

A DAY IN THE LIFE

I thought you might like to take a glimpse into a "day in the life" of three of our interviewees to see if we can pick up some insights about their lifestyle. If you were to see my schedule, by the way, you'd see there is no typical "day in the life." Some days I'm in travel mode, other days I'm preparing for my TV show, other days I'm speaking or hosting an event or doing combinations of things like attending executive management meetings, then speaking, and then maybe hosting a dinner. Of course, e-mail and phone occupies another chunk of my day. I try to be in touch with my husband and children more than once a day. And yes, I do work on weekends.

My life: Brenda Eaton

"I'm up at 5:30 a.m. or 6:00 a.m. It depends on whether I'm running that morning. I listen to the news, and usually start work around 8:00 a.m. I'm happy to say I leave work about 5:00 p.m. In previous lives I worked ridiculously long hours, but young people on the fast track often work long hours. Having said that, it should be a stage in a person's life, not a lifestyle."

"My workday? Let me give you an example from when I was CFO and VP Operations at the Health Authority. I'd usually cycle to work and be in the office by 8:00 a.m. I'll have a one-hour meeting with staff to discuss the most urgent priorities, e.g., hospital room overcrowding, beds, et cetera. I'll then meet for an hour with my direct reports on issues specific to the Health Authority, for example, managing medical records. I'd follow that with a series of meetings with medical leaders and other health care professionals. Then there'd be a working lunch on project issues or strategic concerns, or a cafeteria lunch to meet with medical professionals. Later in the day I'd meet with my Senior Financial Officer, and then my Director of Finance and Budgeting. I'd use weekends as my quiet time, because my weekdays were pretty hectic."

My life: Julie Toskan-Casale

"At 6:00 a.m. I wake up and hug my new Labradoodle puppy. I walk and feed him, while my husband gets the kids' lunches ready for school. I get myself ready, then wake up the kids, have breakfast and drive them to school. I leave the house at 8:00 a.m. Two of the kids go to one school, and the other goes to another school. I share the driving with my husband. I'm in my office from 9:00 a.m. until 3:00 p.m., and home by 3:10 p.m. for my youngest son. I work with him on his homework, and then pick up the others at the station at 4 o'clock. I make dinner fairly quickly, because the kids have either tutoring or hockey or music, and they're often at different times. Hockey's a big-time part of our family. Two years ago, we were in hockey arenas twelve times a week! It got kind of ridiculous. We decided to take a year off and try new things, and have a full and regular dinner together. Yes, there was quite an adjustment period. Now they're back and playing hockey again—and loving it."

My life: Lesley Southwick-Trask

"Three days a week, I get up at 5:40 a.m. to go to the Brahma Kumaris meditation centre. It's a global community in pursuit of peace—on all dimensions. The morning class finishes about 7:30 a.m. (On the other four mornings, I do the class in my home.) Because I live in Halifax, I can get back home in a few minutes to organize my husband's and daughter's health drinks. At 8:00 a.m. I begin my workday with client meetings either at my office or their location. My day is filled with intriguing dialogue, and tough decision-making. If I'm working with professionals such as physicians or lawyers, I meet with them outside the corridor of their 'client day' between 5:00 p.m. and 7:00 p.m. I also squeeze in a fair amount of volunteer work with a number of boards. These days I find myself involved with rethinking what it means to be an active citizen in our changing world. My husband gets dinner ready for the family, and we have conversation and dinner from 6:00 p.m. to 7:30 p.m. Then I try to go for a walk with Greg. Around 9:00 p.m., I sneak down to my office to do e-mails and such until 11:00 p.m. or so, and then bed. Oh, and in the midst of all this stuff, I run my daughter to and from soccer games, her part-time job and a generally chaotic 16-year-old social life."

UNDER PRESSURE

I know when I'm under the gun I perform well. But I need ways to unleash my stress or it will build up to unmanageable levels. My interviewees are a hardy lot. As you might imagine, the majority of them handle stress very well. But not all of them see stress exactly the same way.

"Day-to-day stress I handle very well," says Publisher Sarah Thomson. "I like deadlines because they concentrate the mind. I've suffered excessive stress only once in my life, and I got sick. It happened when my father died."

Trish Kmet also works well under pressure: "It's draining mentally and physically, but I get a lot done. If I have excessive stress in my life I lie down or exercise, and think good thoughts about travelling."

"Now that I'm no longer a skier but a businessperson, I deal with stress by living 'right now,'" says Kerrin Lee-Gartner. "To relax, I might read a mindless thriller because I disappear 100 percent into the pages of the book. Sometimes I have to be snapped out of my trance by my family."

CFO Colleen Johnston deals with stress in a very positive way: "I have a team of seven hundred people behind me. I relieve the ongoing day-to-day stress by walking and by talking to my husband, who gives me a good sense of perspective. I take pride in staying cool under pressure but stress does get internalized."

Ann Kaplan doesn't normally feel stressed, but if it happens, "I confront the issue and find solutions fast," she says. "I find out how I got into that situation and take steps to make sure it never happens again."

We all feel pressure from time to time. It's how we handle it that counts.

FOCUS

When we're significantly out of balance in our lives, at least one of the five F's always seems to get left out. Sometimes it's our friends, sometimes it's our fitness, but interestingly, nearly all the women I interviewed said focus was not one of them. Why is focus so important? If we lose the ability to focus, our lives can slowly unravel without our even knowing it. Here's what a few of our high-achieving women have to say about focus.

"Focus is absolutely *the* most important thing in my work as an interviewer. I'm a very active listener and I always give my guests a 100 percent of my focus. If you learn to listen closely to the full scope of their answers, they'll always give you your next question."
—ANN ROHMER, Broadcaster, Citytv and CP24

"Focus is critically important. To achieve any important goal, you have to be laser-like in your focus. For example, in 1997, I launched WXN and it became an entity for the first time. My goal was to establish WXN in four different centres in four different cities in six months, and we met our target."
—PAMELA JEFFERY, CEO of Women's Executive Network

"I take a long time over things because I want to get it right. I printed a vision statement for the company and put a copy in everyone's

office. I don't shoot from the hip, I need all the info before a decision is made. In a boardroom or on a conference call I'm willing to say 'I don't know, I'll get back to you.' However, I'm not there to please people. As long as I know I've done my homework and thought things through, I don't care what people think, even my children. As your business grows, you become tougher, through experience. I recently did a corporate governance degree because, as CEO, I report to a Board of Directors. I absolutely understand the hierarchy of the board, and I have a lot of respect for them. I treat all my stakeholders with value and respect. Everything must be documented, reported, protocols must be followed."
—ANN KAPLAN, CEO of Medicard

"To me, focus is just one aspect of the total package. Vision, belief, determination and talent are the other keys. For each person the balance may be different. Focus has always been my strength, one of my most powerful tools. However, I never realized just how powerful it was until I suffered a concussion and found I wasn't able to focus the same way."
—KERRIN LEE-GARTNER, Olympic gold medallist

"I have so many things going on at the same time that I've learned to totally focus on the person I'm with or talking to. At work, I often spend ten seconds on each topic, because I have a photographic memory, and I don't forget. I'm currently training my employees in multi-tasking. In my experience, I think women are better at multi-tasking than men."
—DANIELLE IVERSEN, President of That PR Thing

"It's my weakest link. I have so many new ideas I tend to go with the flow. My two assistants help focus me."
—SARAH THOMSON, Publisher of The Women's Post

TIME OUT! CLEAR YOUR MIND
Everyone needs a time out in their lives, whether it's from work or the kids or from family issues. Over the years, I've come to realize there's no better way to get a break than through meditation. In our 24/7

world, relaxation is fast becoming a lost art. But fortunately, meditation is an increasingly popular way to reduce stress and to revive our inner selves.

Artist and teacher Jackie Carroll has long incorporated meditation into her life, with amazing results.

"Simply put, meditation clears our minds," she says. "When we meditate we attempt to 'be in the moment' and free our minds from thoughts/emotions related to the past and future. Consequently, meditation improves our concentration and delivers a calmness that is peaceful and joyful."

Jackie says finding meditation was totally an unexpected happening.

"About twenty-five years ago, I was invited to attend a relaxation response workshop, taught by Eli Bay, in Toronto," she explains. "The workshop attendees were taken through a series of relaxation exercises. The last exercise of the day was a 'guided visualization meditation.' During the guided meditation I experienced a new form of awareness and a sense of calmness that stayed with me for days."

> *"Meditation is less of an event and more of a lifestyle."*
>
> —JACQUELINE CARROLL, Visual Artist and Author

Following the workshop, she researched and read more about meditation and started meditating most days. Her state of mind began to improve and she "moved through each day with increased ease and confidence."

"It was around this time [1980] that I began to paint full-time," she tells me. "It was a natural fit to combine my art and meditation. With meditation before/during my painting, my work would flow effortlessly and unfold easily onto the canvas. Unlike the past, my painting became 'a process' versus 'a product.' Today, meditation is less of an event and more of a lifestyle. Whether it's beginning or ending my day, teaching 'art as a meditation' classes three or four times a week or participating in group meditations or attending retreats for a few days or a few months in Canada and the United States, I've incorporated meditation into each day."

AN INNOVATIVE WAY TO BALANCE YOUR LIFE

Jackie isn't the only one of my interviewees to have discovered the power of meditation. Lesley Southwick-Trask has built a number of healthy habits into her life, including meditation.

"I've made these habits into routines so I don't have to think about them or remember them," she says. "I was highly cynical in the past, and I used to beat myself up a lot. Now, it rarely happens since I started meditating and doing Brahma Kumaris work. When excessive stress comes into my life I find myself responding only briefly like 'the old me' before I switch my thought process to one of letting go (in the ego sense of the term). Perfection for me now is catching myself, rather than deluding myself with false expectations. Good long walks with my dogs are also good therapy!"

> *"Perfection for me now is catching myself, rather than deluding myself with false expectations."*
> —LESLEY SOUTHWICK-TRASK,
> Co-founder of Owl's Head Retreat

Jackie Carroll started to incorporate meditation practices directly into her art classes, and her students love the results.

"It felt like a natural next step to share my findings with others," she says. "I designed my art classes with this in mind. It's incredible to witness the impact of meditation in my students' art and life. A common piece of feedback from students is that 'meditation helps remove my internal critic and allows me to draw freely.' Many students share similar insights when it comes to their day-to-day lives. They actually leave the class viewing life differently."

What types of meditation do you use in your own life?

"The main meditation methods that I practice are Shamatha (tranquility) meditation, Vipassana (insight or mindfulness) meditation and Metta (loving-kindness) meditation," Jackie says. "Shamatha is a technique that encourages tranquility by focusing on an ordinary object such as the breath or the rise and fall of the abdomen. This single pointed focus brings forth tranquility, clarity and a peaceful state of mind. Vipassana is a moment-to-moment investigation of the mind/body process through focused awareness. This method of meditation brings forth insight, wisdom and compassion and helps one see reality clearly.

The three mentioned meditation methods build on each other and help develop a clear mind and an open heart, which empowers the meditator to experience joy, peace and happiness in their daily life."

TIMING IS EVERYTHING

Balance is a very tricky concept. I think by focusing *solely* on one aspect of your life, you can miss an awful lot. But timing is everything in life, and I'm giving a lot to my career right now because I can: my children have grown up.

The work/life balance always comes into equilibrium for me, but not as often as I'd like. Given the extensive travel and the long hours I work, my friends sometimes have to take a back seat, and on occasion, sometimes my family as well. As I mentioned before, I'm an optimist but I'm also a realist. I know it's not a perfect world, but it's a pretty good one most of the time.

I do try to balance things as best I can, and I give and take as best I can. My husband is a senior executive at a multinational corporation. We both constantly work at carving out time for each other. I'm a boomer, I'm of a certain generation of working women with certain attitudes to work and family. Upcoming generations have different values, but as a group, Canadians seem to be experiencing an attitudinal shift about our careers.

Perhaps Aimée Israel expresses it best when she says that, "The number one issue for working parents today is quality in both their work and their life. The notion of work/life balance almost seems too abstract for working parents, because they have so many balls in the air. It's about juggling their shifting priorities and challenges and demands. Men and women today are less willing to make the traditional trade-off at work. They're looking for organizations that are more family-friendly."

CAREER IS NO LONGER THE TOP PRIORITY

Five years ago, Canadians' top life priority was career, followed by family. According to Workopolis.com, those priorities have now reversed, with family ranking first and career second.

Canadians' top priority is family
Five years ago, when asked about their number one *life* priority, their top choice was career (37 percent) followed by family (31 percent).
Today, those priorities have flipped: 44 percent report that family is their number one life priority. Just 31 percent said their career was number one.
Source: March 2006 survey commissioned by Workopolis.com. Used with permission.

YOU CAN'T ALWAYS GET WHAT YOU WANT

The Rolling Stones introduced that song several decades ago, but the words will never become a cliché. Today, some women "want to have it all," while others crave balance. It depends on your life stage, your family and personal issues. You have to make choices, and know that the grass is not always greener on the other side.

In an op-ed letter to the *Globe and Mail*, Allan Mckay, President of the Vanier Institute for the Family, said "Canadians might prefer it if one earner in a family were paid enough to support a financially dependent spouse or that the aging of Canadian society did not compel those of so-called 'working age' to help support the growing numbers of seniors. . . . But most of us are also realists," McKay goes on to say. "Close to seven out of ten Canadians are prepared to see their tax dollars help cover the costs of supplemental child care."

EVERYONE'S DIFFERENT

I think balance can be achieved by establishing priorities, sticking to those priorities and relying on your personal guiding principles to see you through the rough spots. And having a little passion for what you do doesn't hurt. Am I emblematic of my generation, the female boomers? I don't think so at all. Everyone is different. For some examples, let's take a look at Linda Wheler and Kerrin Lee-Gartner.

Whenever her husband got a raise, Linda would cut back on her work hours to spend more time with her children. He wasn't happy about it at first, but he soon came to realize the overall benefits to their family. As a United Church minister, Linda has to care for an entire congregation, but it's important for her to "touch people and make a connection." Linda says that three-fifths of the five F's are in balance—her Faith, Family and Friends. Her Finances and Fitness? "Not so well."

Linda is not only a mom, she has an all-encompassing job. Although she loves what she does, she says, "Sometimes I feel I don't have enough 'play time' for myself. You know, to go for a walk, keep the house, go to the movies, read books. Simple things like that."

"I'm part of the generation that started to go into the workforce," she continues. "The choice was to have a family or go to work. Now, you can have a year off for maternity or paternity leave, so life's rhythm can be maintained. From my conversations, there's definitely more acceptance of the role of family in the workplace."

Kerrin Lee-Gartner left the glamorous life of the downhill skier to become a working mom. She loves her family and spends a lot of time with them, but she admits she's not perfect.

"As a racer, I knew perfection was impossible, I just needed to be the best I could be," she says. "Motherhood is the same. I'm not perfect. I can be crabby sometimes. I'm not an amazing mom every day. I just try to be my best each day."

For Kerrin, the birth of her second daughter came with an unwelcome side effect: back problems, which led to surgery.

"Of all the five F's you talk about, I'm pretty good at all of them," she says. "Family is number one on the list. I understand that absolutely. Fitness might be the weakest one. That may seem strange coming from a gold medal–winning athlete. But we all get older, even Olympians. And along with age and motherhood come

> *"I'm not an amazing mom every day. I just try to be my best each day."*
>
> —KERRIN LEE-GARTNER, Olympic gold medallist

some sacrifices. The biggest sacrifice is me! I miss the little joys I used to have, because I always put myself last on the list. Yes, I know I have to be more of a priority than I am. How am I going to do it? First, I have to get out of denial and recognize the problem for what it is. And second, I have to make the changes gradually, in small steps."

WOMEN IN A MAN'S WORLD

Former fighter pilot Dee Brasseur should know about being a woman in a man's world. She offers this advice: "Go for it, and forget about what those men are saying—the ones who think a woman's place should be in the home." Dee followed her dream and got to tour the world through her job, but things didn't always come easily.

She relates her "coming of age" as a pilot trainee: "I was in my late 20s, and the guys were in their early 20s. There were four women and forty guys. One night I went to the officer's mess for a drink, and I got all kinds of backlash from the senior officers down to the recruits. It was a big issue fitting a woman into the harness, and the seats. I heard it all, like 'You're only doing this for the newspaper coverage,' and 'You should go home and stay in the kitchen.' These comments went on daily! Fortunately, we were all too busy to let it ruin our day, but at some point, the four of us agreed that we'd stop bending over and taking it from these guys and padding their egos by defending ourselves."

Did it work? Did they back down?

"The air never cleared," she admits. "We stopped talking after that. I felt really isolated, yes. We weren't a closely bonded group of women. First of all, we were quite individualistic. And second, we didn't have time. Five or six hours every evening was spent in study, seven days a week, for eighteen months. However, the experience helped me in the long run. It gave me the tools and skills to deal with the 'cream of the crop' when I became a trainer years later. I no longer took things personally, because I realized it was their issue and not mine."

"I no longer took things personally, because I realized it was their issue and not mine."
—DEE BRASSEUR, the world's first female fighter pilot

Although Dee Brasseur worked in a unique, testosterone-filled environment, her experience is by no means unique. Virginia Galt of the *Globe and Mail* reports that the old boys' club is a "fading obstacle" ("'Go for It,' Female Executives Told," June 2004), but she may have been talking to the wrong sector: "When the corporate sisterhood gets together these days, the old boys' club barely merits a mention," she quotes Ethel Taylor, Group Vice President of full-line stores at Toronto-based Sears Canada Inc. "If there are still men, in 2004, who are uncomfortable working with women, ignore them, that's their problem."

Maybe, but retail is one of the more female-friendly sectors of our economy. Women working in the mining sector, oil and gas, the capital markets arena or construction and engineering might have a different story to tell. I've already told you about Jacqui Szeto's experience in capital markets. But things are changing even there. An example relates to her marriage to a fellow TD Securities trader.

"Our marriage is an interesting story," she says. "Brad and I met when we were working for TD overseas. He was TD's overnight trader in Tokyo, and I was based in Hong Kong. I brought in a lot of business, but I was young, and I was given a long-distance mentor. Yes, my mentor was Brad! He complained about me until we finally met. Seven days later he proposed to me. We just knew it was right. We've been married now for thirteen years. We both left Asia and came to work in Toronto. Because of us they changed the HR rules so a husband and wife could work together."

Brenda Eaton believes women bring another dimension to the old boys' network, "but so do younger people and people of ethnic origin," she says.

"I thought the old boys' network would unravel about ten years ago," she says, "but here in western Canada it's still male-oriented. I'm not sure we don't have another wave yet to come. I see the old boys' network crop up when we're looking for a new board member, and ultimately the discussion turns to who knows who and who's a good 'fit.' It's more about finding a team player than about the values that person might bring to the table."

THE BOTTOM LINE IS CHANGING FAST

There's nothing business likes better than a good bottom line, and a January 26, 2004, Catalyst report proves that women are crucial to that bottom line. With offices in Toronto, New York, San Jose and Zug, Catalyst is an independent, non-profit membership organization that conducts research on all aspects of women's career advancement. "The group of companies with the highest representation of women in their senior management teams has a 35 percent higher return on equity and a 34 percent higher total return to shareholders than companies with the lowest women's representation," said the Catalyst report, which was based on data from 353 of the companies on the Fortune 500 list.

So, what about the big question posed throughout this chapter? Can we have it all?

Again and again throughout our lives, we make transformative decisions. Decisions like, "Should I marry now and have children now, or wait until my career is a little more established?" or, "Should I go back to work part-time or full-time?" or, "Should I quit my job to care for my ailing parents?" All of them affect our work/life balance in different ways. But is a trend finally emerging? Maybe. Maybe not. Each woman's definition of balance changes as she enters a different stage in her life. And even the most ardent career woman can change her priorities from time to time. Sarah McLachlan, Canadian folk rock singer and founder of Lilith Fair, decided to end Lilith Fair in favour of having children. McLachlan had a child, named India Ann Sushil Sood, with husband Ash Sood. For three years McLachlan focused on family and philanthropic concerns, but then returned to the business she loved.

A REVOLUTION FROM WITHIN

In an October 2006 *Globe and Mail* article entitled "A Revolution from Within," Ian Brown says women now make up the majority of post-secondary enrolment, and the impact on Canadian society is going to be profound. According to Brown, women outnumber men in all but two fields of post-secondary study—engineering and math. When Brown quotes Serge Blais, Director of the new Student Academic Success Service at the University of Ottawa, things get really interesting. Blais points out that "in the near future the majority of lawyers, judges, scientists, managers, will all be women. Every faculty here is already majority women, except engineering."

"The consequences are gigantic," says Brown, who notes that first-year medical school classes at the University of Montreal are 78 percent female.

I'm looking forward to the next wave myself.

SEVEN

THE
AUTHENTICITY
TRACK

IT'S A BEAUTIFUL MIDSUMMER'S DAY. The ocean glitters brightly as you captain your raft into uncharted waters. A light breeze caresses your face as you look up to an almost cloudless sky marred only by the tiny specks of storm clouds many miles away. You switch on the short-wave radio and hear your favourite song, and as the gentle waves swell against the timbers of your raft you drift into a peaceful trance. But then the sun disappears and you wake up to find the storm clouds are much closer now, puffing themselves out like great grey peacocks, fascinating and repelling you with their hulking majesty. And suddenly you don't feel so secure. You watch in breathless excitement as they scud past and then you breathe a sigh of relief as the sun reappears and as the ocean regains its glitter; the mellow voice of your favourite DJ wishes you happy Canada Day; and you haven't a care in the world as once again you captain your raft towards uncharted waters. . . .

Snap out of it!

I'm sorry, but you're on a little wooden raft in the middle of the ocean, you're drifting along with no direction known like Tom Hanks in *Cast Away*, and who knows how long it'll be before you're rescued. Is that what you really want?

Let's get real, shall we? Do you want to be captain of a wooden raft? Or do you want to be captain of your own destiny? The choice, as always, is yours.

THE SECRET TO *REAL* SUCCESS

Someone once said it's better to always tell the truth because that way you don't have to memorize all your lies. I agree, and I also think that if you follow your truth, you'll always know what your life's passion is. And having passion lights a fire that will never go out. I think that's part of the secret to success—true success, I mean.

To Julie Toskan-Casale, the secret to success is living a meaningful life in which, "I keep working and living in balance; and that means being in alignment with my values."

Pamela Jeffery believes that if you continue to grow and stretch yourself as a person while staying true to your values, you will experience the ultimate inward and outward success.

"We're all so busy, it's hard to do a proper self-assessment," says Jeffery. "Four years ago, my marriage was in crisis. My former husband and I had been going to marriage counselling to try to save the marriage for the sake of our two sons. I had been urging him to seek professional counselling on his own but he had refused. When his mother asked me to get my own counselling, I agreed and what happened was I had a total revelation. I hired my own coach, and she took me through a series of exercises and helped me assess my values and prioritize them. I then realized that my values were not aligned at all with those of my former husband. My former mother-in-law did me a huge favour, giving me the push I needed to self-assess. I continue to see my coach to help me be the best I can be, both professionally and personally."

We may be at the end of this book but we're not at the end of our story. They haven't finished their journey, these twenty-six women. For them, the journey has just begun. Their lives are like rivers that won't stop flowing until they pour into the sea. It's interesting what Lesley Southwick-Trask says about women and the workplace.

"It's like an estuary, a mix of fresh and salt water—there's a new breed of gender roles happening in the workplace," she says.

Maybe nature's alchemist has finally found the authentic formula.

The word "authenticity" may be in danger of overuse, but to me it will always be freighted with meaning. If something's "authentic," it's the real deal, the genuine article. And from experience, I know that authentic people are always the real deal. They're sometimes the object of envy and spite because others have chosen the conformist trap and wish they were on the right track.

What track am I talking about, exactly? It's not the Mommy track and it's not the fast track. The best term for it may be the authenticity track.

THE AUTHENTICITY TRACK

Most people either follow an authenticity track or a conformist track in life, depending on whether they're in or out of alignment with their values or principles. Our interviewees are on the authenticity track, and they're highly unlikely to veer off course. After all, what's the incentive to get off? They believe in themselves, they've accomplished something in their lives and they want to accomplish more.

Our interviewees know the authenticity track is the route to real success. So why don't we all follow it? I think for some of us—maybe a lot of us—the route appears too arduous. I think that's the wrong approach—if anything, it's harder to stay on the conformity track because you're constantly at odds with your values.

The authenticity track begins and ends with you, because it's all about you, yourself and the principles by which you live your life. It's about being real. And if you're truly real, you want to give back.

Always.

That's why my interviewees were more than willing to share advice on their life and career choices. Although their experiences are as varied as their personalities, they realize that knowledge and wisdom are meant to be shared, or they are wasted. Lauren Jawno believes that living an authentic life includes listening to yourself.

"Listen to your gut feelings—they are very seldom wrong," she advises. "I have never made a wrong decision when I have *honestly* listened to my inner feelings and made the decision with sincere intentions, despite being advised differently in numerous situations."

ADVICE TO YOUNGER WOMEN

"If someone wanted to enter my field, I'd highly recommend it," says Brenda Eaton, a former B.C. Deputy Minister under Gordon Campbell's premiership. Her field, public policy, is a magnet for intellectually adventurous women. "It's hugely stimulating intellectually, and it's operationally challenging as well, encompassing social policy to economic policy. Having said that, there's no one path. You need to be open to trying lots of things, taking risks and getting a broad skill set."

"There's no one path. You need to be open to trying lots of things, taking risks and getting a broad skill set."
—BRENDA EATON, Chair of the B.C. Housing Commission

Producer Joan Kelley-Weisshaar is only in her late 30s but she's had a lot of varied careers, from makeup artist to traffic reporter to voice work to video and TV producer to charity fundraiser.

"My general advice for any younger woman is, you don't need to be a superwoman or supermom, and you don't have to be all things to all people," Joan says. "If I were advising someone who wants to become a producer/director? I'd tell them to first set a goal, make sure you don't get distracted from it, get a journalism degree then get a job in a big company. Recognize opportunity when it presents itself and don't be afraid to make a change. But always be true to yourself. Finally, be practical. Take risks but make sure they're calculated risks—in other words, look before you leap. And then work really hard. That's my recipe for success."

"Take risks but make sure they're calculated risks."
—JOAN KELLEY-WEISSHAAR, TV Producer and Director, Founder of Hero Media

Change agent Lesley Southwick-Trask says, "Get inside as many organizations and communities as possible. Get collective experiences, be a 'trekker' of business and community, which means being out there with real people doing real things." However, she offers these words of caution: "If you choose to live and work in certain sectors, you'll be in a man's world, still."

"My advice to any woman wanting to be an entrepreneur is to always have two kinds of support," says Aimée Israel, CEO of LifeSpeak. "One being financial, so that you have some element of comfort in making the leap, and the other being family and friends. When you start a business, it can get intensely personal. A circle of support helps provide a sounding board and a source of reassurance."

Software CEO Jennifer McNeill says it's critical to believe in yourself. "Make sure you don't allow other people to limit you. None of their limiting advice means anything. *You're* the only person who can set limits on your life."

Surgeon Nancy Baxter feels the same way as Jennifer: "Believe in yourself and excel at what you do, and you'll always be valued. If you want to achieve any kind of power, timing is key. It helps to learn to play the game, or at least know what the game is. How? Mentoring helps big time, and a lot of mentors are male. You don't need to be the boss, necessarily, as long as you know how to get things done. That's how I work, at least."

Jackie Carroll is an artist, so she comes at things a little differently.

"My advice to younger artists or self-employed teachers is to be realistic about the financial side of their career," she says. "You must avoid blind faith. For instance, success rarely happens overnight—it just doesn't work that way. So it's wise to have a profession or a supplementary source of income that will give you time and financial stability to pursue your art, writing or teaching career. Part-time work is a possibility. It is important that you believe in yourself, in your uniqueness, and exercise patience and self-love. You must be devoted, steadfast and self-disciplined because there will be hard times as you practice and work at your craft. At the same time, you need to establish your priorities—make some time for your family, friends, your meditation practice (if you have one) and try always to create a balance in your life. Try to be aware of organizations that may be able to give you

> *"Believe in yourself and excel at what you do, and you'll always be valued."*
> —DR. NANCY BAXTER, Surgeon

guidance or provide financial assistance, such as government grants. Also, it helps if you are confident and assertive. For instance, take your work to galleries that specialize in your type of work."

Entrepreneur Julie Toskan-Casale has these words of wisdom for budding entrepreneurs of either gender: "Do your research, know what you're getting into. Give it some time but be prepared to leave it if you're not enjoying it, because life is too short. It takes courage, but it also depends on your circumstances."

Women's Executive Network President Pamela Jeffery says, "If you want to become a successful entrepreneur, I think you should start by talking to entrepreneurs and finding out about business life. I recommend going to business school and getting your business degree. It's absolutely necessary expertise so you can read financial statements, man-

"Be prepared to leave your job if you're not enjoying it, because life is too short."
—JULIE TOSKAN-CASALE, Founder of M.A.C. Cosmetics

age people and learn something about marketing and strategy. For an even richer education, I would get an MBA, but a Bachelor of Commerce from a good school like Ivey is okay. I'm a natural net-worker, so I would also recommend getting peer mentoring. It's a fabulous way to spend quality time with people and obtain counsel on important professional and personal challenges."

Publicist Danielle Iversen suggests young publicists-in-waiting should "intern or work next to a good PR person for an extended period of time. They should plan on working long hours. Unfortunately, most young kids don't. And they need to know how to write and spell and know their grammar."

"You must embrace life and take chances."
—SARAH THOMSON, Publisher of *The Women's Post*

"Yes, I'd say I have a pretty clear sense of direction," says publisher Sarah Thomson. "But you must embrace life and take chances. I'm open to the fact that life may throw me a curve."

"Dentistry is a great career for a woman," says Trish Kmet. "It's very flexible, schedule-wise. It is a very rewarding career, and I don't mean just financially. The relationships with your clients and the care we provide is very fulfilling. And women tend to be a little more nurturing, on average, than men."

"If a woman wants to enter the ministry, I would tell her to go in with open eyes," says United Church Minister Linda Wheler. "It's a wonderfully fulfilling life, but there are lots of demands and lots of evening work. For young mothers, especially, it's a tough occupation."

THE NEXT GENERATION

Our interviewees are very concerned about the next generation, their children and nephews and nieces. It's a big world and the competition seems to get fiercer every year. How will the next generation of women react and how will they forge meaningful careers for themselves?

Brenda Eaton thinks tomorrow's women will see management adapting to them. "It's men that are adapting, not women—they don't have to! Men's and women's work values are truly merging, especially their communications values."

"I think college-age women will have less fear of living life on their own terms," says Akela Peoples. "It's an evolution that's taking place, and it's happening over decades and decades. But there are all kinds of opportunities out there for women today."

Mother and CEO Ann Kaplan sees things happening a little quicker.

"I see the next generation bringing the family back even more," Kaplan says. "All-day babysitting facilities nearer my company or built right in. Maternity, paternity grievances (leaves of absence) will become bigger issues. Although I was back to work three days after all my C-sections, I think the next generation will push for more work/life balance."

> "I see the next generation bringing the family back even more."
>
> —ANN KAPLAN, CEO of Medicard

"I'm a feminist," says Nancy Baxter. "As far as gender inequities go, some are imposed and some are realities. The superwoman concept simply isn't realistic. Gen-Xers won't eradicate the income inequity issue. As long as women are the primary caregivers, I don't think this is going to change."

Lesley Southwick-Trask sees the next generation of young women being much greener.

"I think they are very environmentally active. My daughter, for example, surfs, writes and works in the film industry. She doesn't feel the need to get married, select a single career track and have children. Settling down for Nikki is buying a little house near the ocean from which she will pursue her eclectic hearts' passions. And she will do this from a green and vegetarian set of practices—riding her bike (having sold her car), growing her own food, and generally consuming with a much smaller footprint than her parents."

> "I think they're going to be very environmentally active."
> —LESLEY SOUTHWICK-TRASK, Co-founder of Owl's Head Retreat

Lesley says her generation were pioneers. "But we got caught up in the work-home, home-work dilemma. I remember having to fight to get six months maternity leave at an oil and gas company I once worked for."

"When people ask me about the next generation, I tell them it's becoming more and more acceptable to blend your family life into your work life," says Jennifer McNeill. "In the past, you wouldn't volunteer the information that you were leaving for a while so you could take your daughter to a play at one in the afternoon. Now and in the future, both men and women can talk more freely about taking time off work to do family things."

> "It's becoming more and more acceptable to blend your family life into your work life."
> —JENNIFER MCNEILL, CEO of CipherSoft Inc.

Jacqui Szeto says a sea change is happening.

"This new era of women are going to be super-efficient because they grew up with communications technology and the Internet," she says. "Having said that, if everyone has access to the same information then experience and judgment will be key separators—both for the younger generation and for their older, experienced colleagues. Thinking outside the box will be valued even higher."

Artist and teacher Jackie Carroll thinks women will introduce a unique wisdom to the world—especially the corporate world.

"I think the next generation of women will bring the power of feminine wisdom," she says. "This is not a feminist statement at all, by the way. In the workplace, in the home, in all aspects of life, they can stand in their power and they can share it with other women, and men can have it mirrored back to them as well. Included in this wisdom are spontaneity, a multi-dimensional focus, sensitivity, compassion and awareness of others."

Pamela Jeffery believes the next generation will be more demanding.

"Women will be automatically treated as equals because there is true equality at home and in the workplace," she says. "I'm convinced the upcoming generation will be able to pull it off, and the younger men are going to willingly contribute, big time!"

What does an Air Force Major have to say on the matter?

"I would hope the next generation will bring self-confidence," says Major Dee Brasseur. "Women need a total belief in themselves because there's nothing they can't do if they decide to do it. I've seen a significant change in society since I joined the military. We're getting closer to equality in the workforce, but it will take time as long as the majority of CEOs remain male."

> "Thinking outside the box will be valued even higher."
> —JACQUI SZETO, Vice President and Director at TD Securities Inc. and President of Women in Capital Markets

> "I would hope the next generation will bring self-confidence."
> —DEE BRASSEUR, the world's first female fighter pilot

Aimée Israel, Sarah Thomson, Danielle Iversen, Trish Kmet, Joan Kelley-Weisshaar, Natalie Bean-Sole and Karen Radford are all in their 30s, so they have a different perspective about the up-and-coming college-age generation.

Danielle believes the next generation will harness the power of their superb knowledge of technology.

"They're very computer-savvy and they're more open to new things, but like most people they've got to learn about money," Danielle says.

Trish would like to see less of a focus or obsession with body image, and more of a focus on the mind: "But I wonder if that will happen. I have doubts whether it ever will."

Aimée says the next generation to enter the workforce is going to be the first real "Net" generation.

"The impact of that," she says, "is going to be far-reaching. Because if you're raised in a wired world, interactive, multimedia, fast-paced and mobile is your normal."

"More women are going to know how to get what they want," says Natalie. "They'll have more knowledge because of the Internet, but at the same time competition will be fiercer. I don't agree with conventional wisdom that says advanced degrees are the key to success. To me, real life experience is the great leveller."

> *"More women are going to know how to get what they want."*
> —NATALIE BEAN-SOLE, President of NutritionForeverInc.com

Fast-tracking executive Karen Radford is all of 38, but she says women under 30 will bring a couple of important attributes to the workplace of tomorrow.

"First, I think they'll redefine the leadership model by allowing more distributed control," Karen says. "Second, they'll drive a different kind of entrepreneurship; they'll find new and innovative approaches to running small businesses."

Joan Kelley-Weisshaar sees the next generation bringing more focus, planning and direction to their careers.

"When I was a kid in Wilcox, Saskatchewan, I was afraid to say I wanted to be an actress or a director," she says. "Now that women my age and older have helped pave the way, there are many more role models for younger women to follow."

Sarah Thomson says that because the workforce is shrinking, there will be many more options for men and women.

"I think there will be a more female approach to things; it will be more values-driven, a greater sense of community," she says. "Corporations will become more environmentally focused, but I'm a realist. It's going to be an evolutionary process."

I happen to agree with Dee Brasseur and Pamela Jeffery. I think the next generation will be able to pull it off because they'll have more self-confidence, and the men in their lives are going to be tremendously supportive from a very early age.

MAKING A DIFFERENCE

All the women I interviewed believe in making a difference. It's part of being an authentic person. That's why they engage in various types of volunteer work. It's certainly not because it looks good on their resume. It's because it makes them feel good. These women are already making a difference in their organizations and their communities, but they want to do more. Sarah Raiss has lots of plans for the future.

> "I think there will be a more female approach to things; it will be more values-driven, a greater sense of community."
>
> —SARAH THOMSON,
> Publisher of The Women's Post

"There are twenty thousand things I want to do before I leave this earth," Raiss tells me. "What are some of them? Well, I'd like to spend more time with not-for-profit organizations, volunteering and on boards. I'd like to be on a corporate board, I want to mentor more women and I'd like to help write a book for young women. Because I'm President of the International Women's Chapter in Calgary, the book would cover the success stories of our Calgary members."

Jackie Carroll is planning to write another book.

"This book will be about the power of combining art with meditation," she says.

"I really believe in this teaching process as I see how it empowers others. I want to help people be true to themselves, so I'm planning to spread my teachings to a larger audience. I also often do a painting for the holiday card for the charity Sleeping Children Around the World. This charity gives bed kits to children in underdeveloped countries. I have been on two distribution teams for bed kit distributions in both Thailand and Peru. What a rewarding experience!"

Joan Kelley-Weisshaar has a lot on her plate.

"I'm working with World Vision. I've emceed a number of meetings and panel discussions. I've spoken at fundraising dinners and done videos for them. I serve on committees and I've been to Africa with them. I'll be going more often now. We sponsor twenty-four kids through one program. I've met a couple of the kids and it was an awesome experience! At a special dinner, my husband and I helped raise over $1 million for World Vision. I also work with young moms, HIV/AIDS agencies and kids. I've recently been asked to be a spokesperson for young Cambodian girls who have been lost to the sex trade. We want to try and help them reunite with their families, or help set them up to heal and to be strong individuals."

Julie Toskan-Casale plans to expand the Toskan Casale Foundation and its initiatives around the world, while Pamela Jeffery intends to grow WXN so more women can be a part of it.

"I want to grow it beyond the seven Canadian cities we're now in to other countries," Julie tells me. "And I want to grow WXNWisdom into a truly special mentoring network, matching Canada's Most Powerful Women: Top 100 award winners with young women across Canada in what I think will be truly a groundbreaking program—the first of its kind in the world."

Colleen Johnston says she wants to make a difference in several ways.

"Professionally, I want to do a great job—it's a privilege to be the CFO of a great organization like the TD Bank Financial Group," she says. "Personally, I want to be more supportive of my family—my teenage daughters and my husband. I want to continue to be active in community service. My mother died recently, and I want to be a binding force for the family."

"I'd like to do a little more volunteer work," says dentist Trish Kmet. "My sister and I have gone to schools in third-world countries to treat children who've never had dental care—places like Guatemala and Honduras. I'd like to give back to the community."

LEADERSHIP IN THE TWENTY-FIRST CENTURY

We're well into a new century, and not only are the times a-changing, but so are our organizations. Time and time again, our interviewees have told me that patriarchal leadership styles are in danger of becoming extinct. They believe that the organizations of the twenty-first century will be committed to a more values-based culture that rewards leaders who demonstrate humility and high emotional intelligence. These leaders sound very much like the type of women we've already come to know, don't they? One of Sarah Raiss' favourite quotes comes from Peter Drucker: "Leadership is lifting a person's vision to higher sights, the raising of a person's performance to a higher standard, the building of a personality beyond its normal limitations."

"I use his words as a guide for my behaviour as a leader throughout my career and life," she says.

Denise Bebenek has become a leader, but she had a real eye opener when she started Meagan's Walk.

"I'd never run a business before," she says. "It's been a huge learning curve. I learned you can't run a business on your own, it takes a team. If you have a vision or goal and put your mind to it and find the right people to help you carry it out, then anything is possible!"

I'm a big believer in teamwork, because no individual can manage complexity like a team can. Team building continues to grow in popularity in modern organizations. But to be a truly effective alternative to traditional command and control leadership, team building requires a shared sense of mission, a shared passion.

"I'VE ALREADY ALIGNED MY LIFE WITH MY VALUES"

Okay, you say, "I've gotten to know myself and my values and I've found my passion in life." Well, that's great. "And I'm respectful and respected by others because I've become a great listener who knows how to truly connect with the treasured people in my life." That's even better! "But wait, I'm not finished!" Okay, go on.

> "I'm a collaborator who's learned to take calculated risks. And because I believe in myself, my own opinions still matter. I've even learned to take charge of my money to a certain extent. And yes, I'm careful to make lifestyle changes gradually so they'll

stick and not become yesterday's news. In other words, I've worked hard to align my life with my values."

Congratulations, you've gotten real! But now the question is, do you know how to *stay* real?

BECOME THE LEADER OF YOUR *OWN* LIFE

You need to become the leader of your own life. That's right. Staying the course isn't always easy, as you can tell from the women I've interviewed in this book. You have to work at it almost every day. It's no different than anything else in life. I'm one of the millions who never thought math was a particularly easy subject. But you know something? The more I worked at it, the easier it became.

Medicard CEO Ann Kaplan is a perfectionist—at home.

"My spice rack is in alphabetical order, my towels are in the same direction and the Tupperware containers are all labelled," Ann says. "In some ways I'm like Jack Nicholson's character in the movie *As Good As It Gets*. At work it's a little different. I know there's no such thing as the perfect leader, so I try to surround myself with people who are smarter than me and can get the job done without supervision."

Kaplan's leadership skills are always tested when conflicts arise.

"I make my decisions based on moral values, and if there's a conflict with the business objective, I'll take the moral ground," she says.

> *"I make my decisions based on moral values, and if there's a conflict with the business objective, I'll take the moral ground."*
> —ANN KAPLAN, CEO of Medicard

"I treat people with respect, give them the tools to get better and always listen to my employees with an open mind."

Staying real for a lifetime means forgetting about your position in the hierarchy, because position no longer matters. The only thing that matters is essence. To be and become. It means developing your ability to *be* in alignment, to *be* consistently authentic—or to *become* so.

THE DARK HORSE JUST WALKED IN

At one point or another, we all go through some kind of transformative event. When Ann Rohmer was hit by a car at the age of 14, it changed her life. Up until then, she was a dedicated figure skater, putting in hours and hours at the rink when she wasn't at school. But there was something missing in her life.

"When the accident happened, I developed real doubts about whether I could ever be the best skater in the world," says Ann. "I realized I didn't want to pursue this any more. I wanted to have a normal life; I wanted to date, to have fun. I'd always been a little wild, but I also admired my parents tremendously and how honourably they led their lives. So from then on I decided I wanted balance in my life. I was going to be a 'fun-loving good girl.'"

As a young adult, another serendipitous event happened to Ann.

"I was dating a young man who lived in Florida, and I didn't have the money to shoulder my part of our long-distance relationship," she reveals. "Out of necessity, I decided to try my hand at modelling. But I really wanted to be on television so I auditioned for a show. I had absolutely no experience. Believe me, I was a real dark horse and everyone knew it. After the audition was over, the producer came up to me and said 'the dark horse just came in first.'"

In a way, we're all dark horses, at least until we achieve all our dreams. But no one ever does that. Have you achieved your full potential? None of my interviewees say they have—and they're happy to say it, because it means they're still growing as people. Life is a process of driving toward our potential, but never quite achieving it. That's what makes life so endlessly fascinating, isn't it?

LIFE IS ABOUT *STRETCHING*, NOT LEADING

Not all of us want to be external leaders, or even need to be. But being authentic is always about leading your own life, not someone else's. It's about taking risks and sometimes stretching outside your comfort zone.

However, leadership isn't what it used to be. At the time of writing, the U.S. Securities and Exchange Commission had just filed charges against Nortel Network's former Chief Executive Officer Frank Dunn, former Chief Financial Officer Douglas Beatty, and former controllers Michael Gollogly and MaryAnne Pahapill, accusing them of engaging in accounting fraud to meet earnings forecasts.

Sherron Watkins, the Enron employee who blew the whistle on Jeffrey Skilling at Enron, had so much faith in Enron's leadership that she put her job on the line by informing Chairman Ken Lay that Skilling and Andrew Fastow were engaged in corrupt activities. In a 2004 interview with V. Scott Koerwer of the *Journal of Leadership and Organizational Studies*, Watkins had this telling comment to make about the leadership culture at Enron: "Ken Lay was basically asking executives that had already told him he was wearing clothes if, in fact, he was naked. The executives, if truthful, would have been admitting that they'd been pressured to go along in the past. Also, Ken Lay was known among his executive group as a man who did not like to hear bad news."

In a separate interview with *Time* magazine, Watkins remarked that humble leaders listen to others.

That gets us back to one of the key qualities of the twenty-first century leader: humility. It's not always easy to find "natural-born leaders with humility" because many leadership-type individuals have been fawned over and kowtowed since they were children. It takes a rare individual to want to lead, yet be truly humbled when the opportunity actually appears.

CAN WE HAVE IT ALL?

Can we have it all? Here is an answer, my answer, from a woman's perspective—mine. Yes, we can have it all, if we do it on our own terms, to our own standards and nobody else's. Achievement is not about making some big leap to "the next level." True achievement is about making small, incremental steps that set you up for success. It's about getting real, one step at a time.

However old you are, whatever time it is, wherever you're living, whether you're alone or with people, it's time to get real. That's all our interviewees have been saying. Be yourself. Be nobody else. Get rid of the baggage. It's heavy, useless and just slows you down. Turn off the pressure cooker. Peer pressure, family pressure, career pressure, societal pressure and financial pressure have no place in your life. Be guided by your innermost values, and if you don't know your values, find out so you can really start to get to know yourself and become the leader of your own life.

"I'm a constantly evolving being. I'm continually unfolding my potential. I'm confident I will be wiser tomorrow than I was today," says Lesley Southwick-Trask.

I've made choices in my life, some easy, some hard. I chose my path because I've always wanted a great life, not a good life. I sincerely hope you feel the same way, because it's never too late to get real. And it's never too hard to stay real, as the wonderful women in this book have proven to us. Your choice begins today.

Don't worry, be happy. A trite phrase perhaps, but if you think about it and work at it, it's not so trite. Happiness is elusive because, as we've mentioned before, it's always in the mind of the beholder. So is success, when you get right down to it.

"To me, success is being happy and healthy and surrounded by people I love and who feel the same way about me," says Ann Rohmer. "I have a fabulous job, and I'm challenged all the time in a positive way. I face things full of determination and passion, and I always try to have a good laugh at the end of the day."

On the twin subjects of happiness and success, I'll leave the last words to four of my interviewees.

"To me, happiness is being surrounded by the people I love, and being able to wake up and live for today and make sense of the day. I often think, what can I do today that's going to make my kids happy, and my husband happy? If you doubt you can be happy, just look around you and you'll realize nothing is guaranteed, but everything is beautiful."
—DENISE BEBENEK, Founder of Meagan's Walk

"I'm no happier than I was twenty years ago. I'm not surprised, because money doesn't make me happy. It's about having freedom and independence, and living a full life, and having great relationships with the important people in my life."
—COLLEEN JOHNSTON, CFO of TD Bank Financial Group

"I think happiness and success and passion are closely aligned and intertwined. To me, happiness is all about being true to yourself and helping others be true to themselves. There's never any sacrifice if you're in alignment with your values and deepest beliefs."
—JACQUELINE CARROLL, Visual Artist and Author

"Listen to your heart. Don't reject things out of hand and always be open to opportunities."
—BRENDA EATON, Chair of the B.C. Housing Commission

Oh, there's one more thing my interviewees asked me to tell you. Don't forget to have *fun!*

ENDNOTES

Preface

Page 12:

Valerie Gibson. "Girls Just Wanna Have Husbands?" *Calgary Sun*, March 17, 2004.

———— Gibson highlighted an intriguing U.K. study about women, aged 18–34, and their attitudes to life and career.

www.calgarysun.com/cgi-bin/publish.cgi?p=82697&x=articles&s=lifestyle

Chapter 1: Get Real about Finding Your Passion

Page 23:

Oprah Winfrey. "Lifestyle Makeovers: How to Find Your Passion." Archived show list, Oprah.com, March 2001. www.oprah.com/tows/pastshows/tows_past_20010305.jhtml

———— "Thousands of you recently took an online poll, and more than 70 percent of you told us you have no idea what your life's passion is!"

Page 26:
Eric Quiñones. "Link Between Income and Happiness is Mainly an Illusion." Study conducted by Professors Alan B. Krueger, Daniel Kahneman. News@Princeton archives, June 29, 2006.
—— Two Princeton professors, economist Alan B. Krueger and psychologist and Nobel laureate Daniel Kahneman collaborated on the study with psychologists David Schkade of the University of California-San Diego, Norbert Schwarz of the University of Michigan and Arthur Stone of the State University of New York–Stony Brook.
www.princeton.edu/main/news/archive/S15/15/09S18/index.xml?section=topstories

Page 27:
Martin E.P. Seligman and Ed Royzman. "Happiness: The Three Traditional Theories." July 2003. www.authentichappiness.sas.upenn
—— There are three distinct kinds of happiness: the Pleasant Life (pleasures), the Good Life (engagement), and the Meaningful Life.
www.authentichappiness.sas.upenn.edu/newsletter.aspx?id=49

Page 27:
Richard Handler. "The Science of Happiness." CBC News: Analysis and Viewpoint, December 21, 2006.
www.cbc.ca/news/viewpoint/vp_handler/20061221.html

Page 37:
BBC health reporters. "Why Hard Work Makes People Happy." BBC News Health, January 3, 2006.
news.bbc.co.uk/2/hi/health/4577392.stm
Richard Wiseman. www.psy.herts.ac.uk/wiseman/index.html

Chapter 2: Get Real about Your Relationships

Page 49:
David Niven, Ph.D. "What's Important to You for a Satisfying Relationship?" Special to Yahoo! Personals. personals.yahoo.com/us/static/dating-advice_satisfying-relationship.

Page 52:
F. Ishu Ishiyama "On Self-Validation." *Athabasca University/University of British Columbia Trumpeter*, vol. 10, no. 4 (1993).
———— "Life is a process of self-validation . . . Being criticized or ignored is one of the most self-invalidating experiences, since our life revolves around social relationships and self-concept."

Page 57:
Patricia Ohlott and Marian Ruderman. *Standing at the Crossroads: Next Steps for High Achieving Women*, p. 39. San Francisco: Center for Creative Leadership, Jossey-Bass, 2002.
———— "Women are expected to act as supporters, caretakers, mothers, maintainers of relationships."

Page 67:
Daniel Goleman. "Narcissism Looming Larger As Root of Personality Woes." *New York Times*. November 1, 1988. query.nytimes.com/gst/fullpage.html?sec=health&res=940DE4DC1E38F932A35752C1A9 6E948260
———— "Narcissism is vital for satisfaction and survival; it is the capacity to identify what you need and want."

Page 73:
Patricia Ohlott and Marian Ruderman. *Standing at the Crossroads: Next Steps for High Achieving Women*, p. 61.
———— "Women—who value connection—tend to use participative management."
Keith Ferrazzi and Tahl Raz. *Never Eat Alone, And Other Secrets to Success, One Relationship at a Time*. New York–Toronto: Currency-Doubleday, 2005.

Page 79:
Elizabeth Warren and Amelia Warren Tyagi *The Two Income Trap: Why Middle-Class Mothers and Fathers Are Going Broke*. New York: Basic Books, 2003.
———— "These same two-income families have *less* money to spend than one-income families did thirty years ago."

Page 83:
Valerie Gibson. "Alpha Female & Mr. Mom: What I Need is a WIFE!" *Calgary Sun*, July 21, 2006.
www.calgarysun.com/cgi-bin/publish.cgi?p=147354&x= articles&s=lifestyle

Chapter 3: Get Real about Your Career
Page 95:
Ross Laver, Brenda Branswell, John Demont, Danylo Hawaleshka and Susan McClelland. "Jobs: Best and Worst." *Maclean's*. May 31, 1999.
———— Variety is the spice of life: "Canadians will [work hard] only if they feel the organization values them as much as it cares about customers and shareholders."
www.canadianencyclopedia.ca/index.cfm?PgNm=TCE&Params=M1 ARTM0011964

Page 97:
John Jost. "Women Undervalue Themselves in Setting Pay Rates." Stanford Graduate School of Business (website), August 1998.
www.gsb.stanford.edu/news/research/hr_women.shtml

Page 97:
Jeanne Sahadi. "Want More Pay? Some Disturbing News." CNNMoney.com, October 3, 2005.
money.cnn.com/2005/10/03/commentary/everyday/sahadi/
———— Hannah Riley Bowles is coauthor of a Harvard University working paper entitled, "It Depends Who Is Asking and Who You Ask: Social Incentives for Sex Differences in the Propensity to Initiate Negotiation." Linda Babcock and Lei Lai, July 2005.
www.ksg.harvard.edu/ksgpress/update/winter2006/stories/q_a.htm

Page 102:
Joanne Stanley. CATA WIT (Women in Technology) website. June 8, 2006.
www.catawit.ca/features/news/items/news06080601.asp

—— "The technology sector is an area where women can advance quickly, if we get together and share our strengths."

Page 103:
Ronald Alsop. "Men Do Numbers, Women Do Strategy: Recruiters See a Clear Difference between Male and Female Applicants." *Wall Street Journal*, September 21, 2005, p. R5.
—— "Goldman Sachs' recruiting chief Edith Hunt said that despite generally superior interpersonal skills, many of the women MBAs at her firm don't use those skills to build networks inside the firm."

Page 104:
Anne Fisher. "Five Months of Networking, Still No New Job." *FORTUNE*, May 17, 2006.
money.cnn.com/2006/05/16/news/economy/annie/fortune_annie0517/index.htm

Page 107:
Virginia Galt. "In a Job Rut? It May Be that You're Socially Clueless." *Globe and Mail*, September 30, 2006.
www.theglobeandmail.com/servlet/story/LAC.20060930.RCA-REER30/TPStory/Business

Page 107:
Penelope Trunk. "Social Skills Matter More than Ever, So Here's How to Get Them." Brazen Careerist blog, July 18, 2006.
blog.penelopetrunk.com/2006/07/18/social-skills-matter-more-than-ever-so-heres-how-to-get-them/
—— "Many fields that used to be havens for loners, like programming, increasingly require exceptional people skills."

Page 119:
"Survey of Canadian Attitudes towards Learning, 2006: Early Childhood Learning." A recent joint initiative between Statistics Canada and the Canadian Council on Learning. From the Reports and Data section of the Canadian Council on Learning website.
www.ccl-cca.ca/CCL/Reports/SCAL/SCAL2006ECL.htm

Page 123:
Canadian Council on Learning. "First Survey of Canadian Attitudes toward Learning: Canada's Barometer of Opinions, Perceptions and Beliefs about Lifelong Learning." 2006 Report.

Page 123:
Canadian Council on Learning. "Majority of Parents Can't Help their Children with Homework, Say Canadians." Oct. 10, 2006 press release. www.ccl-cca.ca/CCL/Newsroom/Releases/20061010SCAL2006General.htm

Page 133:
Alix Nyberg Stuart. "What Women Want: In Finance, the Operative Words Are Opportunity, Flexibility, and Balance." *CFO Magazine*, June 1, 2006.
————— "While an overwhelming 83 percent of the male executives *don't* believe the glass ceiling exists, only 44 percent of the women executives agreed with them."

Page 138:
Penelope Trunk. "Career Change Is Inevitable, So Plan for It." The Brazen Careerist. May 7, 2005.

Page 139:
Catalyst.org. "Women Take Care, Men Take Charge. Stereotyping of U.S. Business Leaders Exposed." October 19, 2005 study of 296 corporate leaders (128 men and 168 women). www.catalystwomen.org/files/full/Women%20Take%20Care%20Men%20Take%20Charge.pdf

Chapter 4: Get Real about Your Money

Page 147:
The Vanier Institute of the Family 2006 Annual Report. "Ka-ching! Ka-ching! Can You Hear it Ring!—Debt Ratio Hits 127%." *The Current State of Canadian Family Finances*, February 2007. Quoted with permission.
www.vifamily.ca/library/cft/state06.html#kaching

Page 150:
Financial Planners Standards Council (FPSC). "Test Your Financial I.Q." Chart used with permission. www.cfp-ca.org/public/public_fp_selftest.asp

Chapter 5: Get Real about Your Lifestyle

Page 173:
The Heart and Stroke Foundation. "Is 60 the New 70?" From the 2006 Report Card on Health.
―――― Excerpt: "58% of boomers think their weight has little or no effect on their heart health."

Page 176:
Elizabeth Monier-Williams. "Anxious about Holiday Weight Gain? Don't Look to Others for Social Clues, Study Shows." *News@UofT*, December 14, 2005. U. of T. psychology professors Peter Herman and Janet Polivy examined more than thirty years of research on overeating and obesity. Herman and Polivy study published in *Physiology & Behavior*. www.news.utoronto.ca/bin6/051214-1914.asp

Page 177:
Statistics Canada. *The Daily*, June 15, 2004. StatsCan's Canadian Community Health Survey reported that in 2003, 14.9 percent of adult Canadians were considered obese and 33.3 percent were considered overweight. www.statcan.ca/Daily/English/040615/d040615b.htm

Page 177:
Laurette Dubé. "Marketing Self Care." *McGill Reporter*, vol. 33, April 19, 2001. www.mcgill.ca/reporter/33/15/dube/

Page 180:
Kristin Jenkins. "Why is Change So Hard?" Canadian Health Network, July 15, 2005.

———— "the ratio of pessimistic adjectives to positive adjectives is three to one." www.canadian-health-network.ca/servlet/ ContentServer?cid=1119222324674&pagename=CHN-RCS%2FCHNResource%2FCHNResourcePageTemplate&lang= En&c=CHNResource

Page 185:
"Health Risk Classification According to Body Mass Index (BMI) Chart." Health Canada, Food and Nutrition section, 2003. www.hc-sc.gc.ca/fn-an/nutrition/weights-poids/guide-ld-adult/bmi_chart_java-graph_imc_java_e.html

Page 187:
Harper's Magazine, Weekly Review, March 16, 2004. www.harpers.org/WeeklyReview2004-03-16.html. The full "article" can be found at: www.jaradite.com/thoughts_january2004.html

Page 203:
Darren E.R. Warburton, Crystal Whitney Nicol and Shannon S.D. Bredin. "Health Benefits of Physical Activity: The Evidence." *Canadian Medical Association Journal*, March 14, 2006. www.cmaj.ca/cgi/content/abstract/174/6/801

Page 205:
Heart and Stroke Foundation of Ontario. "How Canadians Feel About Stress (chart)." Just the Facts, 2002/2003. www.sja.ca/bc/pdf/JustFacts_ENG.pdf

Page 209:
Dove. "Campaign for Real Beauty." The website can be found at: www.campaignforrealbeauty.com

Chapter 6: Get Real about Your Life
Page 220:
"The Gangster of Love." 43 Things (blog). www.43things.com

Page 228:
Stephanie Merritt. "The Guilty Party." The Observer *Woman*,
August 6, 2006.
observer.guardian.co.uk/woman/story/0,,1835491,00.html

Page 230:
Timothy Egan. "The Rise of the Shrinking-Vacation Syndrome." *New York Times*, August 19, 2006.
———— Excerpt: "Skipping vacations has become so pervasive that companies are forcing employees to take time off."

Page 230:
Statistics Canada. "Control Over Time and Work-Life Balance: An Empirical Analysis." Labour Force Historical Review. Table 16 (1998). The Canadian Federal Labour Standards Review, November 2005.
www.fls-ntf.gc.ca/en/re-exsum-15.asp
—From a report prepared for the Federal Labour Standards Review Committee by Graham S. Lowe, Ph.D., The Graham Lowe Group Inc., November 3, 2005.

Page 231:
William Michelson and Andrew S. Harvey. "Is Teachers' Work Never Done? Time-Use and Subjective Outcomes." *Radical Pedagogy*, vol. 2, issue 1, Spring 2000. radicalpedagogy.icaap.org/content/issue2_1/02Michelson.html

Page 231:
Human Resources Development Canada. "Work, Family and Community: Key Issues and Directions for Future Research." Labour Program, Human Resources Development Canada. "Women's Incomes are More Important than Ever to the Financial Security of the Household." April 1999. www.hrsdc.gc.ca/asp/gateway.asp?hr=/en/lp/spila/wlb/wfc/05_03.shtml&hs=

Page 239:
"Canadians' Top Priority is Family (chart)." March 2006 survey commissioned by Workopolis.com.

Page 240:
Allan McKay. "You Can't Always Get What You Want: Hopes vs. Realities for Canadian Families." *Globe and Mail*, op-ed page, January 9, 2006. Excerpted from Vanier Institute for the Family Annual Report 2005.
www.vifamily.ca/about/annual_report_2005.html

Page 242:
Virginia Galt. "'Go for It,' Female Executives Told." *Globe and Mail*, June 2004.

Page 243:
Catalyst. "The Bottom Line: Connecting Corporate Performance and Gender Diversity." News release, January 26, 2004.
www.catalyst.org/files/pr/Financial%20Performance.pdf

Page 244:
Ian Brown. "A Revolution from Within," *Globe and Mail*, October 2006.

Chapter 7: The Authenticity Track

Page 260:
V. Scott Koerwer. Feature Interview with Sherron Watkins, former Vice President for Corporate Development of Enron. *Journal of Leadership & Organizational Studies*, p. 7, Summer 2004.
www.allbusiness.com/educational-services/business-schools-computer/290768-7.html
Also on leadership and integrity, Michael C. Feiner, "The Law of the Emperor's Wardrobe." *Ivey Business Journal* (University of Western Ontario). January/February 2005—www.iveybusinessjournal.com/view_article.asp?intArticle_ID=536

ACKNOWLEDGEMENTS

THERE ARE NUMEROUS PEOPLE who have poured their commitment and insight to *Get Real*. I would like to provide a warm-felt thank you to all who have participated in the preparation of the book.

I would like to thank TD Bank Financial Group, who has provided me with an opportunity to share the collection of stories in this book that mean so much to me. In particular, I would like to express my gratitude for the leadership of John See, Executive Vice President, TD Wealth Management. *Get Real* is a symbol of John's drive and vision to educate all investors about achieving their individual life goals.

To the twenty-six women whom we interviewed in the book: Your kindnesses in sharing your stories of success and setbacks with us have made this book come to life. I admire each and every one of you for the perseverance you have made to accomplish your dreams and desires.

To my co-author, Jonathan Verney, who has assisted me in communicating the message of how personal and financial goals are intertwined. Your creativeness has highlighted the women and their stories. They are the true stars of *Get Real*.

To my colleagues at TD who have helped shape the book to the final form: Jean Estabrook, Juanita Soutar, Su McVey and Trevor Yu.

To my family, who has provided me with the support to face the challenge of creating my sixth book: My husband, Jim, and our children Carolyn, David, Jane and Kevin. I cherish the precious time we spend together in the face of my hectic schedule.

INDEX

ABOUT THE AUTHORS

PATRICIA LOVETT-REID, Hon. FCSI, CFP, is a Senior Vice President with TD Waterhouse Canada Inc., a subsidiary of the Toronto-Dominion Bank. She is the host of *MoneyTalk*, a weekly program on Business News Network (formerly ROBtv), and is one of Canada's leading authorities on wealth management. In 2007, she was named one of Canada's Most Powerful Women: Top 100 in the Trailblazers and Trendsetters category by Women's Executive Network. She is the author of six books, including the bestsellers *Live Well, Retire Well: Strategies for a Rich Life and a Richer Retirement*, *Surprise! You're Wealthy: Every Woman's Guide to Financial Independence* and *Retirement Strategies for Women: Turning Dreams Into Reality*. She lives in Oakville, Ontario.

JONATHAN VERNEY is President of Warp Communications Group, the corporate storytellers (www.WarpGroup.ca). He co-authored *Live Well, Retire Well: Strategies for a Rich Life and a Richer Retirement*, has co-written a global marketing report on international executives with Harvard University and The Caldwell Partners, and has created branding initiatives for Canada's largest corporations. He lives in Toronto, Ontario.